ROUTLEDGE LIBRARY EDITIONS: DEVELOPMENT

THE AFRICAN DEBT CRISIS

THE AFRICAN DEBT CRISIS

TREVOR W. PARFITT
and
STEPHEN P. RILEY

Volume 16

Routledge
Taylor & Francis Group
LONDON AND NEW YORK

First published in 1989

This edition first published in 2011
by Routledge
2 Park Square, Milton Park, Abingdon, Oxon, OX14 4RN

Simultaneously published in the USA and Canada
by Routledge
711 Third Avenue, New York, NY 10017

Routledge is an imprint of the Taylor & Francis Group, an informa business

First issued in paperback 2013

British Library Cataloguing in Publication Data
A catalogue record for this book is available from the British Library

ISBN 13: 978-0-415-58414-2 (Set)
eISBN 13: 978-0-203-84035-1 (Set)
ISBN 13: 978-0-415-85358-3 (Volume 16)
eISBN 13: 978-0-203-83989-8 (Volume 16)

Publisher's Note
The publisher has gone to great lengths to ensure the quality of this reprint but points out that some imperfections in the original copies may be apparent.

Disclaimer
The publisher has made every effort to trace copyright holders and welcomes correspondence from those they have been unable to contact.

In Memoriam: Stephen Riley 1949-98

It is more than ten years since the tragic death of Stephen Riley, my co-author on this book. His death robbed us of a superb academic and a good friend. Stephen was a charismatic teacher who is remembered by his students and an innovative researcher. As can be seen from this volume, he was ahead of the game in recognizing the importance of such issues as corruption and what came to be known as good governance in African development. His analysis of them was also a good deal more nuanced than those of the epigones of such institutions as the World Bank. He would abominate the way in which some of them have used the issue of good governance as an alibi for the continued failure of their market fundamentalist policies analysed in the coming pages.

Stephen was not only a fine academic, but also a marvellous friend as those of us who were fortunate enough to know him can testify. He had a generous spirit and I owe him numerous debts that cannot now be repaid. I am delighted that this book is being reissued because it is a monument that he deserves. It also brings me pleasure because it reminds me of the good times we had writing it. Editorial meetings with Steve were not only the occasion of stimulating intellectual exchange, but also of repartee, laughter and the qualities that cement real friendship. They last in my memory as the best of times. I am grateful I had such good times with such a good friend.

Rest in peace Steve.

THE AFRICAN DEBT CRISIS

Trevor W. Parfitt and Stephen P. Riley

(with a chapter on Ghana by Jeffrey Haynes)

ROUTLEDGE
London and New York

First published in 1989 by
Routledge
11 New Fetter Lane, London EC4P 4EE
29 West 35th Street, New York NY 10001

British Library Cataloguing in Publication Data

Parfitt, Trevor, *1954–*
The African debt crisis.
1. Africa. Governments. External debts
I. Title II. Riley, Stephen, *1949–*
336.3′433′6

ISBN 0-415-00441-1

Library of Congress Cataloging-in-Publication Data

Parfitt, Trevor W., 1954–
The African debt crisis / Trevor W. Parfitt and Stephen P. Riley, with a chapter on Ghana by Jeffrey Haynes.
p. cm.
Bibliography: p.
Includes index.
ISBN 0-415-00441-1
1. Debts, Public—Africa. 2. Debts, External—Africa. I. Riley, Stephen P., 1949– . II. Haynes, Jeffrey. III. Title.
HJ8826.P37 1989
336.3′435′096–dc19 88-37898
CIP

Contents

List of tables and figures

TABLES

FIGURES

Preface and acknowledgements

The African debt crisis is a complex and ever-changing phenomenon. In this book we chart many of the dimensions of this crisis. We deal with its causes and consequences both globally and in several African states. We look in particular at the internal political and economic effects of the growing indebtedness of African states, and its international context, through an examination of the role of external powers and institutions such as the International Monetary Fund and the World Bank. We also examine the many potential ways out of the debt trap, and even offer our own solution. The general analysis assesses African indebtedness in the period 1978-87; a postscript examines contemporary developments up to mid-1988.

In writing this book we have ourselves incurred many debts. As a consequence, the authors would like to thank all those who have generously given their help and encouragement. These include our families and friends, numerous helpful Routledge personnel, and colleagues at Huddersfield and North Staffordshire Polytechnics, particularly the Library staffs.

Trevor W. Parfitt
Stephen P. Riley
1988

Introduction

There can be little doubt that the debt crisis has become the bête noire of north-south relations in the 1980s. Whilst Third World debt was recognized as a problem in the 1970s, the sheer volume of money involved has grown to the point whereby it is no longer seen solely as the problem of the less developed countries (LDCs), which sometimes cannot pay for their imports or are unable to meet the next instalment of a loan. Instead it is seen as a threat to the stability of the international economy, the potential cause of a new Great Depression. As such it has stimulated a voluminous literature analysing the causes of debt, its growth, and its effects on the international economy, and speculating on the question as to whether or not the great Latin American debtors (such as Brazil, Argentina, and Mexico) will default and bring the whole house of cards tumbling down.

In this volume we shall attempt to combine a macro-level analysis of the international politics of debt with a concern for the question of how it affects the Third World - in this particular case, Sub-Saharan Africa (SSA). Initially, we shall briefly survey the origins of the world debt crisis before focusing on the dimensions and the nature of SSA commitments. The impact of indebtedness on Africa's position in international politics will then be assessed, particular attention being given to SSA's relations with the most influential international actors in the debt crisis, the IMF and the World Bank. The multifarious effects of this crisis at the national level will be analysed in case studies of Ghana, Sierra Leone, Nigeria, Zaire, and the Francophone states, particularly Ivory Coast.

An OECD survey has suggested that, 'Developing-country debt problems are not all the same'.[1] Indeed, the countries that we shall be examining differ in many ways; in their administrative capacity, the character of political leadership, structure of production, and level and composition of external indebtedness at the very least. We shall seek to demonstrate that whilst there are continental patterns of indebtedness, the local impact of debt can differ quite radically from one state to the next in accordance with the varying socio-political and economic environments. This has important implications for any proposed solution of the debt crisis since it suggests that a complete remedy for debt-related problems must address not only the macro-level of the global economy, but also the micro-level of numerous states facing variegated problems. The related questions of how the various strands of SSA's debt crisis may be solved and whether or not any of the strategies proposed hitherto (for example the Baker Plan) represent a viable solution will be the subject of our final chapters.

Initially, however, we must attempt to trace the origins of the world debt crisis. There is a degree of consensus in the debt literature that the present crisis is attributable to three sets of factors, although different analysts vary in the amount of influence they accord to each factor. They include, first, external shocks in the world economy, such as the oil shocks of 1973-4 and 1979-80; second, economically inefficient domestic policies on the part of debtor states (occasionally creditor states are also accused of adopting such policies); and, third, bad lending policies on the part of the commercial banks to which a large proportion of international debt is owed. How is the blame to be allocated amongst these factors?

The oil shocks have taken a large share of popular blame for exacerbating Third World debt. Hallberg points out that the combined deficit of oil-importing developing countries rose from US$11.3 billion in 1973 to US$37 billion in 1974. It further expanded from US$42 billion in 1978 to US$88 billion in 1980. Many analysts argue that this development lay at the base of the debt crisis since these countries had no option but to fill their deficits by having recourse to loans. However, Hallberg also notes that 'a major part of the expansion of bank lending to developing countries was not coincident with these two periods of increased financing needs'.[2] Bank lending to the Third World was increasing before the first oil shock in 1973. Thus, the debt crisis cannot be blamed solely on OPEC.

Tanzania's ex-President Nyerere has found an alternative explanation for Africa's indebtedness in the long-term trend for the terms of trade for primary commodities to decline. He expands on this theme as follows:

> During the last few years of world recession, the fall in commodity prices has been catastrophic: the World Bank has estimated that from 1980 to 1982, the prices of non-oil primary commodities declined by 27 per cent in current US dollar terms. As a proportion of their

> GDP the result was a 2.4 per cent loss of income for the low income countries of Africa south of the Sahara. Can this kind of thing be regarded as irrelevant to the current economic crisis in Africa?[3]

Nyerere suggests that the tendency for the price of primary commodities to decline has led to 'a regular transfer of wealth from the poor countries to the rich countries', which is a major factor in explaining African indebtedness. However, this does not satisfactorily explain why major oil exporters such as Mexico and Nigeria are amongst the largest debtor states in their respective continents. From 1973-80 Nigerian oil receipts averaged US$25 billion per year and yet the national debt grew apace (see Chapter 3). This can hardly be attributed to declining terms of trade leading to a transfer of wealth out of Nigeria.

The inadequacy of the 'external shock' theses to provide a complete explanation of the debt crisis has led many theorists (often of an economically liberal outlook) to seek an explanation in the policy shortcomings of the debtor states. It has been pointed out that many of the Third World states are highly interventionist and that their growing expenditure has contributed to large fiscal deficits. Often these deficits are filled by printing more money, which contributes to high rates of inflation. Since domestic inflation in such states is usually much higher than world inflation, the exchange rate tends to become over-valued. This gives a disincentive to domestic industry and leads to dependence on artifically cheap imports. These conditions also tend to give rise to habits of conspicuous consumption by the elite, who waste valuable foreign exchange on importing luxury goods. The result is a growing balance of payments deficit, which has to be filled by loans.[4]

However, this line of argument hardly represents a sufficient explanation of the debt crisis since one might have expected that the western banks supplying the loans would have been able to appreciate that the economic policies of the debtor states were unsound. This should have been a clear disincentive to making such loans and yet the banks went on pouring money into states that were to become major problem borrowers. Nunnenkamp criticizes the banks for continuing to lend large sums to oil-importing Third World countries during the early 1980s, when the effects of the oil shocks and inadequate domestic policies had become obvious. He also points to the unbalanced distribution of the loans, observing that certain US banks had loaned the five main Latin American debtors between 140 and 260 per cent of their capital by 1982. The imprudence of these loans is partly explained by the fact that many of them were state-guaranteed and the banks seem to have assumed that the state would foot the bill. If this failed there were still the Central Banks and the IMF to bail them out of trouble.[5] Thus, Nunnenkamp clearly allocates a substantial share of the responsibility for the debt crisis to the banks.

Korner, Maas et al. draw attention to another set of contributory factors to the growth of indebtedness, which are linked to colonialism and neocolonialism. They note that many Third World states were forced to adopt a monocultural, primary-commodity based pattern of development by their colonial masters. Such economies are vulnerable to the vagaries of the world market, in which many primary products are prone to a cycle of boom and slump. On independence the colonial governments handed power to the urban and agricultural elites that had emerged from this economic context. This lent itself to preservation of the monocultural economy since these ruling groups derived their revenue from trade and primary commodity production rather than from industrial investments. Their lack of managerial and technical expertise, together with their orientation towards trade and consumption has led to a dependence on foreign capital to finance some limited economic diversification. Unfortunately this is anti-developmental in the final instance since such investments lead to an outflow of capital in the form of profit repatriation, management and consultancy fees, and so forth. In this way, Korner, Maas et al. relate debt to a colonial legacy that has shaped Third World economies in such a way that they have an in-built tendency towards balance of payments deficits which can only be filled by drawing on loans.[6]

One might also draw on the work of scholars such as Jackson and Rosberg, and Sandbrook, to suggest that the personalized, neopatrimonial nature of rulership in many African states has led to the accumulation of debts.[7] It has often been noted that in many of the new African states political cleavages have often tended to develop along ethnic/regional lines with political factions securing support through means of patronage. Given that the state mechanism represents the greatest single resource in many African countries, there is a tendency for it to become the focus of a spoils system in which different factions compete for control of the national finances in order to fund their patronage networks. This style of rulership lends itself to the misuse and misappropriation of state funds, thus exacerbating tendencies towards indebtedness.

In fact any explanation of the debt crisis must look to a complex interaction of these factors. Initially, it is worth noting that the industries of the developed north were already moving into recession by the early 1970s. Organized labour had pushed up the wage rate and the profit rate was being squeezed.[8] Second, we may point out that the American practice of filling their budget deficit by printing more dollars ensured that the banks were full of dollars seeking a profitable outlet. In other words, the north was faced by the developing contradiction of a surplus of investment capital and the lack of a profitable outlet for it in industry.

The OPEC price hike of 1973 worsened this contradiction in the following ways. First, the recession of northern industry became much more deeply entrenched due to the higher oil price. Second, the OPEC states were flooded with receipts (e.g. petrodollars) that their own underdeveloped economies were unable to absorb completely. Lever and Huhne note that the oil-exporting states' current account surplus increased from US$7billion in 1973 to US$68 billion in 1974.[9] Much of this funding was placed in the very same international banks that already had a surfeit of dollars. All this liquidity was now even less likely to find a profitable outlet in northern industry because of the worsened recession. The situation was exacerbated by the movement of money around the international finance markets, which had the effect of artificially creating more money. Whereas northern governments stipulate a 10 per cent reserve requirement on domestic borrowing, no such limitations apply to offshore lending and so a single dollar on deposit can serve as the base for US$10 or US$100 in loans. DeWitt and Petras have estimated the aggregate amount of offshore deposits at over US$300 billion and argue that the amount created by offshore banks must run into many billions of dollars.[10] In any case the operation of these factors created a huge excess of liquidity for which the international banks were desperate to find an outlet.

As is now known, the outlet was found in the south, where these funds were supposed to provide the impetus for Third World industrialization and development. Such development, together with profits from traditional Third World products (e.g. oil and other primaries), would provide the capital needed to repay the loans. A number of other factors conspired to allay any (in the event well-grounded) fears the banks may have had about the risks involved in making loans to the Third World. The practice of syndicating loans became popular due to the belief that it reduced risk by spreading the investment across a number of banks instead of only one. However, Nunnenkamp points out that this may in fact have had the effect of inducing a number of banks to make unwise loans that they would not otherwise have undertaken. He suggests that many smaller banks joined consortia to finance loans that had been taken on by the larger banks in the belief that the stamp of approval of one of the latter institutions was a solid guarantee of profitability. Unfortunately, this assumption often proved to be mistaken and the only effect of syndication in these instances was to involve more banks in the debt crisis than need have been the case.[11] Lever and Huhne also point to the 'sovereign-risk hypothesis' as a source of complacency concerning the risk attached to Third World loans. This theory held that since any country would certainly own more than it owed, it could not go bankrupt and so the debt would be paid eventually. Lever and Huhne observe that this argument is historically inaccurate, noting that very few of the debts contracted by Latin American states during the 1930s were paid back at par.[12] It can be seen that the banks had recourse to various spurious ideas in justifying the process of recycling OPEC receipts as loans to the Third World. In any event, as Lipietz puts it, 'the bankers laid seige to potential borrowers' between 1974-8 and 'the international exposure of the western banks rose from US$280 billion to US$900 billion'. Indeed, these loans were not entirely without success in terms of stimulating development as was shown by the emergence of the new industrializing countries, such as South Korea, Taiwan, and (more controversially perhaps) Brazil. However, not all the loans were successful either. Lipietz points to Nigeria, Iran, and Turkey as countries that received substantial funding, but which failed to achieve any kind of take-off into development for one reason or another.[13]

It would also be fair to say that during the mid-1970s many Third World states, including several in Africa, seemed to be attractive prospects for investment. Krumm has pointed out that the primary commodity boom of this period led to an expansion in government receipts from such products as cocoa, coffee, groundnuts, and sugar.[14] Many of the states that Korner, Maas _et al._ had identified as vulnerable due to their monocultural dependence on primary goods now seemed to be in a position to finance some level of development due to their increased export receipts. They began to increase their expenditure and to take on loans to complement their export revenues. When the primary commodity bubble unexpectedly burst and boom turned to slump, many of them were unwilling to rein in their spending and continued to take on further loans to finance development programmes that often proved to be unproductive. Lever and Huhne point to the Gabonese example, where US$600 million in guaranteed export credits and US$679 million in syndicated loans were spent on wasteful prestige projects such as a road linking the airport and the presidential palace, the enlargement of government buildings, and purchase of a fleet of commercial jet aircraft.[15] This process, through which many states first wasted their profits from the primary-commodity boom and then took on loans to bankroll unviable schemes, provided one of the bases for debt crisis. In all too many cases the banks seem to have taken little if any care to ensure that their funding was being spent wisely.

Nor can it be said that all of the funding was flowing into development. A considerable proportion of it was spent on simply keeping the weaker Third World economies afloat. Krumm points out that producers of minerals, such as copper and iron, experienced a downward trend in prices throughout the 1970s. However, copper producers such as Zambia and iron exporters such as Liberia and Mauretania were still able to borrow abroad to maintain state spending since it was generally expected that copper and iron ore prices would rise again to historical levels.[16] They also had the impetus to borrow due to the crippling effects of the OPEC price hike. Makgetla argues that rising oil prices combined with declining terms of trade for copper made it essential for the Zambian government to borrow abroad and notes that, 'By 1984, its long- and medium-term foreign debt amounted to US$4,500 million - about one-fifth to private companies and banks, the remainder to foreign governments and multilateral institutions.' In particular, the Zambian government was reliant on IMF assistance to continue paying its debts and to buy necessary imports. It owed the Fund US$600 million by 1984.[17] Zambia's situation is typical of many countries, which have grown increasingly dependent not only on commercial loans, but even more on such agencies as the IMF's oil facilities and its Extended Fund Facility.

By the end of the 1970s, the total debt owed by the Third World as a whole (inclusive of the NICs and those states that were just treading water) amounted to US$445 billion according to the OECD (see Table 1). This represented an increase of over 500 per cent since 1971 when Third World debt stood at a total of US$86 billion. The greatest part of the debt was owed to the north and to multilateral agencies, many of which are dominated by the northern states. Over three-quarters of the debt (US$336 billion) had been lent on non-concessional terms.

This already dangerous situation was made desperate by two developments, these being the second oil shock of 1979 and the decision by many northern states to abandon Keynesian attempts at economic management and to adopt monetarism. The oil price rise severely exacerbated the position of the oil-importing developing countries and on this occasion there was no primary commodity boom to offset the balance of payments problems it caused. Indeed, by helping to push northern industry deeper into recession the oil shock contributed to a reduction in the terms of trade for oil-importing primary commodity exporters as their market contracted. This tendency was fuelled by the response of northern governments, which decided that recession and international inflation could only be cured by the adoption of monetarism. As Lipietz has argued, the two main levers of monetarist policy are the attack on wages in Britain and the USA, and 'the deliberate raising of interest rates in order to slow down the creation of credit money'.[18] The effects of this policy were to give a further impetus to the contraction of northern markets and to transform real negative interest rates into positive real rates of over 8 per cent in the early 1980s. The Third World as a whole suffered a serious fall in their export prices just as monetarism drove interest rates up, making further loans more expensive and raising the cost of servicing existing debts. The Economist Intelligence Unit has noted that:

> Although the developing countries were successful in reducing their aggregate current account deficit from US$100 billion in 1981 to US$25 billion in 1985, global demand was simply insufficient to generate the foreign

Table 0.1 Total disbursed long-term debt of developing countries at year-end 1971-83

US$ bn

Source and terms of lending	1971	1975	1976	1977	1978	1979	1980	1981	1982	1983
1. DAC countries and capital markets	68	131	160	200	255	301	342	381	414	455
ODA	24	34	36	41	49	53	57	57	59	61
Total export credits	26	40	49	64	82	98	110	117	121	127
Total private	18	57	74	95	124	151	175	207	234	267
of which Bank loans[a]	10	46	59	75	98	123	145	175	200	234
Bonds	4	5	6	9	13	13	15	16	16	15
Other	3	6	9	11	13	14	15	17	18	18
2. Multilateral	9	21	26	32	39	46	55	64	75	84
of which: Concessional	6	10	12	14	17	20	24	27	30	33
3. CMEA countries	6	9	9	11	12	15	15	16	17	18
of which: Concessional	5	8	8	9	10	11	12	13	13	14
4. OPEC countries	x	6	8	11	13	15	18	20	21	23
of which: Concessional	x	5	6	8	9	11	12	14	15	16
5. Other LDCs	2	3	3	4	5	6	7	7	7	8
of which: Concessional	1	2	2	2	3	3	3	3	3	3
6. Other and adjustments	1	3	5	5	7	8	8	13	18	18
Total debt	86	173	211	262	331	391	445	501	552	606
of which: Concessional	33	59	65	76	89	99	109	114	121	130
Non-concessional	53	114	146	186	243	292	336	387	431	476

Source: 'External Debt of Developing Countries: 1983 Survey', Paris, OECD, 1984, p.54

a Bank loans other than export credits.

> exchange necessary to meet foreign debt payments and contribute to domestic growth.

The result has been that Third World states have had no option but to take on further loans despite the rising cost of credit. As a consequence developing-country debt rose from US$700 billion in 1982 to nearly US$900 billion in 1985 according to the Economist Intelligence Unit. Some US$425 billion of this was owed to the commercial banks.[19] However, it has been argued that the figures that are usually quoted exclude certain items such as short-term debt. The World Bank's most comprehensive figures indicate total Third World debt to have been US$992 billion at the end of 1985 and projected it to rise to US$1,080 billion in 1987 (see Table 2).

What then are the effects of this problem on debtor nations? Generally, Third World states have encountered foreign exchange shortages due to low commodity prices and debt-servicing problems. Lack of foreign exchange leads to an inability to obtain essential imports, which can cause local shortages of essential goods such as food. It is easy to discern how this chain of events can lead to domestic unrest and instability. The choice facing countries in this position is to take on further loans, to negotiate for the rescheduling of their debts, or default. The traditional objections to the latter course are that the nation in question is likely to become a pariah in the international community, possibly subject to sanctions, and unable to obtain its vital imports (as we shall see this argument may yet require reassessment). As to rescheduling it may be pointed out that many Third World states have had recourse to this option. The period 1982-5 saw the rescheduling of thirty-five countries' debts (beginning with Mexico, whose crisis of 1982 has been perceived as the 'official' beginning of the debt crisis) amounting in total to about US$210 billion.[20] However, the creditor states have been willing to make only piecemeal concessions rather than negotiating the comprehensive agreement that many commentators have argued for. Additionally (as will be demonstrated in the next chapter) reschedulings merely postpone the debt problem rather than solve it.

As we have noted, this has thrown Third World debtors back on the option of taking out further loans to tide themselves over their immediate problems of servicing existing debt and obtaining necessary imports. However, the

Table 0.2 Growth of external debt, 1980-7

US$ bn

	1980	1981	1982	1983	1984	1985[a]	1986	1987[b]
DRS reporting countries	573	666	739	797	833	892	932	972
Long-term debt	430	494	551	630	673	731	775	812
From official sources	162	179	197	221	236	268	290	310
From private sources	268	315	354	409	438	463	485	502
Short-term debt[c]	134	158	167	137	126	124	118	) 160
Use of IMF credit	9	15	20	30	33	37	39	)
Other developing countries[d]	77	83	86	93	96	100	103	108
Long-term debt	59	58	60	67	68	74	77	83
From official sources	17	18	20	17	20	23	24	25
From private sources	42	40	40	50	48	51	53	58
Short-term debt	18	24	25	25	27	25	25	) 25
Use of IMF credit	0	1	1	1	1	1	1	)
Total external debt	650	749	825	890	929	992	1,305	1,080

Source: World Bank, World Debt Tables: External Debt of Developing Countries, 1986-7 (Washington DC, World Bank, 1987, p.8)

a Data for 1985 are preliminary.

b Data for 1986 are estimated and for 1987 are projected.

c Data reflect the known rescheduling of some US$45 billion of short-term debt to banks into long-term debt in 1983-6.

d Includes data for developing countries that do not report through the DRS and for those that report in a form that does not admit publication in the standard tables; excludes debt of the high-income oil-exporting countries.

conditionality attached to such loans can bring problems that are by no means inconsiderable in themselves. According to the Economist Intelligence Unit:

> During the crisis decision-making process, it was determined that the developing countries were suffering from a short-term liquidity as opposed to a long-term solvency crisis, i.e. they needed to realign their spending habits with their shrunken earnings potential. Once this realignment took place balance would be restored and these countries would be able to return to the capital markets.[21]

This analysis led the creditor states and institutions to entrust the management of the debt crisis to the IMF, which was after all designed to correct short-term balance of payments disequilibria. Most debtor states have had recourse to the IMF. Indeed, it might be argued that they have little choice in the matter, since other potential sources of funding (such as bilateral donors and the international banks) have mostly insisted that any potential borrowers must have satisfactorily complied with the conditions attached to IMF loans. These conditions take the form of the well-known stabilization or (some would say more aptly called) austerity programme. Traditionally, such conditions include measures such as public spending cuts and devaluation. Public sector cuts may entail the abolition of price controls and subsidies, the imposition of wage cuts, and rising unemployment, whilst devaluation raises the cost of imports. It can be seen that such measures will have painful consequences for many of the inhabitants of Third World debtor states and that they have the potential to cause substantial unrest and political instability. Indeed, the IMF riot has become a far from rare phenomenon, just two examples being the disturbances in Nimeiry's Sudan after the abolition of the bread subsidy and the riots by rural and industrial workers throughout Brazil after IMF-imposed wage curbs that substantially reduced their living standards.

Furthermore, a question mark arises as to the appropriateness of the IMF's medicine for the debt crisis. It is clear from our analysis that the debt crisis is not a short-term phenomenon that can be solved by bringing debtor states' spending into line with their export receipts. We have already seen that the Third World states have substantially reduced their balance of payments deficits over the period of the 1980s and yet the debt crisis remains one of the most serious of the world's problems. This is because the roots of the crisis lie deep in the structure of the international economic system and in the domestic socio-political structures of the debtor nations. The role of Third World states as monocultural suppliers of primary commodities makes them especially vulnerable to the recession, whilst the reliance of many such states on personalized, neopatrimonial politics leads to a tendency towards growing state spending, often on economically unproductive projects. The question of how far the north's IMF-led strategy for solving the crisis addresses the numerous aspects of the debt problem will be a central concern in the following chapters, where we shall focus more directly on debt in the African context.

1

The nature of African debt

It is now widely recognized that the states of the African continent are suffering the consequences of a particular kind of debt crisis that has emerged in the 1970s, and especially from the second world oil price rises of 1978 onwards. Earlier we have described the origins and general characteristics of the Third World debt crisis, as a consequence of both internal and external factors appertaining to development possibilities and the character of the international economy in the 1970s. But debt is becoming a more generalized phenomenon affecting individuals, states, and corporations alike in both the advanced industrial and peripheral worlds.

The United States is a major debtor nation; so are a number of state socialist societies such as Poland. Multinational companies are also heavily indebted to the international banking system, as are groups of individuals such as American farmers and British consumers. The American farm debt is generally estimated at over US$ 200 billions. In 1986 it was also estimated that private individuals in Britain owed over £27 billion to banks, finance houses, and other money lenders. This consumer debt, which does not include mortgages for house purchases, was growing dramatically.[1]

Though there is a worldwide growth of credit, the indebtedness of African states does however have a number of distinguishing characteristics. African sovereign debt is not particularly large when compared to the debt of major debtor states, but it is large when compared to the economic size and potential of African states. As the 1980s have progressed there has been a growing recognition of the seriousness and specificity of Africa's debt problems. This is now recognized in some unlikely quarters.

In April 1987 the British Chancellor of the Exchequer Nigel Lawson devoted part of his speech to the Interim Committee of the International Monetary Fund to the causes of the Third World debt crisis, and gave special attention to Africa's predicament. Lawson recognized that there were particular problems associated with African indebtedness, and accepted that the general process of adjustment as applied to many Third World countries had caused great difficulties in Sub-Saharan Africa (SSA). As a result of this, the British Chancellor argued that a new initiative for Africa should be developed, which would involve three specific proposals. First, aid loans to Africa should be converted into outright grants. Second, Lawson said that, 'we must allow longer repayment periods of up to twenty years when we are rescheduling other official loans to those countries, providing that they themselves are pursuing appropriate domestic policies'. Finally, it was proposed that creditor countries should join together to reduce interest rates on African external debts to below market levels, provided - again - that debtor countries were pursuing an approved set of economic reform policies.[2]

Lawson's initiative, immediately dubbed the 'Lawson Plan' by journalists to draw parallels with the Baker Plan, is one of the few signs of recognition amongst the western capitalist nations of the seriousness of African indebtedness.[3] (The Baker Plan, which was named after US Treasury Secretary James Baker, would direct more finance into the fifteen largest debtor states.) A selective myopia has been much more common. Considerable public attention, and academic interest, has been directed at the major problems of Latin American debtor states, with some of the largest Third World debts.[4] A voluminous literature has emerged which has tended to focus upon those regimes (such as Argentina, Brazil, and Mexico) with very large external debts, and the possible effects upon the international economy if one or more of them default. There has been some consideration of the peculiarity of the United States as a major debtor nation, and of the debt problems of state socialist societies, such as Poland. However, in recent years there has been a growing international awareness that SSA is also suffering from increasingly severe international debt problems, which are exacerbated by Africa's marginal position within the world economy, and the world recession of the 1980s. The Lawson Plan may be as equally ineffective as the Baker Plan, but it is at least a recognition that

The nature of African debt

Africa's external debt problems are of a different character and scale of severity to those found elsewhere in the Third World. These and many other plans to ameliorate Third World debt problems are discussed later.

Africa's international indebtedness has grown dramatically in the period since 1970, and has become a major problem since 1978. Total African external debts were US$6 billion in 1970; the lowest estimate for 1985 would suggest a continental total of US$82 billion.[5] In relation to GDP Africa's debts are the heaviest in the world. While Latin America has a debt level of 58 per cent of GDP in 1985, the equivalent figure for Africa is 62 per cent. There are, however, varying estimates of the contemporary level of African indebtedness. The World Bank figure at just over US$80 billion does not take into account certain elements of short-term and non-official debt. In addition figures are in dispute, and are not just simply the consequence of recording errors, as we shall see in the case studies. Green and Griffith-Jones have estimated that, if short-term and non-official debt plus trade arrears are added, then total African debt for 1984 was some US$125 billion. The Organization of African Unity (OAU) has suggested a higher figure of US$158 billion at the end of 1984.[6] In global terms these are relatively small figures, but in terms of African economies they are of major consequence.

The estimates of the level of African indebtedness have continued to rise. In December 1987 a major conference on African debt was held in Addis Ababa, Ethiopia, under the auspices of the Organization of African Unity (OAU). The OAU conference has provided a number of more detailed and contemporary assessments of indebtedness. It estimated that debt levels rose to US$200 billion by the end of 1986, the equivalent of 45 per cent of the continent's GDP and 293 per cent of its export earnings.[7] Debts were likely to continue to rise, to US$260 billion by the end of the decade, and to over US$600 billion by the year 2000. The latter debt level would involve an average debt servicing ratio of over 70 per cent, where the debt service ratio is defined as the proportion of earnings from the exports of goods and services required to meet external debt obligations.[8]

The OAU conference documents contained many alarming statistics describing the character and serious consequences of the African debt burden. Debt service obligations had continued to rise. They were now (in 1987) over 40 per cent for the continent as a whole, and in the case of states such as the Sudan, the Comoros, and Zambia, they were over 100 per cent of export earnings. Sustaining such levels of debt repayments was well-nigh impossible, especially as African income from commodity exports had slumped, along with levels of external aid and financial investment. Studies by the United Nations have suggested that the net resource transfer to Africa had declined sharply. The net resource transfer was some US$20 billion in 1978, declining to US$3 billion in 1985. There was a net outflow of resources in 1986, at a time, it must be remembered, of growing hardship on the continent.[9]

Such are the general levels of African debt, which rose from US$6 billion in 1970 to over US$80 billion in the mid 1980s; most commentators are now agreed that the total indebtedness of all the OAU states is somewhere in the region of US$200 billion. The debt level will be at US$260 billion at least by 1990 unless there are major initiatives in respect of debt write-offs or forgiveness. African sovereign debt at US$200 billion is comparable to the size of American farm debt. Its size is not much more than most of the major Latin American debtors. Mexico, for example, had a total external debt of US$110 billion in late 1987, indicating the scale of African debts compared to total Third World debts at over a trillion dollars in 1987.[10] Over fifty African states have external debts which are in total only slightly more than seven times the current private consumer debt of British citizens.

In addition to the comparatively small size of African debt, there are a number of other specific characteristics of the African debt situation. Africa's debts are owed primarily to western governments and to the multilateral institutions such as the International Monetary Fund (IMF) and the World Bank. Latin American governments may owe billions to western commercial banks, but very few African states were regarded as good risks by those banks during the spate of commercial lending in the 1970s. Africa has in general had a low international credit rating. In the period since 1978 commercial bank lending to Africa, already low, has been further declining. For example, in 1983 commercial bank lending to Africa was declining at the same time as overall lending to developing countries was increasing, according to the Bank of International Settlements. Famine and economic marginalization across Africa in the 1980s had resulted in less lending, and, correspondingly, a greater reliance upon other sources of credit. In practice the IMF has emerged as a de facto receiver to African governments, rapidly increasing its commitment to Africa since 1978. The majority of African governments now have stabilization programmes agreed with the IMF, and most are seeking - but occasionally reluctantly - to pursue an agreed policy of economic reform or adjustment, a programme which has found its clearest expression in the World Bank's much debated Berg Report (see pp.30-47).

In sum, African states have a relatively low level of external indebtedness when considered in global terms. Neither individually nor collectively do African states hold much 'debtor power' - the capacity to destabilize the international financial system. A collective default by African states would have comparatively little effect, and it would hurt African states more than their creditors due to the likelihood of retaliation. In terms of their domestic economies, indebtedness has produced a number of serious consequences. It has meant shortages of essential imports, declining production, growing hardship amongst the poor, and pressure to deliver a set of economic reform measures. In some regimes - such as Sudan, Tunisia, and Ghana - there have been politically destabilizing riots as a result. External debt has given bodies such as the IMF and World Bank far greater leverage over African governments than was previously the case. The debt crisis of the 1980s has thus raised the issue of political sovereignty as well as that of economic viability for many African states.

After considering the size of African debt, we now turn to a consideration of the origins of African debt. Why have African states become so seriously indebted?

ORIGINS OF AFRICAN DEBT

As with Third World debt as a whole, the origins of African debt lie in a complex inter-relationship of domestic and extra-African external causes. Debt is linked to the growing economic crisis of African states in the 1980s.

It is now widely accepted that the states and peoples of Sub-Saharan Africa are in the midst of an economic crisis of unprecedented magnitude. The economic crisis has rapidly increased SSA's international indebtedness, and has been caused by both short-term and long-term factors. Domestic food production has been declining, and food imports increasing. This has exacerbated the televised disasters of drought and famine. The recession in western countries has led to a decline in the external demand for Africa's primary product exports. Export volumes and values have decreased overall, producing significant fiscal problems for SSA countries. The resulting foreign exchange shortages have meant a decline in gross domestic product (GDP), industrial stoppages, and an inability to replace infrastructure. The crisis has also led to a significant deterioration in the quality of life of the SSA population, a population already deprived by global standards (see Table 1.1). The GDP of the SSA countries has been declining every year since 1980, and income per head in 1983 is estimated to be about 4 per cent below its 1970 level.[11] The recession is likely to have had unequal effects upon Africa's population; it will reflect the already stark inequalities within African societies. Sutcliffe has pointed out that 'no reliable figures are available about changes in income distribution in Africa'. Nevertheless, the poorest sections of African societies are likely to suffer most, and 'given that even the average living standard appears to be declining, that of the more luckless sections of the population must in some cases be falling quite precipitously'.[12]

One of the consequences of this continental, and global, crisis has been the increasing indebtedness of SSA states. From the perspective of the global economy, SSA debts represent a relatively small percentage of total world debt. SSA debt was estimated at approximately 13 per cent of total non-oil developing country debt in 1983, and the continent's total debt was only the equivalent of that of a major Third World debtor nation. The relatively small size of SSA debt, in global terms, is a reflection of Africa's marginal position in the world economy. The second oil shock and recession have marginalized Africa even further, yet made it more indebted.

While SSA debt may be of little significance in global terms, its level is rather more serious from the point of view of the governments and population of SSA. The major problems of increasing international debt and growing difficulty in debt servicing both contribute to, and are part of, the worsening economic crisis in SSA. The 1970s were years of economic stagnation in most of SSA; but the past five years have been 'catastrophic'. Helleiner summarizes the position in this way:

Table 1.1 Development indicators: Africa compared with all developing countries[a]

Country group	Per capita income 1982 (US$)	Adult literacy 1980 (%)	Life expectancy 1982 (years)	Primary-school enrolment ratio female[b] 1981 (%)
Sub-Saharan Africa				
Low-income	249	38	49	57
Middle-income	777	35	50	70
All low-income countries	280	52	59	81
All middle-income countries	1,520	65	60	95

Source: World Bank, World Development Report, 1984, p. 162

a Averages are weighted by 1982 population.
b Number of females enrolled in primary school as a percentage of all females of primary-school age.

> In Sub-Saharan Africa, stagnation or decline over the medium run, and immediate macroeconomic 'crisis' have become the norms. The shocks of 1979-82 have brought the weakest to a state of near collapse and even the strongest into major economic difficulties.[13]

Even countries which have previously received good credit ratings - such as Nigeria and Ivory Coast - are now facing serious problems. SSA has in general had a low international credit rating and, as a result, commercial bank lending has been substantially lower to SSA than to other parts of the Third World, notably Latin America. Commercial bank lending is low across SSA as a whole, though some countries have had large commercial loans, such as Zaire in the early 1970s, and Nigeria. In the period since 1978 commercial bank lending to SSA was declining at the same time as overall lending to developing countries was increasing, according to the Bank of International Settlements.[14] Despite the assistance to African governments provided - for a fee - by international banking firms such as S.G. Warburg and Samuel Montagu, SSA credit worthiness has apparently been increasingly questioned, and commercial banks are withdrawing from an SSA commitment. Ironically, as Sutcliffe has suggested, Africa's 'debt crisis' has taken an unusual form: 'For other countries the "debt crisis" tends to mean that they are too much in debt to the banks. Africa's debt crisis is in a sense the opposite - it has been unable to get into debt.'[15]

In such circumstances, with growing balance of payments difficulties, it is not surprising that SSA governments have increasingly sought assistance from major public international institutions, especially the World Bank and the IMF. Robert Wood has argued that 'perhaps the most visible and publicized political consequence of the debt crisis has been the increased role of the International Monetary Fund', along with its sister institution, the World Bank.[16]

THE IMF AND AFRICA

The IMF has rapidly increased its commitment to Africa since 1978. African use of IMF funds totalled US$400 million in 1979; by 1981 African borrowing had increased to US$1.6 billion. In 1982, the figure fell slightly to US$1.2 billion, but increased again in 1983 to US$1.4 billion.[17]

Table 1.2 African countries with IMF programmes

Country	Amount (SDR million)	Expiry date
CAR	15.00	9 July 1985
Gambia	12.83	22 July 1985
Ghana	180.00	31 December 1985
Ivory Coast	82.75	21 August 1985
Kenya	425.00	20 September 1984[a]
Liberia	55.00	13 September 1984[a]
Madagascar	33.00	31 March 1985
Malawi	100.00	18 September 1986
Mali	40.50	31 May 1985
Mauritius	49.50	17 August 1984[a]
Niger	18.00	4 December 1984
Senegal	63.00	18 September 1984
Sierra Leone	50.20	2 February 1985
Sudan	90.00	25 June 1985
Togo	19.00	6 May 1985
Uganda	95.00	15 September 1984[a]
Zaire	228.00	26 March 1985
Zambia	225.00	30 April 1986
Zimbabwe	300.00	22 September 1986[b]

Source: Africa Economic Digest (7 September 1984), p.6

a New arrangement under negotiation.
b Suspended, under negotiation

Such a commitment has given the IMF great leverage in SSA, as the Fund has become stricter in its loan conditions since the early 1980s. IMF contacts with African governments have become much more extensive since 1978. In 1978 the IMF signed two new conditional credit agreements with African governments; by 1981 the number of agreements had increased to twenty-one. The majority of African governments now have stabilization programmes agreed with the IMF, or are in the process of negotiation (see Table 1.2). The increase in scale of IMF commitment to Africa was such that by 1981-2 it took back more in total repayments than it had actually lent in 1978-9.[18] As IMF agreements are predominantly short-term balance of payments support, requiring repurchase within three years, this was inevitable. In view of the short-term maturity structure of recent IMF loans and the non-concessional interest rate, it has been calculated that repayments to the Fund will continue to average US$1.4 billion per year in 1985-7,[19] at a time, it may be recalled, of growing economic crisis and deprivation on the continent.

In making these general observations about the origins and consequences of African external indebtedness, it must be remembered that the causes and effects of the debt crisis have been variant across the continent. We have already noted that African states exhibit wide political, economic, and social differences. The causes and effects of external indebtedness in each country will be mediated through these variable factors. In subsequent chapters we hope to contribute to an understanding of the African debt crisis by examining the domestic origins and consequences of debt in several differing African states. In analysing the various ways that debt has manifested itself we shall focus on the following questions: How did each country get into debt? How indebted are they, on what terms, and to whom? What are the political consequences of their indebtedness, both at the international and the local levels? What have been the consequences of external interventions such as those of the IMF? We shall initially turn to a general consideration of the latter question in the next chapter, before embarking on our case studies of debt at the national level.

Table 1.3 Trends in policy and institutional reform amongst African countries

10	countries have decontrolled producer prices
20	countries have frozen hiring or reduced public sector employment
13	countries have eliminated public agricultural marketing agencies or permitted private sector competition
7	countries have turned over import of agricultural inputs to the private sector
14	countries have privatized some state enterprises
21	countries have substantially increased producer prices
14	countries have reduced or eliminated agricultural input subsidies
8	countries have reduced or eliminated food subsidies
16	countries have realigned exchange rates to reflect more closely the real cost of foreign exchange
7	of the 16 countries above have adopted floating market rates

Source: West Africa (30 March 1987), p.645

Figure 1.1 Debt service ratio. Service on medium and long-term public/private debt as % of exports of goods and services

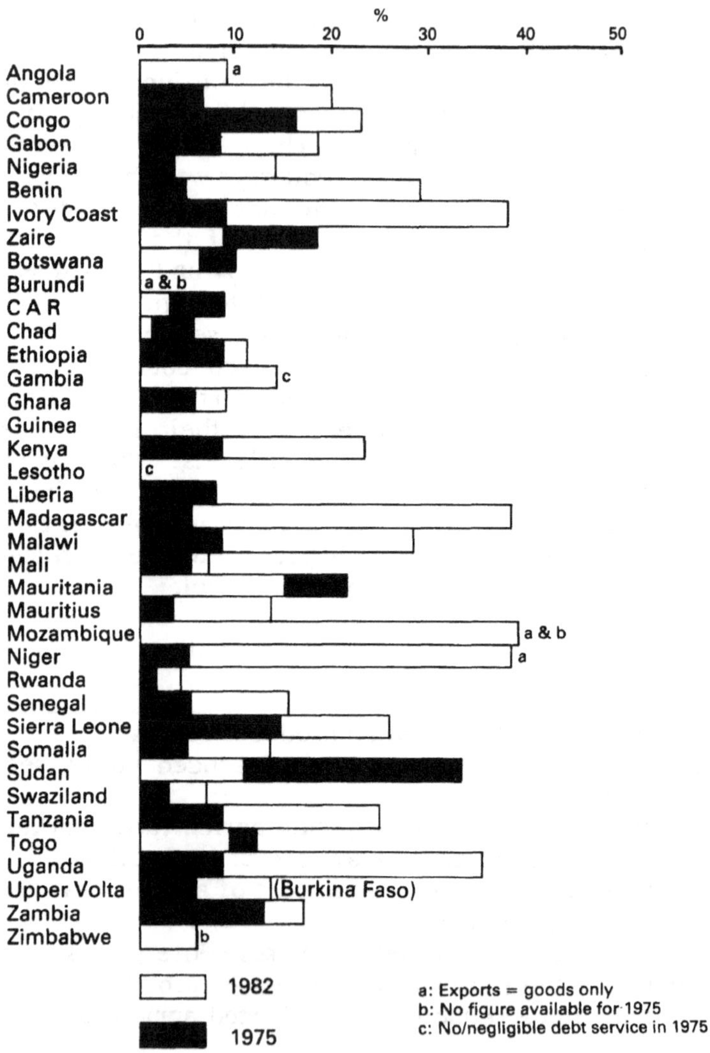

Source: Africa Economic Digest (7 September, 1984), p.11

Figure 1.2 Medium and long-term public and private debt (disbursed)

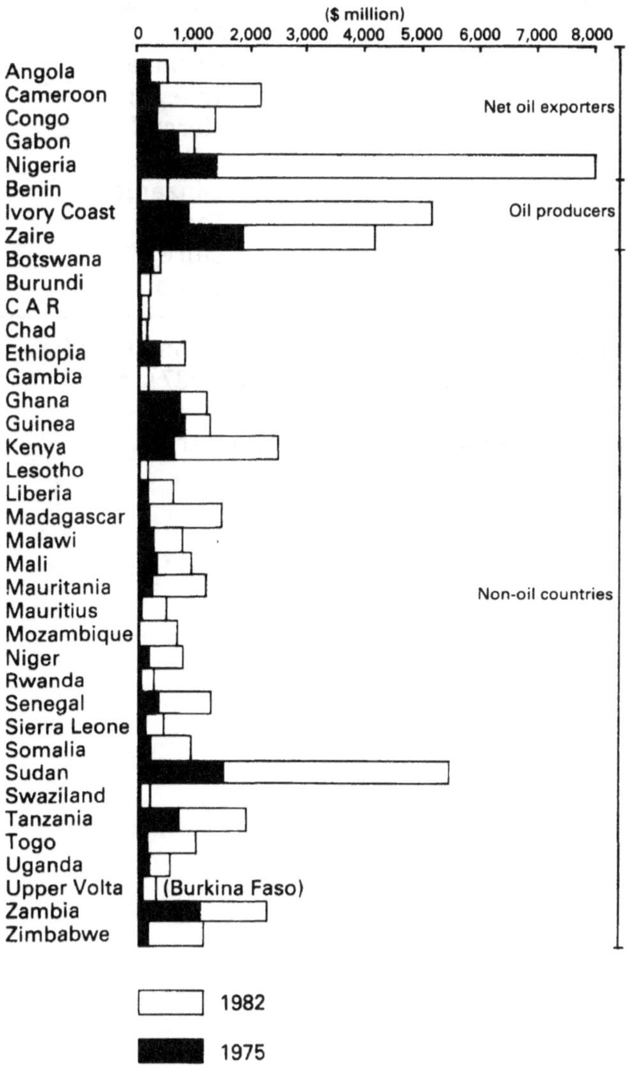

Source: Africa Economic Digest (7 September, 1984), p.11

Table 1.4 African countries[a] with major structural reform programmes planned or underway as of March 1987

Burundi	Mali
Central African Republic	Mauritania
Chad	Niger
Equatorial Guinea	Rwanda
The Gambia	Senegal
Ghana	Sierra Leone
Guinea	Somalia
Guinea Bissau	Tanzania
Kenya	Togo
Madagascar	Zaire
Malawi	Zambia

Source: Overseas Development Council, 'Should the IMF withdraw from Africa?', Policy Focus, 1, (1987), p.6.

a IDA - eligible sub-Saharan African Countries.

2

The politics of external policy direction

Throughout the post-colonial period numerous commentators, including prominent leaders such as Nkrumah and Nyerere, have bemoaned the illusory nature of flag independence in SSA. They have pointed to the economic linkages between imperial metropoles and their ex-colonies, which continue to bind the new states to their former colonial masters. Moreover, they have argued that these ties maintain African subordination to the metropolitan states and render the new states particularly vulnerable to the political influence of the imperialist nations. According to such arguments the debt crisis has served to increase African vulnerability to external policy direction by the metropolitan states and such institutions as the IMF and the World Bank. In this chapter we shall examine the external pressures for policy direction produced by growing indebtedness, paying particular attention to the central role played by the Fund and the Bank in pressing market-orientated policies on often unwilling African governments.

The inadequate flows of private commercial capital to Africa have emphasized the importance of both the IMF and the Bank. However, the Fund in particular has become more than a lender of the last resort. The general weakness of African economies, particularly their disastrous performance since the second oil shock has given the IMF a central role as a _de facto_ receiver to African governments. The IMF can act as a sovereign body and impose mandatory conditions on its members. Africa's weak economic performance has enabled the IMF to act in this manner relatively unchallenged and when African governments are unable or unwilling to comply, support can be suspended.

This can have far-reaching effects, given the propensity of other sources of funding for insisting that potential borrowers must have satisfactorily observed an IMF austerity programme. A typical example is the Paris Club of official government creditors, which has attained considerable influence as the debt crisis has worn on. This organization which is essentially of OECD states, was set up in 1956, and is the central source of debt rescheduling for African states. The World Bank notes:

> The Paris Club requires that debtor countries take prompt and effective measures to address their underlying economic problems; an IMF-supported adjustment programme that will give a country access to the upper credit tranches is, typically, a prerequisite to a Paris Club agreement.[1]

Thus, a loss of IMF support may well imply a loss of support from the Paris Club and most of the major aid donors. Indeed, the IMF's emerging central role in African macroeconomic management has been helped by its ability to endanger or delay other official forms of credit to those African governments it is in dispute with. As ex-President Nyerere of Tanzania has expressed it:

> The IMF has an ideology of political and social development which it is trying to impose on poor countries irrespective of their own clearly stated policies. And when we reject IMF conditions we hear the threatening whisper: 'Without accepting our conditions you will not get any money, and you will get no other money'.[2]

It has been suggested that the IMF and the World Bank act apparently in concert, sharing technical judgements and personnel in the same way that they once shared the same office building in Washington.[3] Helleiner has argued that the IMF can also have considerable influence over bilateral aid donors.[4] Given the small, and decreasing, level of commercial lending to SSA and in view of its increasing influence over multilateral and bilateral aid donors, the IMF's central position is substantially enhanced.

IMPERIALISM OR REFORM?

What, then, is the nature of the conditionality that the IMF is imposing on SSA? As we have seen, Nyerere argues that it represents a particular 'ideology of political and social development'. His Planning Minister, Kighoma Malima went further in claiming that:

> As a condition for assistance, a developing country is often required to scrap public enterprises and hand them over to the private sector; to abandon price controls, agricultural subsidies, free medical and other social services; to take these things away from a population which everyone agrees is already too deprived. The political and ideological slant of such conditionality is beyond doubt.[5]

The thesis that the IMF promulgates a specifically capitalist and inegalitarian mode of development has been most fully explicated by Cheryl Payer.[6] The main burden of Payer's argument is that IMF conditionality is designed to open up recipient nations' economies to international capital, largely at the expense of the workers and peasants in those countries. She notes that IMF insistence on the abolition or liberalization of exchange and import controls serves to enforce free trading on recipients, often at the expense of domestic industries that had relied on protection. Furthermore, deflationary policies serve the purpose of reducing inflation, thus creating a stable business climate, but only at the cost of declining wages and living standards for ordinary people. This unfortunately combines with another IMF condition, that of devaluation, which raises the cost of essential imports at a time when wages are falling. The final element of IMF conditionality is an insistence upon greater hospitality to foreign investment, which simply reinforces other conditions designed to open up the economy. As we have seen, the overall effect of these packages is to destabilize the recipient nations as the populace rebels against the combination of rising prices and declining wages and public services. In this context one may recall the anti-IMF riots in Sudan after the abolition of the bread subsidy and the unrest that developed in Tunisia and Morocco in the wake of IMF programmes involving the removal of food subsidies.[7] This critical view of the IMF has been reiterated by numerous left-wing commentators. A typical example is EA Brett, who has asserted that:

> Although the IMF always presents its policies as non-political, and based entirely on scientific economic

> theory, there can be no doubt that their recommendations correspond to the policies favoured by large-scale international capital and its supporters in Third World countries.[8]

Thus it is implied that the Fund is at the head of a capitalist conspiracy for the economic domination of Africa.

Naturally, there are alternative analyses, not least that put forward by the Fund's own officials. Zulu and Nsouli, both employees of the IMF, have argued that the stabilization programmes applied in SSA during 1980-1 were designed 'to promote economic growth, to reduce inflation, and to improve the current account position of the balance of payments over the medium term'. According to Zulu and Nsouli measures to phase out or streamline public enterprises were necessary on grounds of efficiency, whilst 'reduction in the scope of price controls and subsidies' was designed to promote growth in the private sector. Deflationary measures, such as wage restraints, restrictions on public expenditure and closer scrutiny of new government hiring, were essential to restore financial stability. Substantial devaluations of the exchange rate were often recommended because an over-valued currency 'generates cost-price distortions that have a negative effect on consumption and investment as well as on the trade balance, as it tends to reduce the profitability of export-orientated and import-competing activities in the country'.[9]

Indeed, there seems to be a high degree of donor consensus that such market-orientated policies represent the cure for SSA's multi-faceted crisis. The document that has probably been most influential in creating this consensus is the 1981 World Bank report, Accelerated Development in Sub-Saharan Africa (the Berg Report). The Report attributes Africa's growing indebtedness and declining economic growth in large part to three critical domestic policy inadequacies.

> First, trade and exchange rate policies have over-protected industry, held back agriculture, and absorbed much administrative capacity. Second, too little attention has been paid to administrative constraints in mobilizing and managing resources for development; given the widespread weakness of planning, decision-making, and management capacities, public sectors frequently became over-extended. Third, there has been

> a consistent bias against agriculture in price, tax, and exchange rate policies.[10]

Thus, Africa's desperate economic situation is attributed to the growth of a large public sector that swallows resources and uses them inefficiently; the use of trade controls that are supposed to protect industry, but which are costly to apply (and often ineffective); and the widespread practice of overvaluing the exchange rate. This is a disincentive to farmers, who 'obtain less in their local currencies for their export crops, while the price of food imports is reduced'.[11] Given this analysis it is hardly surprising that the Berg Report's policy recommendations to achieve growth include less use of trade controls and other protective practices, tighter control over public expenditure with a view to leaving more room for private capital, and devaluation to give farmers a greater incentive to produce for the local market and for export. The similarity of this package to the typical IMF programme is striking. Certainly, the Berg Report also recommended a strategy for agricultural growth, involving better price incentives, improvement of infrastructure, research and better pest control. However, the temptation to regard the Berg strategy as a derivation from the typical IMF stabilization package remains strong.

Notwithstanding this, many donors and analysts, including those of the left such as Sender and Smith, have endorsed many or all of the Berg Report's policy analyses and prescriptions. Sender and Smith berate analysts such as Colclough for criticizing the Berg recommendations by comparing them with IMF conditionality, insisting that much of the left condemn the Fund as a bogey without giving sufficient reason for such disapprobation. This is to ignore Payer's thesis which gives considerable reason for condemning the IMF as a bogey. However, Sender and Smith also put forward important arguments in favour of the Berg/IMF prescriptions. We shall proceed with an analysis of the various debates centring on the strategy propounded by the Fund and the Bank.

ROLLING BACK THE STATE?

Sender and Smith concur with many of the arguments put forward in the Berg Report for a reduction of the public sector. Suggestions that the state plays an important role in redistributing income are dismissed by reference to evidence demonstrating that Tanzania, a socialist state, has been inegalitarian in its distribution of social services such as health and education, concentrating on the urban population at the expense of the rural sector.[12] Numerous analysts have commented on the pattern of urban bias in state spending that seems to be prevalent across much of SSA, a pattern that seems likely to persist so long as African state mechanisms are dominated by largely urban-based elites and are fearful of growing potentially restive urban populations. Bates has assembled considerable evidence to show that numerous African governments have intervened in the rural sector to keep the prices of agricultural commodities low for a variety of reasons. One of their central concerns has been to maintain a supply of cheap food for the urban populace in order to prevent potential unrest and to stave off wage demands from employees in the industrial sector. It should be noted that the state itself has a direct interest in keeping wage demands low as a major urban employer. Another explanation for low agricultural prices is to be found in the attempts of many states to boost their own resources by levying an indirect tax on agrarian produce. Bates cites many examples of African governments using the monopsonies held by parastatals to compel farmers to accept low producer prices for commodities that have been sold on the world market at a profit. They have appropriated this profit in order to finance development (usually in the industrial sector), or to lubricate the governing elite's network of patrimonial power.

Farmers have tended to respond to such policies by reducing their participation in the official market and selling increasing proportions of their produce in the parallel market.[13] This, together with the tendency to overvalue the exchange rate, has led many states to become increasingly dependent on food imports to satisfy urban demand. Thus, state intervention can be seen not only as inegalitarian and biased towards the urban areas, but also as actively detrimental to the rural sector. In this context, conditionality, designed to trim an overmanned and often inefficient or corrupt public sector, appears quite desirable since it might conserve resources that are currently being wasted on perquisites for the elite, or on subsidies to provide cheap food for the urban populace. It will also limit the ability of the state to intervene harmfully in the agrarian sector.

However, Bienefield has criticized Bates, arguing that investments in public goods such as education, health, and infrastructure will bear fruit only in largely non-quantifiable forms over the long term. Consequently, such investments are unlikely to be made if development is dictated solely by the logic of the market. For Bienefield this suggests that state intervention to provide such investments is necessary and that some (though not excessive) taxation of agriculture to finance them is desirable.[14] Indeed, there is evidence to show that many African states succeed in producing some level of public policy output (albeit minimal in many cases) which reaches the rural as well as the urban areas.

Some states have made a deliberate attempt to deliver educational and health services to the rural areas. Both Mozambique's Frelimo regime and the Mugabe government of Zimbabwe have tried to counteract patterns of urban bias in the distribution of social services that were caused by the white supremacist policies of their predecessors.[15] Public sector retrenchment can do real harm in such countries. Davies and Saunders have compiled considerable evidence to show that stabilization measures have had a marked and adverse effect on child health in Zimbabwe. They note that a 1982 agreement with the IMF resulted in a wage freeze, substantial food price rises and cutbacks in health expenditure. In that year the Ministry of Health found that out of a sample of 1,776 children between the ages of 0 and 3 the proportion of underweight children in the rural areas was 18-22 per cent. A survey of July 1984 showed that 48 per cent of children between 12 and 59 months of age were underweight. Despite the differences between the two samples Davies and Saunders conclude that the rise in the proportion of undernourished children is so sharp that it reflects a real deterioration in child nourishment between 1982-4, a development that they feel to be related to declining real incomes brought about by the stabilization measures of those years.[16] Clearly, indiscriminate public sector cuts can have adverse effects on those states that have set out to improve conditions in the rural areas.

Even in countries that have a reputation for patrimonial diversion of resources there are indications that public sector retrenchment can have harmful effects. This is the case in Zambia, a state which Bates identifies as particularly unsympathetic to the rural sector due to the fact that its nationalist movement was dominated by industrial workers. Chambers has argued that even though the effects of recurrent budget cuts are often unseen they can be gauged with reference to the following example from the Zambia Basic Needs Report:

> A woman who lives 15km from the nearest health centre has a sick child. The difficulties of travel are such that her decision whether to take the child to the health centre is in the balance. If she hears that the centre is short of drugs and occasionally out of them altogether, she may not risk a fruitless journey. The child may then suffer avoidably, or die. If, on the other hand, she knows that the health centre is always adequately stocked, and all comers are in consequence treated, she may decide to go. The child may then suffer less, and live. It is innumerable, individual, unseen ways like this that the benefits of adequate recurrent allocations reach the poorer, weaker and more remote people (sic). Those who make the allocations can never know the wide ramifications of their decisions: but imagination can suggest the costs and benefits of those decisions to those who are unseen.[17]

In fact imagination can be complemented by the findings of Mutemba, who has revealed that over the period since 1973, when the IMF began its interventions, the Zambian diet has deteriorated in response to the country's economic decline. This has led to a higher incidence of ailments such as anaemia, malnutrition, malaria, and diarrhoea.[18]

Cuts may not only have unintended adverse effects on African people. It must be remembered that the IMF usually sets only macro-economic targets for operating, which recipient governments are supposed to observe. It does not generally specify where cuts must be made. This leaves patrimonial governments with the option of safeguarding those areas of the economy that finance their clientelist power networks at the expense of more efficient and essential services. Our case study of Zaire shows that Mobutu Sese Seko's corrupt government has used precisely this tactic to minimize cuts in the sectors from which he and his cronies draw their 'informal' income. Thus, Mobutu fought hard to protect the corrupt parastatal sector from IMF cuts, but was quite willing to pare the already underfunded health and educational services down to the point where they were robbed of any minimal efficacy. All this suggests that IMF spending cuts may not lead to an efficient exercise in trimming fat from the body politic, but to destructive amputations. Clearly, if donors wish to stipulate public expenditure cuts as a condition for aid, they should try to ensure that such cuts do not adversely affect public policy output either by accident, or by the design of unscrupulous leaders.

Another question mark over public sector retrenchment policies concerns how the space left by the retreat of the state and the parastatals will be filled. The Berg Report suggests that the private sector might take over some of the functions previously reserved for the public sector. In particular, it is argued that the marketing functions of agricultural parastatals could be privatized in order to break the state monopoly, which pays farmers low producer prices. Whilst acknowledging that private traders have proved exploitative in the past, the report argues that the only way to raise producer prices is to encourage competition between buyers in the private sector. However, this assumes that there will be entrepreneurs in a position to move into marketing and, as the Overseas Development Institute points out, this is not the case in every African country.[19] Schatz has argued that even in those states which have a considerable business sector, entrepreneurial effectiveness is severely limited by shortcomings in education, skills, training, experience, and so forth. Additionally, they have to contend with irregular supplies of inputs, inadequate infrastructure and inexperienced staff. For Schatz there are major factors in the failure of African entrepreneurs to provide a major developmental impetus.[20] This would seem to suggest that even where there may be entrepreneurs to take over the role of the parastatals they are unlikely to be paragons of market efficiency. It appears that a number of unfortunate scenarios could well result from privatization. Where there is an absence of entrepreneurial talent it might simply create a vacuum, or a private monopoly might develop in which exploitation will continue, but with the profits flowing into private hands rather than state coffers. Even where there is competition the effects of this on producer prices may not be as spectacular as some commentators seem to hope, given the infrastructural and other difficulties that stand in the way of profitable operation.

Evidently the Bank has recognized some of these problems, noting that policy reforms will be successful only 'if pursued in the context of more comprehensive policy packages'. Schatz summarizes these as follows:

> The Bank specifically mentions the need for such major and difficult programmes as the development of a more effective system to provide inputs to agriculture; the daunting task of reforming the marketing system; the expensive undertaking of improving transport, usually the most costly part of any economic plan; and other measures which might induce a quick supply response to price incentives.[21]

Such pronouncements go some way towards recognizing the problems identified by Bienefield and indicate that even market-orientated policies require a substantial level of state intervention. However, as the Bank makes such theoretical recommendations for public investment, the Fund, abetted by the Bank's practice, has continued to force policies of retrenchment on Third World governments.

It is also worth pointing out that although Sender and Smith agree with the Berg Report's criticism of inefficient public sector activities (e.g. excessive taxation of imports, inflationary monetary policy and urban bias) they are certainly not thoroughgoing exponents of laissez-faireism. A central element of their thesis is that 'the state in late-industrializing countries must intervene to co-ordinate an import-substituting industrialization strategy'.[22] They assert that 'World Bank analyses of the determinants of success or failure in Sub-Saharan Africa, which suggest that "undistorted" market forces have been a sine qua non of economic success, are incoherent and historically inaccurate, given that state initiatives have been crucial in all accumulation processes, not only throughout post-independence Africa, but also everywhere else'.[23] Development for Sender and Smith depends on achieving 'appropriate balances between major macro-economic variables: between foreign exchange requirements and foreign exchange availability; between the rate of growth of total real wages and the availability of wage goods; and between public sector investment and non-inflationary means of financing such investment'.[24] Not only must the government make public sector initiatives, it must also play a role in ensuring the availability of wage and incentive goods. Clearly, Sender and Smith go some way beyond the Bank's views on the role of state intervention. Whereas the

Bank sees the state essentially as a means of filling infrastructural and other gaps left by the market, Sender and Smith see its proper role as involving direct intervention in the market.

The problems that are likely to beset either of these alternatives lie in the patrimonial nature of the African state, which results in governments having to allocate resources in accordance with such considerations as 'ethnic arithmetic' rather than economic efficiency. Charney has provided an interesting synthesis of clientelist and Marxist literature on the nature of the state, which throws some light on the subject. According to Charney, 'lineage-type' discourses are the hegemonic device used by transnational capital (the hegemonic class) and the indigenous petty-bourgeoisie (the reigning class) to maintain control over subordinated classes in Third World states. Such states cannot rely on an unadulterated capitalist hegemony since commodity relations are not universal. In the west, the predominance of commodity relations disguises the exploitation of wage labour as a transaction between equals, with wages and profits being seen as determined by the impartial and impersonal forces of the market. In this context the state is legitimated as 'impersonal, neutral, and above the fray'. Consequently, it is able to purvey an ideology of popular nationalism, which helps to keep class struggle under control. By contrast, commodity production is far from universal in Africa and:

> A large proportion of reproduction takes place within domestic, or lineage relations, rather than through commodity sales. Furthermore, much of production is organized around personal relations of direct dependence between peasant, or worker and chief, merchant, marabout, or bureaucrat, rather than through an impersonal market.[25]

Therefore, state hegemony must be based on the use of lineage relations and effected through clientelism. Whilst this serves to secure the compliance of the subordinate classes it also leads to economic inefficiency as seen above. This analysis suggests a severe contradiction for capitalist development in Africa, since it means that patrimonialism is on the one hand an essential source of social control, whilst on the other hand it is a major obstacle to the adoption of capitalist economic rationality.

Indeed, the debt crisis has severely exacerbated this contradiction, bringing several states to the point of a social breakdown. It is a firmly established tenet of the clientelist literature that neopatrimonial relationships will become difficult to maintain if patrons run short of resources to distribute to their followers, or begin to make unbearably heavy exactions on them. It may be argued that IMF public sector cuts have induced just such a crisis in many states. As we have seen, the abolition of food subsidies has been the trigger for riots in Tunisia, Sudan, and Morocco. One of the most recent (and one of the most serious) of such crises occurred in Zambia when the withdrawal of the maize subsidy on 5 December 1986, followed by a concomitant doubling of the maize meal price, led to severe riots throughout the Copperbelt. Apparently, disturbances involving over 10,000 people began on 9 December forcing President Kaunda to impose a dawn-to-dusk curfew on all Copperbelt towns and to dispatch troops to contain the rioting.[26] Such was the severity of the crisis that he felt obliged to restore the subsidy, a measure that involved costs in excess of US$42 million. The Fund responded unsympathetically to Kaunda's difficulties, presenting him with a set of macro-economic objectives that took no account of the restoration of the subsidy. According to one Washington source the IMF refused to acknowledge that Zambian inability to fall in line with their strictures might be 'a question of political feasibility'.[27] Finally, Kaunda broke with the IMF largely due to its insistence that Zambia should follow its policies of economic rationalization irrespective of any political damage they might cause. In the face of IMF intransigence and the consequent threat to his government's stability from the urban populace Kaunda was forced to revert to the clientelist policies so objectionable to the Fund and to restore the food subsidy.

It can be seen that the policies of public sector retrenchment and laissez-faireism currently favoured by many Western analysts carry with them a number of severe problems for Africa's debtor states. Certainly, public sector cuts have some potential for improving state efficiency and saving resources that would otherwise be wasted. However, the IMF practice of setting macro-economic targets can allow ruling elites to allocate cuts in accordance with their patrimonial interests rather than economic efficiency (as in Zaire). Furthermore, there is some evidence to suggest that most African states produce some level of public policy output, however minimal it may be. It would seem that the imprint of clientelism is variable from one state to the next. Some states, such as Zaire, are characterized by extreme waste, corruption, and a concomitantly low output of social services, whilst others, such as Mozambique, are relatively untouched by clientelist patterns of waste and have an impressive record in producing such services. Most states lie between these two extremes and manage to produce some services despite their variable levels of clientelism. The mechanistic application of public sector cuts to all these states takes little or no cognizance of the differences between them and, in many cases, results in the reduction of productive services that benefit ordinary Africans. Clearly, rolling back the state is an inexact way of attempting to curtail the waste of resources associated with patrimonial politics. There is no guarantee that it will eliminate clientelism and, in many instances, it severely reduces living standards for workers and peasants. In fact, history suggests that some level of state intervention is necessary to ensure the success of any development strategy. This indicates that Africa's recovery from its present crisis is more likely to be contingent on reforming the state than on enforcing laissez-faireism. Such a reform would have to involve ending the clientelist patterns of government that obstruct a more rational allocation of resources. To revert to Charney's Marxian terminology, the patrimonial state hegemony of the governing elites must be broken. We shall be arguing that this goal can be attained only by a widening of political accountability to the general populace rather than to selected clientelist groups. It might well be argued that IMF austerity programmes are more likely to hinder progress to such reform than assist it, given that they tend to engender fierce political pressure from the urban populace on the state to reverse the policies that have eroded their standard of living and to restore clientelist, urban-biased measures such as food subsidies (e.g. Zambia).

SOME MARKETS ARE FREER THAN OTHERS

Having dealt with the IMF/Berg proposal on public sector retrenchment we may now turn to an interrelated set of proposals for devaluation and increased primary commodity exports. The Berg Report expresses concern that other developing regions had managed to increase their exports, while Africa's had fallen. Consequently, the report recommends that 'Africa's share of world trade in most commodities could be increased with relatively small effects on prices'.[28] Sender and Smith concur with this view, premising their recommendation of an import-substitution strategy on the need to expand primary commodity exports. They dismiss the argument that demand elasticities for many such commodities are so low that a rise in African exports would lower the world price, arguing that:

> Even if Africa's market share was 50 per cent, one would have to assume a price elasticity of demand with respect to exports of less than 0.5, if one wishes to argue that an increase in volume of Africa's exports would lead to a reduction in Africa's export earnings.[29]

Further support for their contention is gained by quoting Godfrey to the effect that only two commodities, coffee and cocoa, have large enough market shares combined with low enough price elasticities (-0.24 and -0.3 respectively) to bring this about.[30] However, it might also be argued that African producers could have difficulty with groundnut oil and sisal, both of which are likely to have low elasticities due to SSA's high share of the world market, and with beef and bananas, commodities over which SSA faces overwhelming competition from the EEC and Latin America (or, rather, the corporations, like United Brands, which dominate Latin America) respectively.

This is not to deny the central point made by the Berg Report, and Sender and Smith tht SSA could put more effort into boosting its exports, for it is undoubtedly true that Africa has been losing markets over the last decade. In a reappraisal of the report named after him Berg argues that:

> Not all countries will follow counsel to expand primary exports. So those that do will capture the market of those that do not, regardless of their respective comparative advantages. Given this reality, those who stand on the sidelines and urge African states to shun the export sector are in fact handing over market shares to Brazil or Malaysia or Indonesia.

Berg goes on to add that, 'It may not be very rewarding to expand primary product exports in the face of gloomy predictions about future market conditions, but there may be no better option now at hand.'[31] These are compelling arguments. However, where possible, African states should try to identify commodities with a high enough elasticity to maintain prices at a level where increased exports will be rewarded with increased receipts. Gulhati et al. cite unpublished studies by World Bank staff identifying a number of opportunities for diversification in countries such as Zambia, Malawi, and Madagascar. Thus, they suggest that Malawi diversify into rubber, wheat, cashew nuts, and coffee, as well as rehabilitating traditional exports such as tobacco, cotton, and groundnuts; Zambia should move into beef, coffee, tobacco, and groundnuts; Madagascar should rehabilitate coffee, vanilla, and cocoa, whilst moving into coconut, cashew, nutmeg, etc. Clearly, there are opportunities for diversification and expansion of exports.[32] Nevertheless, African states would be well advised to heed Loxley's advice that they should 'check out the kind of advice the Bank is giving to primary producers elsewhere in the world' before deciding to boost any particular commodity, because IDA and World Bank advice led to overproduction of tea and tobacco and a consequent fall in prices.[33] Indeed, we may note that it advised Malawi, Madagascar, and Zambia to adopt several products identified as having, or likely to have, low elasticities, such as coffee, cocoa, and beef.

A related IMF-Berg proposal is devaluation of the exchange rate with a view to improving a country's competitiveness, both in its domestic and export markets. Such a measure should also save foreign exchange by making it more expensive. A number of analysts have denied the beneficial effects of devaluation, arguing that it is more likely to spark a stagflationary downward spiral than to improve Africa's competitiveness. Certainly, there is evidence to suggest that many of the devaluations imposed by the IMF in SSA have resulted in inflation. In the Zairean case a 77.5 per cent devaluation agreed in December 1983 resulted in the doubling or tripling of prices for essential items such as fuel and staple foods. The Sierra Leonean case is also revealing, with the flotation of the leone in July 1986 resulting in hyperinflation of more than 300 per cent. This led to a severe shortage of petroleum products and substantial rises in the prices of local foods that have to be transported from the countryside. Most notably, the price of rice, the staple food, quickly rose beyond the reach of the average Sierra Leonean. Clearly, such developments do not give any kind of incentive to domestic agriculture, or industry. Additional evidence comes from Sudan, revealing that successive IMF-dictated devaluations caused declines in output, because of shortages of necessary imported inputs, and that inflationary pressures were increased.[34] Clearly, there is considerable evidence to the effect that devaluations in several African countries have led to substantial domestic price inflation and to declining agricultural and industrial output.

Colclough points out that if devaluation is to be effective in changing the relativity between import prices and the prices of domestic produce in such a way that the latter are given an incentive, then domestic prices must not adjust upwards to the extent that they fully counteract the devaluation. It would seem that most African countries are unable to meet this requirement and Colclough notes many cases in which inflation 'has more than negated the effects of devaluation'. In the cases of Kenya and Mauritius, inflation has apparently been caused by employers using devaluation as an opportunity to raise prices and maximize their profits, while the self-employed, including agricultural producers, gained little or no benefit and wage earners had to bear the main burden.[35] There is evidence of a similar pattern of events in Sierra Leone, where it was felt that the Lebanese-dominated commercial stratum was hoarding goods in order to force up the prices.

Gulhati et al. argue that devaluation can be accomplished without sparking off massive inflation by combining it with a policy of budgetary restraint. They also point out that devaluation will increase the local currency value of import and export tax receipts and financial aid. Although they are undoubtedly right in identifying the latter benefit the other suggestions are of dubious value. The increment to import and export taxes will be offset by the IMF and World Bank preference for free trade, which leads them to press governments for the elimination or reduction of their trade barriers. It may also be remembered that any IMF stabilization programme will combine devaluation with reductions in government spending. Despite this, many African countries have suffered high rates of inflation on implementing the Fund's recommendations for devaluation and public sector retrenchment. Part of the explanation for this is to be found in the structural factors underlying inflation. Gulhati et al. note that government spending incorporates an import component that can be quite high. They found that in their sample of nine countries the median share of imports in government spending was 24 per cent.[36] The local currency value of such expenditure, together with that of external debt will be increased by devaluation, thus boosting inflation. Moreover, much of agriculture and industry is dependent on imported inputs such as petroleum, machinery, tools, and fertilizers. Devaluation will raise the cost of these imports to local producers, who will consequently tend to raise their prices rather than take a substantial profit cut. Clearly, there are strong imperatives towards inflation.

Gulhati et al. are aware that 'devaluation and related policy reforms under conditions of overall economic decline will impose a heavy strain on the political leadership'. They conclude:

> It is of the utmost importance, under these circumstances, to inject additional external resources into the economy and thereby reduce the interval between the introduction of the reform and the arrival of the social dividend which all groups can share.[37]

Certainly, increased aid and private investment would enable the government and private business to maintain spending and production without passing on the cost to the consumer, thus containing inflation. As we have seen, this need for external resources is far from being fulfilled. Private capital is in full retreat from Africa whilst aid inflows are insufficient to compensate for the costs of debt servicing. Obviously, there is a desperate need for an increased input of resources into SSA.

Even if devaluation is accomplished in such a way that inflation does not raise domestic prices to an uncompetitive level there is still no guarantee of rising agricultural production. Schatz has argued that aggregate farm production shows only limited responsiveness to price increases. He cites Bond's study, which 'shows a median short-run elasticity for nine countries of 0.13'. The long-run elasticity would be little better with a mean of 0.21 and a median of 0.15. Schatz concludes that increased agrarian output of 5 per cent over a period of a year would require a doubling of agricultural prices. In assessing the ramifications of this conclusion it is worth remembering that price rises for a single crop can be effective in raising production primarily because farmers will shift resources from other crops.[38] This suggests that a possible viable option might be specialization in production of a staple food or an export crop. Sender and Smith also point out that getting the prices right will not suffice to improve production in the absence of adequate infrastructure and inputs such as tools, fertilizer, and storage construction materials. They also point to the constraints on production caused by labour shortages attributable to flight to the city and the demands of alternative employment. Possible solutions to these problems include attempting to improve the attractiveness of agriculture compared with competing activities and wider provision of the social services that often attract the rural populace to the towns.[39]

It would seem from our analysis thus far that it is feasible for African states to attempt to boost their exports, with the proviso that they will be best rewarded by focusing on products with relatively high price elasticities. A policy of boosting production by 'getting the prices right' through devaluation will show results only if financial transfers to SSA are enhanced in order to counteract stagflationary tendencies.

However, there are still a number of important structural factors to consider. It must be remembered that the success of Third World exports is dependent on the buoyancy of the market for them in the developed states, which is in turn largely dependent on the rate of growth in those nations. Lever and Huhne point out that many authoritative commentators seem to be agreed that a minimum growth rate of some 3 per cent is needed to maintain sufficiently healthy northern markets for the Third World to be able to finance its debt repayments.[40] In fact, as Schatz points out, northern growth rates between 1980-5 were only 2-3 per cent.[41] The World Bank has summed up the situation as follows:

> The pace of growth in the developed world is too slow to stimulate rapid expansion of developing countries' exports or bring about a reversal of the long decline in commodity prices that is needed for these countries to achieve sustained faster growth. Based on present policies, it appears that industrial-country growth will continue at no more than its 1986 rate of well below 3 per cent. The prospects for reducing the current, very high levels of unemployment in the developed world,

> especially in Europe, are not encouraging. In these circumstances, markets for developing-country exports will continue to be difficult, and protectionist sentiment, which remained active in 1986, may gain new footholds that would then prove very hard to dislodge.[42]

In fact northern growth rates for 1987 have been estimated at 2.3 per cent.[43] A recent World Bank report suggests that continued slow growth in the industrialized world will keep commodity prices low for the foreseeable future. It predicts that 'real non-fuel commodity prices in the year 2000 may not yet have recovered to the low levels of 1985' and that consequently per capita incomes in SSA 'will probably not exceed their 1980 levels much before the end of the century'. The report also points to the problems of diversification, noting that Zambian attempts to move into the production of sugar and coffee are adding to a world glut of both crops, whilst moves by Cameroon, Gabon, Congo, and Zimbabwe into rubber and palm oil are running into difficulties competing with the plentiful supplies of such traditional producers as Malaysia.[44] At the time of writing there are signs that the stock market crash of 1987 may worsen commodity prices. There are fears that the slight recovery in prices experienced in the months prior to the crash will be reversed. For example, the bull market for copper has declined despite the fact that stocks are at their lowest for ten years.[45] Whilst Berg, and Sender and Smith may be correct to argue that African states have no viable alternative strategy to export orientation, it would be a fatal error to underestimate the difficulties they face in trying to sell their commodities in a stagnant market which shows signs of further deterioration.

A concomitant difficulty is posed by the protectionist tendencies identified by the World Bank (see above). Its World Development Report for 1987 has revealed that although successive rounds of the General Agreement on Tariffs and Trade (GATT) have reduced tariffs Third World states now have to face an increasing battery of non-tariff barriers (NTBs) including quotas and voluntary export restraints. Apparently, the proportion of North American and European imports affected by NTBs has risen by above 20 per cent between 1981-6. These restrictions particularly affect agricultural goods and textiles. The developed states protect and subsidize their agrarian sectors. Thus, the EEC subsidizes sugar beet production to the extent that it is massively overproduced and then dumps it abroad so that the world market is depressed and other producers suffer. Certainly, it is true that the African, Caribbean, and Pacific (ACP) signatories of Lomé Conventions with the EEC are granted a quota on the European market under the terms of the Sugar Protocol. However, the price they are paid is continually being squeezed and their exports outside Europe suffer due to EEC dumping practices. (The Lomé Conventions are trade and aid treaties between the EEC and the grouping of EEC members' ex-colonies known as the African, Caribbean and Pacific states (ACP). The first Lomé Convention was signed in 1975 and it was renewed in the form of a second convention in 1980. The third Lomé Convention commenced in 1985 and is due to be renewed in 1990.)

Third World textile exports have been adversely affected by a series of increasingly restrictive Multi-Fibre Agreements (MFAs). Whilst it would be true to say that the chief losers under the MFA have been newly industrializing countries like South Korea and Hong Kong, African states have also suffered. Mauritius was forced to conclude a 'voluntary' export restraint agreement restricting its textile exports to the EEC (particularly the United Kingdom and Ireland) despite the fact that exports from the ACP states constituted only 0.8 per cent of Europe's textile imports.[46] This presents a stark contrast with recent events in Ivory Coast, where World Bank insistence on a 40 per cent reduction of Ivorian tariffs has led to the virtual collapse of the chemical, textile, shoe, and automobile assembly industries in the face of foreign competition.[47]

Even more disturbing are the reports of undue influence being exerted on the Bank by a heavily protectionist US Congress and American Treasury Secretary James Baker. It has been argued that in lobbying Congress for additional capital the Bank has fallen into the trap of modifying its own decisions in accordance with American protectionist interests. Apparently, the Bank's president, Barber Conable, has decided that support for steel projects should be limited to technical assistance, thus blocking loans to India and Pakistan. He also blocked a US$12 billion loan for Zambia to restructure its parastatal, Zambia Consolidated Copper Mines, apparently due to managerial fears of alienating the Reagan administration. At the time of writing trepidation has been expressed about a study of agricultural lending, (particularly in surplus areas such as wheat and palm oil) which has been mounted in response to complaints by US farm groups that the Bank's policies were harming their members. Whilst the Bank claims that it is gathering information to confound its critics, there are others who fear it will lead to a curtailment of loans to countries that compete with the USA.[48] It would seem that the Bank is coming dangerously close to discrediting itself as an advocate either of development, or free trade, as it imposes disastrous laissez-faire policies in the Ivorian context, whilst winking at (if not aiding and abetting) protectionism in the USA. Certainly, such activities place severe obstacles in the path of African states that wish to develop an industrial capacity behind tariff walls, or to sell their products in stagnant and increasingly protectionist northern markets.

CONCLUSIONS

Where does this analysis leave the IMF/Berg prescriptions for Africa's debt crisis? We have seen that policies of laissez-faire and public sector retrenchment, though superficially attractive, are not in the final instance an appropriate solution to the waste of resources associated with the variable imprint of clientelist politics in SSA. Spending cuts will tend to damage those services that the state actually produces, whilst failing to eliminate the cause of such waste, namely clientelism. It has been seen that devaluation is a risky course of action in Africa, because it often leads to stagflation. The present context of low world growth also bodes ill for African exports that have to face stagnant and often protectionist markets. Berg, and Sender and Smith would tend to object to this analysis in so far as it puts an emphasis on structural blocks to Africa's development. They argue that such explanations have caused many states to eschew the export strategies that are vital to their development and to blame external factors for their own policy failures. Certainly, it is not the intention here to whitewash the patrimonialism endemic in African state mechanisms, or to discourage such states from trying to maximize their export receipts. However, it is difficult to avoid the conclusion that Africa's full recovery from the present crisis can take place only in a context of reflation and growth.

3

Nigeria: the circuitous path to stabilization?

Nigeria is an important test case of the socio-political effects of debt in Sub-Saharan Africa for a variety of reasons. First, its level of indebtedness is greater than that of any other nation on the continent. Second, its oil wealth brought it a degree of influence in international relations, as evidenced by the leading role played by Nigeria in negotiating the first Lomé Convention. It seems eminently possible that Nigeria may also have a leading influence in determining the reaction of other African states to the debt crisis. Third (and significantly in view of the latter point), Nigeria has taken what many regard as an independent line in dealing with its debt obligations, preferring to keep the IMF at arm's length. Fourth, it has helped to pioneer the use of techniques such as countertrade and conciliatory default in the management of its debt crisis. In the following pages we shall briefly survey the politics of Nigerian debt, with a view first to assessing what light it throws on the merits and demerits of the IMF medicine for indebtedness and, second, to determine whether or not it has produced any viable alternatives to this medicine. Initially, however, we shall examine the origins and proportions of Nigeria's debt in order to attain an understanding of the exact nature of the problem to be solved.

The exact amount of Nigeria's debt is a matter of dispute. Most creditors and some Nigerians place the total at over US$20 billion. Indeed, the most recently deposed head of state, Major General Buhari, acknowledged debts amounting to 19 billion naira (US$22.6 billion) in his budget speech for 1985.[1] However, the current administration of President Babangida has thrown some doubt on the validity of this figure. The then finance minister, Mr Kalu, placed debt at N11.4 billion (US$12.3 billion) as at 31 October 1985.

The latter estimate is lower because it only takes account of N1.1 billion of trade arrears (at an exchange rate of N0.9225 to the dollar), whereas creditors' claims amount to some US$7 billion.[2] The Babangida administration has been wary of accepting responsibility for all these commitments in view of the dubious nature of some of the transactions, particularly those involving Johnson Matthey Bankers (JMB). The most recent total that has been placed on Nigeria's external obligations is that given by the current finance minister, Chu Okongwu, in the 1987 budget statement, when he announced, that debt stood at US$18.5 billion at the end of November 1986.[3]

Notwithstanding question marks over the exact amount of the Nigerian debt, it is clear from the breakdown of the debt given in Table 3.1 that Nigeria's commitments are amongst the largest in SSA. We can also be sure that the main growth in these commitments took place over the last decade. According to World Bank figures, gross external liabilities jumped from US$5.1 billion in 1978 to US$9 billion in 1980. With the advent of the Second Republic the debt began to soar upwards, reaching US$19.7 billion in 1983 (though this figure includes some of the aforementioned disputed trade arrears). The scale of the problem is illustrated by the fact that the ratio of debt (outstanding and disbursed) to exports grew from 32.5 per cent in 1980, at the beginning of the Second Republic, to 179.1 per cent in 1983, whilst the debt service ratio rose from 10.5 per cent in 1980 to 30.1 per cent in 1983. In the latter year Nigeria's reserves were sufficient to cover only one month's imports. Not only did the Second Republic oversee a massive rise in Nigeria's debt, but it left a problematic legacy for successor governments in the shape of debt service. Ugochukwu has pointed out that the debts contracted by the Second Republic 'were not only mostly unwise, but also their maturity pattern was not co-ordinated and properly structured', with the result that 'there is a three year lump (1985-7) in debt service'. In 1985 the debt service ratio stood at 44 per cent and before his overthrow Buhari estimated the figure for 1986 at some 57 per cent, with a similar figure for 1987.[4]

It might be asked how Nigeria fell into such dire straits given the massive wealth that flowed into the country during the oil boom years of 1973-80, when sales of petroleum products brought in US$25 billion per annum.[5] A variety of explanations has been offered, but they all agree

Table 3.1 Nigeria's external loan profile

Loan type	Original commitment US$m	Cumulative drawn down less repayment 1.1.86 US$m	Drawn down 1986 US$m	Repayment 1986 US$m	Balance 1986 US$m
International organizations (multinational)	3,028.79	1,633.64	239.81	66.34	1,807.11
Bilateral credits	1,154.14	373.43	79.51	4.03	448.91
Federal direct debts:					
Export credits	5,301.07	3,582.18	157.17	15.61	3,723.74
Syndicated loans	3,481.22	1,546.07	-	2.40	1,543.67
Uninsured supplier credit	1,318.01	1,027.64	-	94.53	933.11
Guaranteed debt:					
Export credit	2,862.74	1,716.12	32.29	5.13	1,744.28
Syndicated loans	1,979.61	1,369.62	0.40	11.00	1,359.02
Uninsured supplier credit	303.23	148.67	-	18.77	129.90
Sub total	19,428.81	11,397.37	510.18	217.81	11,689.72
Foreign exchange approval	2,079.44	1,061.12	-	222.34	38.78
Short-term arrears claims	6,045.00	1,923.00	1,502.00	-	3,425.00
Estimated current letter of credit	2,500.00	-	2,500.00	-	2,500.00

Source: West Africa, (12 January 1987) p.80

on one point, this being that in one way or another the Nigerian state is guilty of wasting enormous amounts of resources. Rimmer, for example, is scathing about Nigeria's 'gross government', arguing that, 'In good times as well as bad, Nigeria is administered excessively, inefficiently, corruptly, and often ineffectively'.[6] Certainly, all these were well-documented failings of the Second Republic. Ekwe-Ekwe identifies the project of building a new capital at Abuja as an example of the Shagari government's profligacy. Between 1980-3, the government spent N2 billion and yet the period did not even see the construction of a coherent infrastructure on site.[7] Such projects regularly suffered from cost inflation due to the ubiquitous '10 per cent factor'. Corruption became so rife that at the fall of the Second Republic the NET building (the tallest building in Africa), the Ministry of External Affairs and the Accounts section of the Federal Capital Development Authority, Abuja, were all burnt apparently to conceal widespread fraud.[8]

However, corruption and profligacy were not the sole preserve of the Second Republic. Similar accusations were levelled against the First Republic, Gowon's military regime, the Buhari regime and the current administration of General Babangida.[9] It must be asked why corruption and financial mismanagement have been such common characteristics of Nigerian politics. Analysts such as Williams and Turner, and Forrest, explain this phenomenon in terms of the nature of Nigerian politics, which takes the form of a spoils system.[10] They point to the low level of capitalist development in Nigeria, which has meant that the commercial and bureaucratic strata are the dominant social groups. The weakness of the bourgeoisie has meant that the state has become the leading force in the economy. The economic centrality of the state combined with the patron-clientelist networks that permeate Nigerian politics has resulted in the state becoming the focus for capital accumulation. In this context politics consists essentially of the competition between different factions, often ethnically based, for control of the state and its economic resources. Many commentators have attested to the centrality of such uncontrolled competition, especially along north-south lines, in the collapse of the First Republic. Othman and Ekwe-Ekwe point to the influence of a loose-knit, but powerful elite group known as the Kaduna Mafia in this competition. Ekwe-Ekwe refers to the 'Mafia' as 'Nigeria's "unofficial government" '. He argues that it utilizes the state as a key element in its accumulation process. It pressured the Shagari government to undertake the Abuja project and construction of a multi-million naira oil refinery in Kaduna, so that its members could make money out of the contracts arising from these ventures. They also benefited from government funding made available for the Green Revolution.[11]

The impact of the oil boom in the 1970s was to make the state an even richer prize and thus an even more important focus for economic activity. Falola and Ihonvbere identify the Nigerian polity as a rentier state subsisting off huge oil rents. The patron-clientelist nature of Nigerian politics led to overwhelming pressures on the state to increase its oil production so that it could maximize its public spending. Indeed, the state has concentrated on petroleum production to the extent that oil revenues account for about 70 per cent of government revenue and some 95 per cent of total export earnings.[12] Public spending as a proportion of GDP also rose from 9 per cent in 1962 to 55 per cent in 1979.[13] The predominance of commercial and bureaucratic strata has meant that little of this spending has been in productive agricultural and industrial ventures since such activities are not the basis of these groups' power. Instead the bulk of the oil rents were used to import manufactures, food, consumer goods, and armaments, often at highly inflated prices incorporating a kick-back for one or more members of the ruling strata, which Falola and Ihonvbere identify as a *comprador* group. So long as the oil rents remained sufficiently high this unproductive accumulation process could continue unabated. However, the oil glut of the early 1980s brought production levels and prices down. Nigerian production fell from 2.058 million barrels per day (mbd) in 1980 to approximately 1.367 mbd in 1984, while the price per barrel fell from US$35.20 in 1980 to US$28 in 1984.[14] Declining oil production and prices were reflected in falling export receipts, which were reduced from N12.8 billion in 1980 to N7.5 billion in 1983. In marked contrast imports rose from their 1979 level of N7.1 billion and peaked at the height of the oil glut, hitting N11.3 billion in 1981 and 1982 as the *comprador* group made the most of its ascendancy. This contributed to a current account deficit of N12 billion (about US$17 billion), which was financed by foreign borrowings, running down the foreign exchange reserves and accumulating trade arrears.[15] Such were the origins of Nigeria's debt crisis.

It is clear from this analysis that Nigerian indebtedness is in large part a result of the profligate nature of the rentier state. The process of capital accumulation is not contingent on productive activities, but on control of the state and its revenues, which are subject to large-scale misappropriation of one sort or another. Thus, the oil rents have been frittered away without producing any substantive economic development and a large debt has emerged. In considering the various strategies that have been proposed for alleviating debt we must ask how far they address the roots of the problem, which lie embedded in the Nigerian political economy.

THE IMF: FOR AND AGAINST

In 1983 President Shagari's government approached the IMF for a loan. Nigeria was offered US$2.4 billion contingent on the successful performance of a typical IMF stabilization programme consisting of public sector retrenchment, elimination of import controls and a 60 per cent devaluation of the naira. Shagari rejected the loan because he objected to the conditions stipulating devaluation, removal of import controls and abolition of various subsidies including one for petroleum products. This signalled the start of the long-running debate as to whether or not Nigeria should take the IMF loan. The IMF debate has been a central concern in Nigerian public life, although it had to go underground when the Buhari government outlawed all political debates in July 1985. However, the ban was soon lifted after the Babangida coup in August of the same year and the debate acquired a new impetus when the new government gave it official sanction. Numerous commentators argued the pros and cons of accepting the loan.

The main objections to the loan have been itemized as follows:

> i) A relaxation of import controls would discourage local domestic firms from using local raw materials as imported raw materials would be cheaper. It would result in foreign firms based in Nigeria being even more competitive with local firms. Moreover, any further extension of credit lines to importers would perpetuate the country's chronic foreign indebtedness.

ii) A devaluation of the naira would raise the cost (in naira) of imported foodstuffs, industrial raw materials, and other capital equipment, exacerbating inflation. Moreover, the advantage of a devaluation, in so far as external demand is concerned, would be minimal, since 95 per cent of Nigeria's exports consist of crude oil which is valued in dollar terms. A devaluation would also increase the value of the country's outstanding foreign debts which are fixed in terms of the creditor nation's currencies.

iii) The Fund's insistence that fuel subsidies should be reduced, if not entirely removed, together with a review of current prices for public utilities, which are considered too low, would ensure that transport and production costs generally would rise, again exacerbating inflation.

iv) An open-door investment policy, allowing a free inflow and outflow of foreign capital, would undermine local industries and entrench foreign concerns, stifling the development of indigenous technology.

v) The Fund's proposed loan is short-term and designed only to accommodate current debt servicing requirements. It would make the country more dependent, rather than independent, of foreign capital, benefiting foreign businesses based in Nigeria rather than indigenous businesses.[16]

Clearly, the case against the loan mobilized most of the well-known left wing objections to IMF conditionality. Devaluation and removal of subsidies were condemned as inflationary, whilst relaxation of import controls and an open-door investment policy were seen as attempts to enforce a neo-colonial development process on Nigeria.

However, other commentators rejected these arguments. Rimmer argued that devaluation is desirable on a number of counts. It would increase petroleum export receipts in naira terms, thus ameliorating the government's budget deficit. Furthermore, it would give an incentive to Nigerian agricultural production by making food imports prohibitively expensive, whilst traditional cash crop exports would become more competitive in the world market. Similarly, he suggested that the abolition of subsidies would benefit the rural sector. Subsidies covering goods such as petrol were of most benefit to the urban areas. Thus public funds were being spent to subsidize consumption in the towns, whilst the rural sector was ignored. Abolition of the subsidies would release these funds for agricultural investment.

Undoubtedly, there is substance to these arguments. Overvaluation of the naira has made imported food artificially cheap with the resut that such imports have become a substantial drain on the balance of payments. Rice imports from Thailand cost US$1.1 billion in 1984-5.[17] However, many African countries have found that devaluation tends to exacerbate inflation and the prices of domestic products can be driven so high that they remain uncompetitive with imported goods.[18] It is also dubious to argue that devaluation will help Nigeria to recapture export markets for some of its traditional cash crops. Whilst it is true that such exports have declined substantially over the 1970s and 1980s, it must also be remembered that the demand elasticities for many of Nigeria's traditional products, such as cocoa and groundnut oil, are extremely low.[19] Any substantial increase in exports of these goods could result in a reduction in prices. Clearly, devaluation was potentially a painful measure for Nigeria to undertake.

Ugochukwu took a different line of argument from Rimmer in advocating acceptance of the loan. He pointed out that although Nigeria had failed to come to terms with the IMF over devaluation, trade liberalization, and abolition of the petroleum subsidy there were fourteen other conditions on which agreement was reached.

> These include reduction in government expenditure and the budget deficit, introduction of stricter budgeting discipline, review of ongoing projects, reduction of subsidies to parastatals, restructuring of parastatals, with commercial potential to make them more profit oriented, stoppage of grants to state governments, rationalization of customs tariffs, an increase in interest rates and reduction of monetary expansion, phased removal of fertilizer subsidies, a review of industrial incentives and policy, an export drive to broaden the export base, an upward adjustment of producer prices for agricultural commodities, strict external debt control and management, and improvement in the efficiency of the revenue collection agencies.[20]

Ugochukwu goes on to point out that there had been massive

retrenchment in the public sector; state governments had been told to dispense with external loans and not to exceed their statutory allocation of revenues; subventions to parastatals had been reduced; and subsidies for fertilizers, education, and health had been cut. Indeed the value of the naira against the dollar has been allowed to float downwards throughout the 1980s. However, it has been argued that any real depreciation was more than counteracted by the high Nigerian rate of inflation.[21] Nevertheless, Ugochukwu was able to argue with some validity that about 75 per cent of the IMF's conditions had been accepted and implemented by successive Nigerian governments. On this basis he suggested that Nigeria had little to lose by implementing the few remaining conditions and much to gain in the shape of US$2.4 billion from the IMF and US$3 billion from the World Bank, which had been withheld due to refusal of the loan.

Despite these arguments the Babangida regime rejected an IMF loan in late 1985. This came as something of a surprise since it had been thought that Babangida was a pro-IMF man. However, the debate mobilized such widespread anti-IMF feeling that Babangida obviously felt unable to continue negotiations with the Fund, noting that, 'This is clearly the will of the majority of our people on this issue'.[22] Indeed, the IMF debate reached all sections of society. On one occasion a corporal in the army told a member of the Armed Forces Ruling Council (AFRA) that 'he and his mates did not want the IMF'.[23]

It might be asked why Babangida opened the issue up to a public debate if he wanted to accept the loan, rather than simply going ahead and negotiating a settlement with the IMF. In explaining this it is worth bearing in mind the unpopularity of the IMF throughout Africa. As we have noted above, the Fund's austerity programmes have lowered standards of living and caused unrest in all parts of the continent. There have been instances in which leaders have been deposed in what were essentially anti-IMF coups. In this context it is understandable that Babangida would wish to be sure that he had the backing of the Nigerian populace for any action he might take regarding the IMF.

Furthermore, it is worth noting the circumstances under which the Buhari regime was deposed in trying to understand Babangida's tactics. As we have seen, most of the conditions set by the Fund were accepted by the Nigerian government under Buhari's leadership and put into implementation. Public sector retrenchment increased unemployment, whilst the ending of subsidies in education and the health sector reduced living standards. Such measures were introduced in a very authoritarian manner. The government launched a programme known as the War Against Indiscipline (WAI) under the auspices of which Draconian and repressive measures were taken. For example the government passed the State Security (Detention of Persons) Decree, No 2 in February 1984. Under this decree people could be held indefinitely without being charged, if suspected of acts prejudicial to the nation's security, or of having contributed to the country's economic adversity. This led to numerous people being detained.[24] Not surprisingly such measures made the Buhari government very unpopular and helped to create the conditions for Babangida's takeover.

Given that Babangida was essentially in agreement with Buhari and the IMF on the need for austerity measures, it can be seen that he faced a problem in trying to carry the Nigerian populace with him whilst delivering the same economic medicine that helped to bring down his predecessor. It would appear that Babangida's solution has been to change the political element of Buhari's formula. Instead of trying to force his economic programme through with a political clampdown he employed the apparently democratic device of consulting the people's opinion through the IMF debate. The skill of this manoeuvre lies in the fact that Babangida was able to convince substantial numbers of Nigerians that he was giving them a genuine say in deciding policy, thus rallying a certain level of support for his regime. In fact the people were given a choice as to whether or not the IMF loan should be taken, but it was always clear that austerity policies would be imposed irrespective of acceptance or non-acceptance of the loan. Babangida was also skilful in mobilizing the chauvinistic element in the anti-IMF line of argument in favour of his own programme. Thus, he argued that, 'We must by ourselves, and on our own terms, do all these things which will help to restructure our economy, no matter what pains are involved.' For Babangida the value of the IMF debate lay in the fact that, 'It has helped to awaken the conscience of the nation and raise our democratic ideals in a way no other public issue has done in recent times'.[25] It gave his regime the democratic veneer that was so notably lacking in the Buhari government and allowed him the opportunity to portray his economic policies in a nationalistic light, despite the fact that they are substantially the same policies that were found so objectionable when demanded by the IMF and when implemented by Buhari. The IMF debate played an essential legitimating role for Babangida.

A NIGERIAN SOLUTION FOR A NIGERIAN PROBLEM?

Given the conviction of the Babangida administration that the cure for Nigeria's debt will be provided by the austerity measures favoured by the IMF and Buhari, we must examine whether or not this strategy represents a viable solution to Nigeria's debt problem. As we have noted Buhari took a number of deflationary measures. These 'resulted in the sacking of thousands of workers, cutting subsidies for education, health, and other subsidies, increasing taxes in the form of ubiquitous levies and the shelving of a number of core projects.'[26] All these measures fell very much in line with the standard IMF programme and they also had the standard results of declining living standards combined with rising prices, which in turn caused political discontentment.

However, there were a few differences from the IMF model in Buhari's programme. The Nigerians elected to undertake the crucial task of controlling their imports through use of the import controls so detested by the IMF rather than by means of devaluation of the naira. Unfortunately, Nigeria's controls had exactly the same effect that devaluation normally has on the recipients of IMF loans. They caused a shortage of imported in-puts. This hamstrung Nigerian manufacturing industry, which is about 70 per cent dependent on imported raw materials. In 1984 about fifty factories were closed and 50,000 workers were laid off according to Oladapo Fafowora, the executive director of the Manufacturers Association of Nigeria. Other companies had to resort to short-time working and extended holiday closures. Nigerian manufacturing companies were operating at only 30 per cent capacity.[27] Manufacturing output fell by 18.2 per cent in the year, whilst industrial output fell by 11.7 per cent. It might be expected that the ensuing shortages would add to the inflationary tendencies created by the abolition of subsidies on such goods as fertilizers. Indeed the composite consumer price index rose 36.9 per cent in 1984, compared with 23.2 per cent in 1983. However, this was apparently due to shortages of food caused by supply problems.[28] Inflation stood at 39.6 per cent during 1984.[29]

It would seem that the Nigerian decision to use import controls did not prevent the high inflation rate that is often associated with devaluation. It seems all too possible that the actual reason for retention of the controls was that they provided a ready opportunity for the misappropriation of state funds. During the Second Republic fortunes were accumulated through the misuse of import licences. One report states:

> The allocation of import licences had been a perennial source of corruption. Its manipulation could shift the wealth of the country from one point to another and could wipe out a business or create new millionaires overnight. Though it must be admitted that the flagrant abuse of import licences was minimal (under Buhari), the economic sabotage that restricting imports was supposed to arrest none the less persisted. Smuggling is still rife, and the August seizure of sixty containers stuffed with mud and rubbish shocked the nation and questioned the efficiency of the three import pre-shipment inspection firms.[30]

The same report notes that although a permanent secretary to the Ministry of Finance was found guilty of wrongfully awarding contracts by a tribunal of inquiry in Niger State, the Buhari regime promoted him to the Ministry of National Planning where he was responsible for preparing the costly Fifth Development Plan. It seems by no means impossible that members of the Buhari government were using import controls illicitly to make profit, albeit on a smaller scale than the Second Republic. Indeed, such suspicions played a part in rousing public discontent with the Buhari regime. Diamond quotes a Financial Times report which referred to the Nigerian public's:

> Widespread scepticism ... about the army's claims to have reduced corruption. Not only were senior ministers alleged to be making fortunes in the time-honoured fashion - from kick-backs on contracts and import licence allocations - but suspicion was also aroused by big oil barter deals in which middlemen in or close to government were alleged to have made fortunes.[31]

As we have seen, the Babangida regime opted to continue

the austerity programme when it came to office on 27 August 1985. On 1 October the AFRC announced a national economic emergency and this was followed by the announcement of pay cuts of between 2.5 per cent and 20 per cent for the armed forces. Officers of brigadier rank and above lost 20 per cent whilst corporals and lower ranks lost 2.5 per cent. Employees in the public sector also suffered pay cuts of between 2 per cent and 15 per cent. Further austerity measures included the banning of rice and maize imports and the recalling of 30 per cent of Nigerian diplomats from abroad in order to save money.[32] The 1986 budget continued this trend. The Federal Government tried to balance the budget by means of funds raised through cutting the petroleum subsidy (thought to be worth N900 million), salary and income cuts (worth N500 million) and imposition of a 30 per cent general levy on all imports (worth N1 billion). In addition subsidies to parastatals were cut by 50 per cent and this was followed by abolition of the marketing boards.

Perhaps the most fundamental element of Babangida's austerity programme has been the abolition of import controls and their replacement by a Second-tier Foreign Exchange Market (SFEM) to bidders (e.g. bankers), which involves auctioning foreign exchange on the free market, thus allowing market forces to determine the value of the naira. This was widely interpreted as a disguised devaluation of the naira, which was expected to fall from its official rate of N1.47 to the US dollar (the rate in early September 1986, immediately prior to the introduction of the SFEM) to a rate much closer to that extant on the parallel market, N4 to the dollar. Consequently, the SFEM was subjected to similar criticisms to those aimed at devaluation, notably that it would lead to inflationary price rises, wipe out small companies, and that the market might be cornered by a few businessmen who would then sell their foreign exchange on the parallel market. By contrast advocates of the system argued that SFEM would give an impetus to local production of food and industrial inputs by making imports prohibitively expensive. It would also give an incentive to new foreign investors since their capital would be converted to naira at a realistic rate, whilst giving a disincentive to established investors to repatriate capital at current rates since their profits would be much reduced in foreign exchange terms.[33]

What then have been the effects of the SFEM? Certainly, it brought about something approaching a 60 per cent devaluation of the naira, which has fluctuated between a rate of N3-5 to the US dollar (see Table 3.2). This has indeed resulted in the price rises that were feared by the scheme's detractors. Many traders hoarded goods in anticipation of being able to sell them at high post-SFEM prices and this sent the cost of items such as milk, sugar, meat, soap, detergent, cigarettes, and beer soaring upwards even before the new exchange regime had been introduced. However, the Central Bank of Nigeria has tried to defuse these inflationary tendencies by withdrawing the naira used to buy foreign exchange through the SFEM from circulation. In this way N6 billion have been withdrawn from the economy.[34] Unfortunately, this seems to have done little to restrain price rises, especially in public services.[35] Furthermore, the shortage of naira has caused a squeeze on bank credit, which limits the ability to finance productive investments.[36] This situation has been exacerbated by the tight credit restrictions in the 1987 budget, which limit growth in lending to the private and public sector to 8.4 per cent and 1.5 per cent respectively.[37] It is unlikely that this will allow a sufficient rate of growth to fuel Nigeria's economic recovery.

SFEM also poses problems for Nigeria's overwhelmingly import-dependent industrial sector. Industry was already in trouble, as shown by the Central Bank's Half-Yearly Report which noted that production costs for the first half of 1986 had risen 77 per cent in naira terms, from N364.5 million in the first half of 1985 to N645.2 million in the first half of 1986. Shortly after the introduction of the SFEM, the Manufacturers Association of Nigeria (MAN) sent a pre-budget memo to the government in November 1986 stating that, 'The economy is still sluggish, and the basic objectives of the 1986 budget have not yet been attained.'[38] In the event there was little comfort for manufacturers in the restrictive monetary strategy of the 1987 budget, which MAN condemned as 'conducive to depression and no growth'.[39] The difficulties of the manufacturing sector are reflected in the situation of the motor industry. Prior to SFEM, Nigeria's eight vehicle assembly plants were already operating at a fraction of capacity due to shortage of foreign exchange and the depressed local market, which had resulted in demand for commercial vehicles sinking to about 7,000 a year, as compared with production capacity of 70,000. The SFEM and the consequent depreciation of the naira led to a sharp increase in the cost of inputs and therefore the assembled cars, which has led in turn to a further depression of demand. Consequently, two of the country's largest vehicle assembly plants at Ibadan and Kano have been permanently closed. The Ibadan plant had employed 1,700 people in 1984. According to the chairman of the Bompia branch of MAN, some nineteen companies closed in Kano alone during May to October 1987. In this way it can be argued that SFEM is damaging the economy, causing closures and unemployment. The government view is rather different, explaining the effects of SFEM in terms of rationalization in order to achieve economies of scale. It is critical of assembly plants because they have failed to increase their use of local inputs. A target of 75 per cent local sourcing was set for 1987, but none of the companies have managed over 30 per cent. The companies themselves complain of the high price, low quality, and irregular supplies of local inputs and argue that the closure of plant damages the capital base.[40] Clearly, the rationalization and local sourcing the SFEM is meant to encourage will not come about easily or quickly, whilst the closures and unemployment that it is also causing may lead to lasting economic damage.

Furthermore there are questions as to whether or not the SFEM actually represents a genuine use of market forces in determining the value of the naira due to the numerous interventions in the operation of the system by the government and the Central Bank. In the first instance the rate of the naira to the dollar was derived from an average of the successful bids. However, the bankers bidding for foreign exchange complained that this led to an unduly low valuation of the naira. Indeed, it was at this early stage that the naira hit its lowest rate of five to the dollar (see Table 3.2). Consequently, the system was changed so that the marginal bid rate (the lowest successful bid) set the value of the naira. Subsequently, the official rate of the naira increased, but the Central Bank has felt obliged to intervene to set its value on various occasions. The auction of 11 December 1986 set a marginal bid rate of N2.9 to the dollar, which the Central Bank deemed too high, altering the rate to N3.20 to the dollar. Subsequently, the Central Bank intervened to prop up the naira when the rate appeared to be falling towards four to the dollar. The most recent intervention in the operation of the SFEM at the time of writing was in the auction of 12 February 1987, when the Central Bank adjusted the marginal rate of N3 to the dollar down to N3.50 to the dollar, only to be countermanded by the government, which restored the higher rate as the value of the naira for that week.[41] These events throw considerable doubt on the proposition that the SFEM allows the free market to set the value of the naira. Both the government and the Central Bank seem determined to limit the extent to which the naira is devalued and this still leaves room for the operation of a parallel market. It is worth noting that when the naira hit its lowest rate of N5.1 to the dollar in October 1986 it was close to the black market rate of N5.2 to the dollar. However, as the naira has appreciated since that time it has grown further away from the black market rate, which was N4.7 to the dollar in February 1987.[42] This raises the possibility that the SFEM will become a conduit to the black market for foreign exchange, although the tight money policies enforced by the Central Bank may limit this tendency. Nevertheless, there is a danger that the SFEM will replicate the undesirable effects of devaluation, such as giving an upward twist to inflation and depressing production, whilst failing to produce the central benefits that are attributed to devaluation, these being the elimination of cost-price distortions and the parallel market.

The 1987 budget continued the austerity programme with the aforementioned limits on credit and restrictions on the growth of the money supply to 11.8 per cent.[43] The government allocated 47 per cent of the capital budget of N6.757 billion to productive investments in agriculture, water resources, and mining. It has also bitten a very difficult bullet for any military government, substantially reducing its defence allocation. Capital spending was almost halved from N164 million in the 1986 budget to N92 million in 1987, with recurrent spending being reduced from N742 million in 1986 to N717 million in 1987. Rather more disappointingly for many Nigerians health and education were the subject of cutbacks, but this was counter-balanced by a new N100 million job creation programme.[44]

We might ask if Nigeria's austerity measures have borne any fruit in the form of economic growth. Certainly, we may note that during 1985 GDP rose by 2.4 per cent in real terms after an absolute decline in the years 1982-4 (see Table 3.3). With regard to external transactions the current account stood at a surplus of N1.109 billion in 1985, this being a substantial improvement on the previous year's surplus of N264 million. However, this was largely due to oil

Table 3.2 SFEM's Rates for major currencies

	Week 1 26.9.86	Week 2 2.10.86	Week 3 9.10.86	Week 4 16.10.86	Week 5 23.10.86	Week 6 30.10.86	Week 7 6.11.86	Week 8 13.11.86	Week 9 20.11.86	Week 10 27.11.86
US dollar	4.6174	5.0839	3.4999	3.9101	4.1775	3.8525	3.6000	3.4993	3.4599	3.4945
Pound sterling	6.6269	7.3462	4.9151	5.6305	5.9801	5.4225	5.1408	4.9848	4.9590	5.007
Deutsche mark	2.2578	2.5180	1.7517	1.9807	2.0661	1.9095	1.7450	1.7332	1.7426	1.7578
Swiss franc	2.2784	3.1056	2.1492	2.4915	2.5504	2.3055	2.0912	2.0879	2.0920	0.5368
French franc	0.6900	0.7688	0.5353	0.6048	0.6420	0.5841	0.5353	0.5298	0.5321	2.1077
Dutch guilder	1.9972	2.2278	1.5503	1.5134	1.8592	1.6856	1.5477	1.5358	1.5406	1.5549
Japanese yen	0.0299	0.0330	0.0227	0.0267	0.0267	0.0241	0.0221	1.0218	0.0215	0.0214

Table 3.2 Cont.

	Week 11 4.12.86	Week 12 11.12.86	Week 13 18.12.86	Week 14 8.1.87	Week 15 15.1.87	Week 16 22.1.87	Week 17 29.1.87	Week 18 5.2.87	Week 19 12.2.87
US dollar	3.0050	3.2000	3.3000	3.4250	3.5369	3.6817	3.8719	3.9215	3.0000
Pound sterling	4.2998	4.5696	4.7648	5.0433	5.3213	5.6072	5.9647	6.0005	5.3148
Deutsche mark	1.5238	1.5932	1.6546	1.7760	1.9291	2.0003	2.1710	2.1721	1.9230
Swiss franc	0.8301	1.9042	1.9602	2.1142	2.3012	2.3854	2.5908	2.5734	2.2713
French franc	0.4652	0.4863	0.5008	0.5333	0.5779	0.5997	0.6504	0.6511	0.5776
Dutch guilder	1.3482	1.4091	1.4619	1.5757	1.7116	1.7240	1.9258	1.9324	1.7031
Japanese yen	0.0185	0.0197	0.0204	0.0217	0.0232	0.0240	0.0256	0.0258	0.0100

Source: West Africa, (23 February 1987), p.359

exports. The slump in oil prices in 1986 saw the price per barrel decline from US$28 at the beginning of the year to US$10 by the middle of the year, recovering only slightly to about US$15 by the end of the year. This caused Nigeria's current account surplus to evaporate, leaving a deficit of N763 million for 1986.[45]

Table 3.3 Growth of gross domestic product, at 1977-8 market prices

% per annum

1976	1977	1978	1979	1980[a]	1981	1982	1983	1984	1985
10.0	7.6	-7.3	2.4	2.6	-2.6	0.2	-8.8	-6.6	2.4[b]

Source: Economist Intelligence Unit, Nigeria: the Dilemmas Ahead - a Political Risk Analysis (Special Report 1072 by S. Wright), (London, The Economist, 1986), p. 35

a In 1980, Nigeria changed its accounting year from April-March to the calendar year.
b Real growth of GDP at factor cost.

Nigeria's continued reliance on oil receipts throws doubt on the sustainability of any recovery. The Babangida administration places emphasis on boosting agricultural production as the cornerstone of development. The government has abolished the market boards due to their practice of paying inadequate producer prices and (as noted above) has banned imports of maize and rice in the hope of stimulating production. Whilst these may give an impetus to higher production there are still problems to be dealt with such as improving access roads throughout the country and providing inputs such as insecticides, tractors, drugs for livestock and fertilizers, all of which have to be imported. The 1986 budget increased the allocation to agriculture in the attempt to provide an answer to these problems. However, this was supposed to be financed largely by oil receipts, a calculation that became entirely redundant with the oil collapse. In other words, Nigeria is in a 'Catch 22' situation in which falling oil receipts impede development in other economic sectors, thus maintaining dependence on oil. Although oil prices rallied to about US$18-19 per barrel in March 1987 due to OPEC's agreement of December 1986 to cut production, there were doubts as to how long the agreement would hold, given that Iran and Iraq had dissociated themselves from it. Certainly, most of the long-term forecasts at the time of writing suggest that the prospects for the oil price are less than optimistic.[46]

The aforementioned abolition of the marketing boards has also had mixed effects. Although free marketeers have argued that farmers would benefit from deregulation of the agrarian sector and the determination of prices by the operation of the market, this has not always proved to be the case. The 1987 harvest produced a one million ton grain surplus, which depressed grain prices to under N400 per ton, which is below the N450 per ton guaranteed price that was paid by the now defunct Nigerian Grains Board. It was suggested that this might prompt farmers to plant less, thus causing future shortages. There have also been reports that farmers in Sokoto state were left with a large surplus of cotton for which they had no marketing outlet due to the demise of the Nigerian Cotton Board.[47] Even when deregulation has resulted in higher producer prices there have been problems. For example the prices for cocoa rose to between about N3,500 and N5,000 per ton at the start of the 1986-7 season, which compares very favourably with the old official price of N1,600 per ton in 1985-6. However, bankers argue that these high prices indicate that certain interests are utilizing cocoa exports as a conduit for transferring capital out of Nigeria. Even though world prices for cocoa are low, they will still gain in excess of a 10 per cent premium on the exchange rates extant on the Second-tier Foreign Exchange Market. The intervention of such interests in the cocoa market has meant that less attention was paid to quality controls, with the result that Nigerian cocoa lost its traditional premium in the London market. Thus, Nigeria's cocoa boom has had contradictory effects. Whilst farmers have benefited from higher producer prices it has to be recognized that quality declined and cocoa exports are indicative of a drain of capital out of the economy.[48] It must also be noted that by mid-1987 food exports had increased from a low base by 100 per cent and receipts had reached N254.9 million. However, this has made little impact on the overall structure of exports, with oil providing over 90 per cent of receipts.[49] In order to effect a substantial increase in agrarian exports it will be essential to improve rural infrastructures. Clearly, recourse to the free market does not represent an unproblematic solution to Nigeria's problems.

Given this context the Nigerian government faces a complex economic problem. If it continues with its austerity policies, it is likely to encounter many of the difficulties that are commonly associated with IMF stabilization programmes. The abolition of subsidies caused a rise in inflation as did the SFEM, although this may have been held in check to some degree by tight money policies. The partial devaluation associated with the SFEM has also adversely affected many industries by making their imported inputs more expensive. The liquidity squeeze has adverse effects on industrial production. Austerity has taken its toll on those who have suffered wage cuts, or who have lost their jobs, just as prices were rising. The International Labour Organization has conservatively estimated that some three million people are unemployed in Nigeria, many of whom are concentrated in the urban areas.[50] Nor has deregulation delivered all the benefits that have been claimed for it. The Keynesian lobby of Nigerian academics, bankers, and officials claim that reflationary monetary and credit policies could bring about growth. However, the government can reasonably argue that such measures could simply let inflation rip and give an impetus to transactions in the parallel market. The problem then is that deflation tends to stand in the way of growth, whilst reflation might simply cause burgeoning inflation.

In the event it would appear that the government is determined to persist with its stabilization programme, whilst trying to soften the effects on the general populace by limiting inflationary tendencies. Notwithstanding their efforts, unemployment and rising prices have combined to produce discontented groups, especially in the towns. Already, Babangida has had to face down an attempted coup. Public consensus on this is that it was undertaken by a group of discontented officers led by a personal rival of Babangida, one Mamman Vatsa, and that their primary motive was a desire for spoils. In any event, their coup attempt failed when they were arrested just before Christmas 1986.[51] More seriously, the government has had to face the consistent opposition of the Nigerian Labour Congress protesting at the declining living standards of its membership.[52] Babangida also raised the ire of many Nigerians by releasing ex-President Shagari and many of his lieutenants without punishment. Perhaps a more serious threat than these is posed by the apparently religiously motivated riots in Kaduna, which have stirred traditional hostilities between Northern Muslims and Eastern Christians. Many commentators felt that Babangida had committed a gaffe in joining the Islamic Conference Organization and it would appear that religion still has the potential to cause violence in Nigeria. Yet, various members of government have argued that the Kaduna riots were not entirely religious in character, but have a clear political significance. Babangida himself has said that some of the later incidents 'were fomented by a group of ambitious power seekers'.[53] Fears have been expressed that the riots presage worse struggles for power between north and south when the army step down. It is probably such considerations that have motivated Babangida to postpone the return of civilian government, originally scheduled for 1990, until 1992.[54] This measure, combined with public discontent at the inefficiency with which the 1987 local government elections were held, may exacerbate tensions and create the conditions for a coup.[55]

Furthermore doubts have emerged as to the probity of the Babangida regime. The release of Shagari and many of the stalwarts of the Second Republic has given rise to suspicions amongst numerous Nigerians that the Babangida regime is also prone to corrupt practices. Indeed, a report on the early days of the regime by Hall indicates that instances of corruption are still quite common.[56] Whilst the austerity programme has meant that pickings are not quite as rich as they were during the heady days of the Second Republic, according to Hall 'bribery was everywhere, kick-backs the rule'. The same report refers to an incident where a customs official examined a container that was supposedly full of spare parts for Peugeots, only to find a white Mercedes. He was bought off and the Mercedes was sent through customs. Hall also found evidence to suggest that corruption still goes up to the highest level of Nigerian society. In asking questions about the JMB scandal and its connections with Nigeria, Hall was advised 'by a man who should know' not to ask too many questions, as he 'could get too close to some big names'. Moreover the motivations behind the Vatsa coup attempt indicate that members of the armed forces still tend to associate government with the opportunity to accumulate money. The continued influence of such ideas suggests that the Nigerian polity is still vulnerable to misappropriation and misuse of state funds, which can be ill afforded in the present context.

Nigeria: stabilization?

In the face of all these problems we must ask how Nigeria has attempted to manage a debt crisis in which repayments were scheduled to hit a peak in 1986 and 1987. One tactic has been to use countertrading deals to conserve scarce foreign exchange. Barter deals with countries such as Brazil, France, and Italy were concluded under the Buhari regime through which Nigeria exchanged oil for industrial inputs (see Table 3.4). Although these deals succeeded in saving foreign exchange, the Babangida administration questioned their usefulness because of suspicions that Nigeria had been paying inflated prices for the goods it was importing. The government set up a commission on countertrade, which reported in November 1985. Although the commission affirmed the principle of countertrade deals it recommended that any future agreements had to be carefully monitored and implied that many officials had used previous deals as an opportunity for misappropriation. Subsequently, senior civil servants argued that some 30 per cent of Nigeria's oil could be marketed through countertrading, although there were questions as to whether this would be attractive to prospective trading partners since the country could no longer offer the incentive of a price discount due to the low oil price.[57] It was also suggested that countertrade could be expanded to cover Nigeria's non-oil exports such as coal, columbite, bitumen, cocoa, rubber, processed wood, fibre, and beer.[58]

Another tactic used by Babangida to manage debt repayments has been to limit the amount to be spent on servicing to 30 per cent of the foreign exchange earned by the country. This measure was introduced in the 1986 budget and continued in 1987.[59] The advantages of this tactic are that it can be used to hold repayments at a manageable level and yet it does not represent a complete repudiation of debts, which would provoke considerable hostility and possible retaliation by creditor nations. Indeed, it may prove to be a useful tactic for putting pressure on creditor states for concessions. Whilst it is clear that the western states are concerned about the prospect of Nigeria defaulting on a proportion of its debts, they have evidently decided to take a conciliatory line in view of the government's adherence to an orthodox austerity programme.

Indeed, the IMF endorsed the government's policies in September 1986, thus signalling to other donors that Nigeria had a clean bill of health to receive further financial assistance. This has led to further loans (see Table 3.5).

Table 3.4 Countertrade agreements, 1984-5

Country	Date	Value ($m)	Major commodities imported
Brazil	Sept 1984	500	Volkswagen car kits, manufactured goods, sugar
France	May 1985	500	Peugeot car kits
Austria	May 1985	200	Capital goods, steel, building materials
Italy	June 1985	400	Fiat spares
Malaysia	June 1985	77	Palm oil

Source: Economist Intelligence Unit, Nigeria: the Dilemmas Ahead - a Political Risk Analysis, Special Report 1072 by S. Wright, (London, The Economist, 1986), p. 35

Table 3.5 Loans to Nigeria agreed in 1986

	$m	
World Bank	450	
Western Central Banks	250	quick-disbursing
Commercial Banks	320	
	1,020	
World Bank	4,280	project loans over three years of which about half will be quick-disbursing

Source: West Africa, (20 October 1986), p. 2197

Although this new funding is badly needed, it has to be noted that Nigeria's commercial creditors in the London Club drove a hard bargain despite the fact that the criteria set by the Baker Plan should qualify the country for favourable treatment. The Nigerians had requested the rescheduling over twelve years of debts worth US$6 billion, which were to fall due in 1990. They managed to obtain agreement to the rescheduling of medium-term debts worth US$1.5 billion over ten years and the restructuring of short-term debts worth US$2 billion into medium-term debts. The London Club charged Nigeria higher interest rates for this privilege than Mexico had obtained on its recent rescheduling deal (the Nigerians have to pay US$15 million more in interest on their US$3.5 billion of rescheduled debt than the Mexicans would have been required to pay on a similar amount) and a renegotiation fee of 0.5 per cent (i.e. US$17.5 million) was also charged. Whereas the Nigerians had asked for US$600 million in new money over 1986-7, the banks would supply only US$320 million at an interest rate of 1.25 per cent above Libor (London Inter-Bank rate) plus a negotiation fee of 0.5 per cent and a commitment fee of 0.5 per cent on undrawn balances.[60] The mean-mindedness of this deal moved even the IMF to complain that the 'short-term collateralized nature of the proposal is consistent neither with Nigeria's minimal financing need nor with efforts made in other cases in the recent past' (e.g. Mexico). Not content with this it would seem that the banks are delaying the issue of their US$320 million in order to try and pressure the Nigerian government into accepting responsibility for the aforementioned disputed trade arrears.[61] Agreement with the London Club led to an accord with the Paris Club to reschedule some US$6.5 billion of official debt. Subsequently, a number of states, including Britain, France, West Germany, and the USA began to promise Nigeria new export credits. France, in particular, has ambitions to establish a market for its services in Nigeria and has taken a flexible negotiating position in establishing the terms for its credits. The Nigerians also seem to have won a favourable settlement of their hotly disputed commercial debts amounting to some US$3.25 billion. A private meeting of Nigeria's creditors at the Wembley Conference Centre on the 14 January 1988 voted in favour of a scheme to reschedule these debts over 22 years. This represented a victory for Nigeria, given that the creditors wanted a maximum rescheduling period of 15 years. However, several of the creditors have complained that they were intimidated by being told that the Nigerian government would be informed of how they voted and that they would try to overturn the result. Consequently, we cannot be sure that this agreement will be implemented at the time of writing.[62] Although these agreements will undoubtedly be welcome it has to be remembered that rescheduling represents only a postponement of debt repayment, and in the absence of adequate financial inflows there is a real danger that they will only lead to an even worse debt crisis in the future.[63]

We must also note that agreement with the IMF and the World Bank has had potential costs in the form of the abandonment of the countertrade policy. The Fund and the Bank object to countertrading as the practice does not accord with their views on the proper operation of the free market and impedes control and monitoring of a country's foreign exchange holdings. Nigeria was threatened with the freezing of its stabilization agreement with the Fund and withdrawal of a World Bank trade policy loan worth US$5 million if more countertrading deals were agreed. This resulted in the Babangida regime renouncing this policy in April 1987.[64]

Perhaps the most optimistic recent development is the proposal by two major banks to agree debt-equity swaps with Nigeria. Under these proposals an investor might purchase entitlement to certain Nigerian obligations at a discount and then sell them to the Central Bank of Nigeria for naira to be invested in an approved project. This could prove to be an effective means of killing two birds with one stone in that it would fulfil some of Nigeria's debt obligations whilst providing some much needed investment in the local economy.[65]

In conclusion, Nigeria has a long distance to travel before it achieves any final solution to its debt problems. The IMF debate was not in fact the great exercise in democratic government that it initially appeared to be. It was the means through which the Babangida government rallied popular support (or at least acquiescence) for an austerity programme that essentially followed on from the economic policy of the Buhari regime. Whilst this strategy arguably falls some way short of the classic IMF stabilization programme, particularly in as much as it has not brought about a full devaluation of the naira, it has been orthodox enough to win the endorsement of the Fund. It has also had many of the same effects as one of the Fund's programmes with subsidy cuts leading to higher inflation, whilst wage retrenchment policies and public spending cuts are reflected in declining living standards. What it has failed to do is stimulate growth in an overwhelmingly oil dependent economy. Hopes have been expressed that agriculture will be stimulated by abolition of the marketing boards and the devaluation of the naira, but so far the results of these measures have been minimal. Furthermore, it is questionable whether the government will be able to provide sufficient finance to stimulate development in the face of an uncertain oil market. Whilst IMF approval of the austerity programme has brought about further inputs of finance it is doubtful whether these will prove sufficient to meet Nigeria's needs. In the face of this scenario of economic decline, it is hardly surprising to note that the Babangida regime is showing signs of instability as evidenced by growing religious tensions and rumblings from the discontented labour movement. On the positive side there is a clear potential for the use of tactics such as countertrade and creeping default payments to wring concessions out of creditors. Equally significantly, Nigeria has won the support of the IMF and the World Bank, which have been known to exert pressure on creditors to give favourable terms to certain debtor states. It remains to be seen whether or not such forces can effect an alleviation of the terms of Nigerian debt so that the country will have a genuine chance of recovery.

4

Zaire: debt in an absolutist kleptocracy

The history of Zaire's debt crisis is a chequered one. In the late 1970s and early 1980s, Zaire earned a reputation as the 'sick man of Africa' due to its increasing inability to meet its debt obligations and its all too apparent unwillingness to adhere to IMF austerity programmes. During this period Zaire attained an almost unparalleled notoriety for economic mismanagement and disaster. However, in 1983 all this changed as Zaire mended its bridges with the IMF and its western creditors. Zaire's subsequent faithfulness to the IMF's dictates earned it a new and contrasting reputation as the Fund's model pupil in Africa. More recently, however, Zaire has broken with the IMF yet again. This chequered development raises a number of questions. We might start by asking what Zaire's role in these events has been? Is Zairean debt attributable to the mismanagement and profligacy of the Mobutu regime as many commentators insist, or is it the result of adverse developments in the world economy? How are we to interpret Zaire's off-on-off relationship with the IMF? Is Mobutu's reconciliation with the Fund in 1983 to be seen as the reform of a reprobate ruler? Is this simply a return to his former profligate ways, or is it to be seen as reflecting some element of dubiety about the efficacy of the IMF cure for indebtedness? We shall attempt to answer these questions by describing the origins of Zaire's debt and the progress of its relationship with the IMF.

ORIGINS OF THE ZAIREAN DEBT

It has become the norm for analyses of the Zairean political economy to begin by focusing on the contrast between the country's potential wealth and its actual status as the fourth poorest nation in the world.[1] Despite having plentiful stocks of mineral resources such as copper, cobalt, uranium, and diamonds, Zaire's GNP stood at an appallingly low US$140 per capita in 1984 and its external debt is one of the largest in Africa.[2] According to World Bank figures, the disbursed total was US$4.8 billion at the end of 1985, up from US$4.2 billion in 1984. However, these figures exclude various short term, non-guaranteed and other (e.g. IMF) liabilities. The more comprehensive OECD figures put the total debt at US$5.9 billion at the end of 1985, a 17 per cent increase on the previous year's total of US$5 billion (see Tables 4.1 and 4.2). Moreover, a considerable proportion of this debt had been borrowed from private banks on non-concessional terms. Wood notes that the terms agreed for Zaire were considerably worse than those agreed for loans in thirty other countries. The terms for Zaire (other countries in brackets) were: interest rate 6.9 per cent (2.6 per cent), maturity 14.9 years (30.7 years), grace period 4.4 years (7.8 years) and grant element 20.6 per cent (57.2 per cent).[2] About two-thirds of this debt is owed to Paris Club official creditors, whilst some US$350 million is owed to London Club commercial creditors.[3] Debt service represents a major obligation, having risen from 10 per cent of the national budget in 1982 to 44 per cent in 1985.[4] The World Bank has projected a rise in debt service from US$750.6 million in 1986 to US$755.0 million in 1987, falling to US$713.2 million in 1988 and then gradually declining to some US$500 million in 1993.[5]

The explanation for Zairean poverty and indebtedness lies with various factors. In part Zaire was the victim of a number of developments that were beyond its control. The decline in the world price of copper was a particularly heavy blow. Having reached a peak of US$1.40 per pound in April 1974 the price slumped to the mid-sixty-cents range in 1976. Young and Turner note that the fall in copper prices played a major role in causing a US$600 million decline in the purchasing power of Zairean exports in 1975. They also point to the effects of the rising oil price which caused oil import costs to quadruple between 1973-7. By 1977 Zaire was spending US$200 million a year on oil imports, which accounted for 20 per cent of available foreign exchange. The Angolan civil war also played its part in Zaire's economic disaster since it brought about the closure of the Benguela railway in August 1975, this being the cheapest

Table 4.1 External public debt[a] according to the World Bank

	1980	1981	1982	1983	1984	1985
Total (incl undisbursed)	5,084	4,843	4,735	4,991	4,944	5,650
Disbursed total of which:	4,288	4,213	4,083	4,384	4,240	4,825
Official creditors	2,685	2,864	2,830	3,404	3,396	4,063
Multilateral[b]	467	463	512	571	585	693
Bilateral	2,216	2,401	2,318	2,833	2,812	3,370
Private creditors	1,603	1,349	1,253	980	844	762
Net flows[c] of which:	333	230	111	113	34	27
Official creditors	157	196	118	129	76	63
Multilateral[b]	93	21	51	79	46	64
Bilateral	64	175	67	51	30	-1
Private creditors	176	34	-7	-17	-42	-36
Net transfers[d] of which:	135	104	40	17	-169	-193
Official creditors	52	146	87	105	-52	-90
Multilateral[b]	82	10	41	66	33	50
Bilateral	-30	137	46	39	-86	-140
Private creditors	84	-42	-47	-87	-116	-103
Total debt service[e]	365	195	135	186	320	341
as % of exports of goods and services	16.7	11.9	8.7	11.2	...	...
Disbursed debt/GNP (%)	74.1	82.7	80.1	99.7	137.0	...

Source: Economist Intelligence Unit, Country Report: Zaire, Rwanda, Burundi, 1, (London, The Economist, 1987), p.19

a Including publicly guaranteed private debt; maturity over one year
b Excluding IMF
c Disbursements less amortization
d Disbursements less amortization and interest payments
e Principal and interest.

Table 4.2 External debt and liabilities[a] according to the OECD

	$m (year end) 1984	1985
OECD countries and capital markets		
Official development assistance	640	781
Non-bank trade claims	2,219	2,671
of which: Long-term	2,188	2,643
Guaranteed bank claims	175	101
Other bank claims	577	698
of which: Long-term	388	417
Non-bank deposits	-	-
Multilateral		
Concessional	486	575
Non-concessional	99	118
Other claims	260	238
Use of IMF credit	585	721
Total	5,041	5,903

Source: Economist Intelligence Unit, Country Report: Zaire, Rwanda, Burundi: 1, (London, The Economist, 1987), p.19

a Total debt, including short-term and non-guaranteed trade and other claims

and fastest route to the Shaba copperbelt. These difficulties were compounded by the Shaba incursions of 1977 and 1978.[6]

However, Zaire's debt problems cannot be blamed solely on unfortunate world developments. We must also note the misconceived development policy, which put an emphasis on expensive and ultimately unproductive prestige projects. During 1973-5 Zaire contracted US$2.6 billion in loans to finance ambitious ventures such as the Maluku Steel Mill and the Inga-Shaba powerline.[7] The Maluku Steel Mill could only produce steel at about eight times the cost of imported steel and it never operated at above 10 per cent of its 250,000 ton capacity. It had effectively ceased operations by 1980.[8] The Inga-Shaba powerline was similarly disastrous, contributing to a total Zairean capacity of 1,750MW, of which only 350MW found a use.[9] In the attempt to find customers for this excess capacity the Zairean government has set up the Zofi industrial free zone on the River Zaire estuary. Amongst the incentives being offered to foreign investors is cheap power.

According to many analysts, the most influential factor in Zaire's economic crisis has been the corruption, which in Delamaide's words, 'reaches an intensity in Mobutu's Zaire that goes beyond shame and almost beyond imagination.'[10] In Brussels it is rumoured that Mobutu's personal holdings in Swiss bank accounts amount to some US$5 billion. Those who are close to Mobutu also take a substantial share of the spoils. Loyal lieutenants are given spectacular gifts, such as Mercedes cars and houses, and are free to misappropriate state funds at will. Callaghy points to the Shaba Regional Commissioner, who grossed US$100,000 a month in 1975 of which only 2 per cent was his salary, whilst in the same year 'a prominent general reputedly had a monthly salary of 45,000 Zaires plus numerous informal payments, including 8,000 Zaires a month paid to him out of a special account in the Banque de Kinshasa.'[11] Indeed, a parallel economy based on gross corruption gained increasing importance, with activities such as coffee smuggling attaining a huge scale.

Callaghy attributes this high level of corruption to the patrimonial nature of the Zairean state, which he sees as an African variant on the European absolutist state. He points to a number of levels on which Mobutu's regime fits the absolutist typology. Mobutu was careful to dismantle all inherited structures at his accession to power in 1965, banning all political organizations and depriving the legislature of any independent power. Complementary to this was Mobutu's attempt to gain control over autonomous sources of power such as the trade unions and the press. Having curbed any potential source of opposition Mobutu proceeded with a complex of processes designed to consolidate his rule. He has manoeuvred to ensure his control of coercive power in the form of the military. He also proceeded in the construction of a unitary state in which power was concentrated in his own person. Thus, the state was merged with Mobutu's party, the Mouvement Populaire de la Révolution (MPR), which was declared the supreme institution in the country in 1970. Mobutu's domination has been underpinned through promulgation of the state ideology of Mobutuism, which has the advantage of enabling Mobutu to change the official political line at will. Central to Mobutu's consolidation process was his patrimonialization of power and the development of what Callaghy terms a political aristocracy through which Mobutu rules. All the positions and perquisites of power are controlled by Mobutu and he distributes them to his loyal lieutenants. In this way, he has surrounded himself with a 'court', or 'aristocracy', consisting of influential members of the state mechanism, the parastatal sector, and his family. He rules through this aristocracy by means of a complex network of patron-client relationships. Callaghy thus sees Mobutu's rulership as absolutist in that it is based on a centralized, authoritarian state, which extends its power through patron-clientelist relationships.[12]

This system is essentially unproductive since Mobutu's patronage power and, in turn, that of his 'aristocracy' is dependent on the booty they have plundered from the state mechanism, or the country at large. An example of their activities is provided by the 'Zaireanization Programme' of 1973, under which various foreign-owned enterprises were nationalized, but were distributed amongst Mobutu's cronies rather than being taken under state control. The programme was an economic disaster. Young and Turner recount that the *acquéreurs* (those members of the elite fortunate enough to be awarded some share of the spoils) for the most part had little or no business experience, a quality that was reflected in their management of their new enterprises. Many *acquéreurs* simply engaged in asset-stripping when it became plain that their businesses were failing. As a result the Zairean commercial infrastructure became severely depleted and this in turn caused shortages of many basic products. The resultant inflation motivated many *acquéreurs* to resort to hoarding which gave a further impetus to the upward spiral of inflation. Other *acquéreurs* attempted to avoid business failure by retaining the previous owner as a manager, which also led to higher inflation since both owner and manager would attempt to maximize their returns at the expense of higher prices. Furthermore, numerous *acquéreurs* simply refused to pay taxes and would not honour the debts that their new businesses had been committed to prior to Zaireanization. Within a short period the Zaireanization Programme had become a notorious fiasco and the government had little option but to begin returning those concerns that had not been bankrupted to their former owners, in order to avert even worse economic disaster.[13]

Unfortunately, there are many more examples of gross corruption. For a long period, the major source of illicit funds was Sozacom, the parastatal responsible for marketing copper and cobalt. The Zairean elite used Sozacom's right of access to foreign exchange to make money on the black market. It is estimated that about US$1 billion was misappropriated in this way.[14] Such activities did great damage to the Zairean economy. According to one estimate some 20 per cent of the budget was lost through corruption.[15] One group of thirteen members of the Zaire parliament wrote to Mobutu in December 1980 noting that if even a quarter of the elite's illicit earnings were returned from their foreign bank accounts it would be sufficient to pay off Zaire's debts. Mobutu did not appreciate the advice and all thirteen were arrested.[16]

Given these circumstances it is easy to see how Zaire has attained its unenviable status as one of Africa's most indebted countries and one of its most notorious kleptocracies. In the remaining sections of this chapter we shall examine how the Mobuto brand of absolutist kleptocracy has attempted to deal with the problem of debt.

ZAIRE VERSUS THE IMF

The Zairean debt ran out of control in 1975 in the wake of the OPEC price hike, the collapse of the copper price, and the recession. It was at this stage that Zaire stopped paying any principal or interest on its commercial bank debt, which amounted to US$700-800 million at that time. The IMF first intervened in March 1976 when it agreed a stabilization programme, the first of five, with Zaire. All of the so-called 'Mobutu Plans' adhered to normal IMF conditionality, involving measures to raise tax revenues, reduce state spending, limit corruption, and ensure that debts were repaid on time. In fact the first two plans lapsed very quickly because of Zairean failure to meet the IMF's terms. Apparently, Mobutu and his aristocracy 'had no intention of living up to the agreements', since they 'do not view international organisations and aid agencies as sources of development assistance but rather as channels for access to more resources, particularly foreign exchange.'[17]

After these failures Zaire's commercial creditors became increasingly concerned and the IMF insisted on installing one of their own teams in the Zaire Central Bank to run the nation's financial affairs as a precondition for more aid. The leader of this team, Erwin Blumenthal, a retired Bundesbank official, decided to enforce tight limits on credit and foreign exchange facilities in December 1978. He actually denied access to such facilities to several of Mobutu's closest associates, including Mobutu's uncle, Litho Mobutu.[18] This badly undercut the patronage power of Mobutu and his lieutenants, which is to a considerable extent dependent on the very free availability of these resources. The ensuing conflict between the Zairean elite and the IMF team resulted in a decisive defeat for the latter. The team was small, subject to frequent personnel changes and to unremitting harassment from Mobutu and his 'aristocrats'. On one occasion soldiers under the command of General Tukuzu, Mobutu's father-in-law, threatened Blumenthal with sub-machine guns because they could not get access to foreign exchange for their general. By the end of his stay in Zaire Blumenthal was sleeping with a shotgun under his bed and he had a radio to keep him in touch with the West German and US embassies. He later commented on his year in Zaire in 1978-9 saying that it was:

> alarmingly clear that the corruptive system in Zaire with all its wicked and ugly manifestations, its mismanagement and fraud, will destroy all endeavours of institutions, of friendly governments, and of the commercial banks towards recovery and rehabilitation of Zaire's economy. Sure, there will be new promises by Mobutu, by members of his government, rescheduling, and rescheduling again of a growing external public debt, but no (repeat: no) prospect for Zaire's creditors to get their money back in any foreseeable future.[19]

With the departure of Blumenthal in 1979, the IMF team was effectively tamed and it never took such controversial actions again.

Subsequent attempts to control the Zairean debt also foundered. In 1979 Zaire hired a team of investment banking firms, including Lazard Frères, Lehman Brothers, Kuhn Loeb, and S.G. Warburg to handle negotiations with the IMF, the World Bank, western bilateral donors, and the London and Paris Clubs. However, the Zairean 'aristocracy' remained intransigent when faced with the prospect of having to meet conditions that conflicted with their interests. Delamaide notes that:

> A US$1.2 billion IMF programme worked out in 1979 led to a single payment of $200 million in 1980, before the IMF suspended the programme because Zaire failed to meet the targets for cutting the budget deficit.[20]

A programme agreed in 1981 with some US$1.06 billion (SDR 912 million) was suspended after two drawings (worth a total of SDR 175 million), again due to failure to cut the budget deficit.[21] In late 1982 the team of bankers that had helped to negotiate these deals lost patience with Mobutu and severed their contract with Zaire. Callaghy suggests that the Zairean leadership had consciously used the bankers to provide international legitimacy, whilst they pursued their own interests in the normal corrupt manner.[22]

It is arguable that up to this stage the heavily indebted Zairean state was winning its battle with the IMF hands down, a course of events that directly conflicts with the account of those commentators who saw Zaire's relations with the IMF as an example of debt-induced Third World dependency. However, Zaire's successful resistance of the Fund was not attributable to the availability of alternative private sources of finance, as was the case with certain of the wealthier Latin American states. By the late 1970s, the private banks were becoming increasingly unwilling to lend to Mobutu.

In order to understand how Zaire has managed to hold off its creditors we must examine the following factors. First, Delamaide points out that the banks and northern countries were willing to show endless patience with Zaire in order to avoid the prospect of a default. Although this would not have constituted an insurmountable financial disaster, they wanted to avoid setting a bad precedent for other debtor nations.[23] Zaire was favoured with five reschedulings of its debt by the Paris Club and successive IMF programmes despite repeated failure to live up to the conditions set for aid. Second, Mobutu has shown great skill in manipulating external forces and alliances to his own advantage. As Callaghy notes, he has invariably been willing to acquiesce in externally-induced changes in order to acquire aid, only to renege on promises that did not suit his purposes when the situation allowed (e.g. when the external pressures were reduced, or when a political/military crisis such as the Shaba Wars allowed him to divert attention from financial issues.[24] He has been allowed to get away with this because of Zaire's abundant resources and concomitant strategic value to the western states. The importance that the USA attaches to keeping Zaire in the western sphere of influence was reflected in the leading role taken by the Kinshasa CIA station in arranging the 1965 coup that replaced the unstable Tshombe regime with Mobutu's military regime. Since that time the western states have repeatedly intervened to protect Mobutu from any radical threat. Prime examples are provided by the role of the French government in the two Shaba conflicts. During Shaba One, the French provided military transport planes to airlift in Moroccan troops to put down the invaders. They took an even more direct role in Shaba Two, providing paratroops, who together with Belgian forces, were responsible for retaking Kolwezi. The Americans also played a part, providing air transport.[25]

Mobutu repays his external guarantors for this support by taking care to align himself with their political wishes. Thus, he acts as a bastion against communism in Africa. He supported the FNLA against the Marxist MPLA in Angola and has more recently rendered signal assistance to UNITA in their continuing campaigns against the communist government in Angola. Mobutu has also won American plaudits for his opposition to the anti-Israeli stance promoted by Arabic states in international form. Young and Turner quote the then Ambassador to the UN Vance's comment on Mobutu's 'rather gallant' opposition to Arabic condemnations of Zionism at the Lima non-aligned conference in 1975.[26] Mobutu was one of the first in the recent rash of Black African leaders to have recognized Israel. In 1982, Mobutu earned the direct praise of President Reagan for sending 2,700 troops to Chad to fight against Libyan incursions into that state. He has also campaigned for an all-black Organization of African Unity, a measure that would also help to reduce the influence of Libya, America's prime enemy in North Africa.[27] Perhaps the most exceptional of Mobutu's diplomatic manoeuvres was the OTRAG deal of 1976 under which he ceded sovereignty over a large area of Zaire to a West German rocket company. According to some accounts, the deal was a cover story for an arrangement whereby the West German government was to be allowed to test cruise and intermediate range ballistic missiles in Zaire. Young and Turner have recently argued that there are no grounds for suggesting that the deal was anything other than a commercial transaction and conclude that its only diplomatic significance lay in Mobutu's wish to give the West Germans a stake in the survival of his regime.[28] Nevertheless, it is eminently clear that Mobutu is willing to go a long way to maintain the support of his western allies. It is this that has allowed him an unusual degree of autonomy in the economic sphere.

THE IMF TRIUMPHANT?

The year 1983 saw an apparent transformation in Zaire's relations with its creditors and the IMF. The economy was in even direr straits due to falling world prices for Zaire's main exports, such as copper, cobalt, and other metals. This left Mobutu with little option but to approach the IMF for funding yet again. Assistance was forthcoming in the shape of a compensatory finance facility of SDR 114.5 million and a fifteen month standby loan of SDR 228 million. However, these facilities were only agreed in December 1983 after Mobutu had proved his serious intent to carry through the reforms that the Fund had previously tried to force on him unsuccessfully. Thus, 1983 saw cuts in government spending, a tightening of budgetary controls, the beginning of price liberalization, devaluation of the zaire by 77.5 per cent and, significantly, the abolition of the notoriously corrupt Sozacom (though apparently the latter measure was undertaken in the face of fierce resistance from Mobutu).[29] These actions, together with the way in which Mobutu scrupulously observed successive stabilization programmes, wrought a profound change in Zaire's relationship with the IMF. The one-time sick man of Africa had become the Fund's 'model pupil'. Mobutu's somewhat unexpected acquiescence to IMF demands may have been attributable to a perception that his country's economic ills were becoming increasingly desperate, combined with a sense that the threat of a Zairean default was no longer such an effective blackmail weapon compared with the similar threats then being made by the large Latin American debtors. In this context he could no longer rely on the endless patience of his northern creditors and he therefore had to make some efforts to satisfy their demands.

Certainly, Mobutu gave every appearance of being serious about applying a programme of economic reforms based on the market-oriented tenets favoured by the Fund.

After the 1983 devaluation the zaire was floated and allowed to find its own level. The government sought to reduce public spending with a succession of austerity budgets and a policy of privatization. Thus, it reduced the staff of the notoriously inefficient parastatal, Air Zaire by 6,500 to 2,500 and announced its willingness to sell 40 per cent of the equity of both this company and the state maritime company CMZ. Additional measures included the abolition of Petrozaire's (another parastatal) monopoly over imports of petroleum and the use of credit controls to reduce government borrowing, thus limiting monetary growth and curbing inflation.[30]

It can be argued that Zaire's new-found economic probity bore some fruit. The flotation of the zaire went a long way towards wiping out the black market, reducing the differential between the official and the black market rates to between 5 and 10 per cent (previously the official exchange rate had placed the zaire at five times its black market value). This has in turn reduced the incentive to smuggle, which raised exports by 20 per cent in dollar terms in 1984, with diamond output rising 55 per cent. The decontrolling of agricultural producer prices led to price rises ranging from 100 to 200 per cent, which stimulated increases in production in some parts of the country of certain food and export crops, notably coffee.[31] The IMF also expressed some satisfaction that the budget deficit fell as a percentage of GDP from 10.5 per cent in 1982 to 3.6 per cent in 1984 whilst GDP itself showed a modest growth of 2 per cent in 1984. According to the National Statistical Institute (INS), a government body, inflation registered a substantial decline from 101 per cent in 1983 to 14.3 per cent in 1984.[32]

Zaire's creditors were sufficiently impressed with this good behaviour to reward Mobutu with further aid and reschedulings. With the conclusion of the December 1983 IMF standby loan, further agreements were signed covering April 1985 to April 1986 (worth SDR 162 million) and the 22 months beginning in April 1986 (worth SDR 214 million). The Paris Club also awarded successive reschedulings, the first covering about a billion dollars of debt falling due in 1983-4, the second covering US$305 million due to mature in 1985 and the first quarter of 1986, whilst a third dealt with US$100 million falling due between April 1986 and March 1987. In September 1985 the World Bank's representative in Kinshasa announced that the Bank planned to commit

US$550 million to Zaire in 1986-8, including US$300 million from International Development Association and US$150 million from the special fund for Sub-Saharan Africa.[33]

Unfortunately, all was not as well as these indicators would seem to suggest. Although government sources suggested that inflation had fallen during 1983-4, alternative figures gathered by the Economic and Social Research Institute (IRES) an independent university body, indicated that inflation had, in fact, risen from 42.3 per cent in 1983 to 76.7 per cent in 1984.[34] Whilst it would probably be wise to take both the INS and the IRES figures with a pinch of salt the evidence from Zaire does tend to suggest that inflation rose after 1983. According to Callaghy, the impact of the December 1983 stabilization programme 'was quickly felt by most of Zaire. The price of oil, other fuels, the key food items rose between 200 and 300 per cent over the next three months.'[35] Indeed, various analysts have noted that large devaluations tend to be inflationary. It must also be noted that whilst GNP grew by 2 per cent in 1984, population rose by 3 per cent, which meant that per capita income had fallen.[36] Nor was Mobutu's agricultural price liberalization uniformly successful. Zaire is a huge country (four times the size of France) with less than 12,000 kilometres of regularly usable roads, of which less than 3,000 kilometres are all-weather roads. This means that many farmers are too isolated to take advantage of the new incentives to market their surplus. It has been calculated that farmers receive only 20 to 40 per cent of the retail price of their produce due to high transport costs. In some areas farmers are at the mercy of the only operator in the region who owns a truck. Even where the price rises have succeeded in raising production, there are doubts as to whether the benefits will be lasting. For example, increased coffee production was brought about by smallholders who have no access to credit or training in improved farming methods. Neither the state nor private capital have shown much interest in providing these services and so the prospects for long-term development look bleak.[37]

Indeed, it might be argued that the austerity programme compounds such difficulties in various ways. By keeping a limit on wages whilst raising prices, austerity encourages government officials to indulge in the common practice of making private arrangements with the taxpayers that allow them to evade tax. With revenues thus reduced there is an incentive for the government to raise money by levying taxes against business instead - although it is the business sector, which it is supposed to be encouraging. Austerity has also meant that the government is unable to budget sufficiently for investment in physical and social infrastructure. The investment budget for 1985 was set at an already low Z2,600 million (US$65 million) only to be reduced to Z2,000 million (some US$40 million) in April. No disbursements were authorized during the first half of the year and the depreciation of the zaire reduced the budget to a foreign exchange equivalent of US$38 million by November. This was not only inadequate to provide needed investment in the severely run-down transport network (see above), but also meant that the government was unable to meet its counterpart funding obligations on numerous development projects. (Most aid donors insist that recipient nations provide some portion of the cost of an aid project, usually those costs incurred within the recipient state itself. This obligation is known as counterpart funding.) The World Bank was able to disburse less than 50 per cent of its commitments to Zairean projects during the three years up to 1985 due to inadequate government counterpart funding for agreed programmes. Furthermore, the liberalization of capital movements undertaken as part of the austerity programme freed foreign businesses in Zaire to repatriate their profits, a development that is certain to enhance capital flight out of the country.[38]

In addition to all these problems, it must be remembered that debt service is projected to rise until 1988 and then to decline only gradually until the early 1990s. The numerous reschedulings accorded to Zaire tend only to exacerbate this situation. According to an authoritative source cited in the Financial Times, the 1983 Paris Club rescheduling added US$1.2 billion to the debt service falling due in the period 1985-91. Zaire's inability to meet these commitments has been proved by its resorting to further reschedulings, which simply postpone the necessity for repayment. It has to be noted that in spite of these arrangements Zaire's debt repayments for 1984 amounted to US$191.5 million more than the aid it received in the year. Mobutu's three closest western allies, the USA, France, and Belgium, received debt service payments over US$110 million in excess of fresh aid that they gave during the year (the USA made no disbursements at all in 1984). Over the three years to 1986 there was a net outflow of US$800 million due to debt services. A leading aid donor has calculated that even if sufficient Zairean debt is rescheduled to keep debt service down to 20 per cent over the next five years, minimum aid of US$430 million per annum would be needed to keep net transfers at zero.[39] This fails to take into account the fact that Zaire suffers an outflow on services of between US$850-1,000 million per annum (see Table 4.3). Clearly, these circumstances are most unconducive to any form of development.

Table 4.3 Balance of payments, 1980-4

$m

	1980	1981	1982	1983[a]	1984[a]
Exports (fob)	1,988	1,475	1,454	1,523	1,787
Imports (fob)	-1,436	-1,269	-1,124	-1,114	-1,170
Trade balance	552	206	329	409	617
Services[b] (net)	-883	-864	-870	-898	-966
Net transfers/non debt[c]	183	240	172	177	120
Current account balance	-148	-418	-369	-312	-229
Public capital[d]	-22	-166	-156	-226	-187
Private capital; errors and omissions	-80	-145	-128	74	-55
SDR allocation	20	19	-	-	-
Overall balance	-230	-710	-653	-464	-471

Source: Banque du Zaire; quoted in Economist Intelligence Unit, Zaire to the 1990s: Will Retrenchment Work? (Special Report 227 by Gregory Kronsten) (London, The Economist, 1986), p.46

a Provisional
b Includes interest and investment income
c Public and private unrequited transfers
d Net medium and long-term borrowing

Consequently, it is essential to mobilize private capital to finance Zaire's development. This is reflected in the 1986-90 development plan, which premisses its assumptions of 4 to 6 per cent average annual growth on an estimated private sector investment of US$1.86 billion. The public sector contribution is put at Z260.2 billion in 1985 prices, but projects are to be prioritized on the basis of a projected total financial resource availability of Z150 billion. As Table 4.4 shows, the latter figure will not be sufficient to cover all the transport projects, which are costed at Z152.4 billion. Clearly then the Zairean government is basing its hopes on increased private investment. Domestic capital is not sufficiently developed to provide a sufficient rate of investment to maintain the plan and is, in any case, predominantly dependent on the quick returns to be had from commerce rather than the longer term benefits to be gained from industry and infrastructure. As to the prospects for foreign capital, it has to be noted that there has not been one foreign investment since independence of more than US$50 million. Although the austerity programme motivated businessmen such as Adnan Khashoggi and Tiny Rowland to pay visits to Kinshasa, it did not persuade them to make any hard guarantees of investment. Nor has the Zofi free trading zone succeeded in attracting any major investment, despite offering an attractive programme of tax and energy pricing concessions.[40] Despite Mobutu's recent efforts it would seem that private capital still remembers Zaire as the sick man of Africa.

The implementation of Zaire's austerity programme has also had adverse effects on lower and middle income Zaireans. It would, of course, be true to say that the lower strata of Zairean society have always suffered under the kleptocratic system run by Mobutu and his lieutenants, which has traditionally produced very little in the way of public policy output. Nevertheless, the evidence suggests that austerity measures have made their situation still worse. We have already noted that the 1983 devaluation triggered price rises of key food items of between 200 to 300 per cent over the next three months. This was at a time when wages increased by only 20 per cent.[41] In the wake of the devaluation the zaire continued to float downwards and prices have continued to rise, whilst wages have remained largely stagnant. In early 1986 it was reported that a sack of maize, which will feed a family of five for a month, cost Z700, whilst a teacher was paid only Z1,000 a month. It was also calculated (very approximately) that the average Zairean salary was Z15,500 per annum (less than US$300 at the November 1985 exchange rate).[42] Austerity has meant not simply wage stagnation, but also massive lay-offs in the public sector. During the first year of the programme, the number of teachers and civil servants employed by the state fell from 260,000 to 178,000.[43] This involved the

Table 4.4 Five-year development plan, 1986-90[a]

Z bn; 1985 prices

	PRINT projects[b]	Other projects	Total	Share of total	Budget	Self-financing	Foreign	Total	Share of total	Proportion of Programme
				%					%	
Agriculture	13.6	9.5	23.1	8.9	4.0	7.0	19.0	30.0	20.0	130
Mining	18.5	4.4	22.9	8.8	-	15.0	8.0	23.0	15.3	100
Electricity/water	9.3	11.0	20.3	7.8	5.0	5.0	13.0	23.0	15.3	113
Transport	9.1	143.0	152.4	58.6	4.0	36.0	17.0	57.0	38.0	37
Education	0.4	12.6	12.9	4.9	3.0	1.0	2.0	6.0	4.0	47
Health	1.3	3.1	4.4	1.7	3.0	1.0	4.0	8.0	5.3	182
Other	3.0	21.2	24.2	9.3	1.0	-	2.0	3.0	2.0	12
Total[c]	55.1	205.1	260.2	100.0	20.0	65.0	65.0	150.0	100.0	58
%	21.2	78.8	100.0		13.3	43.3	43.3	100.0		

Source: Economist Intelligence Unit, Zaire to the 1990s: Will Retrenchment Work? (Special Report 227 by Gregory Kronsten) (London, The Economist, 1986), p. 32

a Including only projects for which finance is expected to be available
b Programme intérimaire de réhabilitation economique 1983-5 (PRINT)
c Figures may not add due to rounding

elimination of several thousand fictitious names from the payroll. However, it has to be noted that highly placed government functionaries tended not to be affected, whilst essential services such as health and education were cut to the bone. In certain instances it would appear that headmasters elected to keep fictitious staff on the payroll so that they could appropriate the salaries, whilst dismissing their actual staff. Not surprisingly, the results of retrenchment were disastrous. It was reported that in one Kinshasa secondary school a teaching staff of around forty were reduced to five and similar reports were received from all over the country.[44] Higher education has also been badly affected with students having their right to free board and lodging withdrawn, a measure that tends to penalize the lower strata.[45]

Indeed, it would be fair to say that the ordinary people have been the main victims of austerity. It is notable that Mobutu has allowed wages to stagnate, prices to soar and basic services to collapse and has put up resistance only to the IMF demands that might adversely affect the perquisites of his 'aristocracy' (e.g. the abolition of Sozacom). Certainly, he has not allowed the clean-up of the bureaucracy to reach any of his lieutenants. Clearly, Mobutu is determined that if his northern creditors have to be paid their pound of flesh it will not be himself or his cronies who have to pay, but the ordinary people of Zaire.

In response to these increasing demands the lower strata have little option, but to resort to their own survival strategies. For Zaireans this tends to mean having recourse to the ubiquitous parallel market. MacGaffey points out that in the face of scarcity and exploitation, 'people have organized their own production and distribution of foodstuffs, systems of export and import, and even the necessary infrastructure to make them work'. She cites instances of rural farmers sending their foodcrops to urban kin in exchange for items such as cloth, kerosene, and manufactures.[46] However one might also expect that this uneven distribution of the burdens of austerity would provoke discontent and unrest amongst the disadvantaged groups. Such fears were expressed in a document of 19 July 1985 signed by the first vice-president of the legislative council, Kakume Mwana Kahambwe, on behalf of 20 members of the Zaire parliament. It complained that many civil servants had not been paid and that the alleged successes of the austerity programme had not filtered down to the general populace. Consequently, it argued, internal security was at risk.[47] Support for this view was provided by instances such as the strike of workers at the harbour of Matadi and on the Zaire River during January 1985. They brought all commercial traffic to a halt as they struck for a 50 per cent wage rise, in direct opposition to the 25 per cent wage limit then in force. Mobutu had to step in so as to persuade the strikers directly to accept 25 per cent.[48] Evidently Mobutu was well aware of grass roots resentment of the austerity programme and he is reputed to have commented to one Western minister that, 'Kinshasa is a powder keg.'[49]

It would seem that Mobutu hoped to contain discontentment with his usual methods of repression and there is some evidence to suggest that he was supported in this course of action by certain of his creditors. West Germany provided military aid of DM2.5 million to set up a new Civil Guard numbering 20,000 men, one of whose duties was designated as crowd control. The USA played its part by promising to increase military aid by 50 per cent. It was suggested that 'a US-West German axis has been emerging in which the Americans provide finance and the Germans hardware and know-how.'[50] Indeed, there was speculation that Mobutu timed the arrest of seven members of an opposition party, the Union for Democracy and Social Progress in December 1985 to coincide with IMF talks, in order to demonstrate to his creditors that he could quell discontent and make the austerity programme stick.[51] Apparently then Mobutu's plan was to keep Zaire on the path of austerity using a rod of iron.

BREAKING POINT?

Despite Mobutu's apparent determination to press on with austerity the signs that a breaking point was being reached began to emerge in mid-1986. Both Mobutu and his prime minister, Kengo Wa Dondo, pleaded for more external funding to assist Zaire through its travails.[52] This was followed by Mobutu's decision of May 1986 to raise public sector wages by up to 150 per cent according to grade, breaching the 25 per cent limit agreed with the IMF, to lower the price of water by 75 per cent, and to nationalize the Bank of Kinshasa (allegedly to boost savings).[53] These developments culminated in the declaration of October 1986 that debt service repayments were to be limited to 10 per cent of export receipts and 20 per cent of the national budget from January 1987. Other proposals included suspending flotation of the zaire and restoration of its parity with the SDR; reduction of bank rates; increasing the capital budget by 20 per cent; raising provision for salaries by 20 per cent; increasing central and regional administrative budgets by 35 per cent; limiting internal debt service to 5 per cent of the budget; and a priority system for the allocation of foreign exchange. Mobutu also dismissed Kengo, who had been very much associated with the austerity programme and elevated a critic of the IMF, Mabi Mlumba, to the post of finance minister.[54] Although these activities betokened a substantial departure from IMF orthodoxy, Mobutu was careful to ensure that he did not break with the Fund completely. Whilst noting that the austerity programme had led to a transfer of capital out of Zaire rather than badly needed investment Mobutu also commented as follows:

> Any future programme with the IMF should be seen as a supplementary aid to national efforts, and concluded with a view to a real launch of the Zaire economy, and no longer simply as a programme of austerity and stabilisation.[55]

Evidently, Mobutu was not rebelling against the IMF in order to tread his own path. Rather, he was manoeuvering for a more advantageous deal with the Fund.

Mobutu had prepared the ground for this gambit when he sent Nguza Karl I Bond to take up his ambassadorship to the United States. Nguza's speech upon presenting his diplomatic letters of credence to President Reagan ran as follows:

> Zaire is a large country, and when one considers the geopolitics of Africa, it stands out as a country that must be taken into account as regards policy in Africa in general, and in Central and Southern Africa in particular. Fortunately, this great country is a friend of the USA.[56]

A State Department survey of voting patterns at the United Nations General Assembly underlined Nguza's point, noting that Zaire was one of the USA's most loyal allies at the UN, supporting the American position on 23 per cent of resolutions.[56] It is thought that Nguza's appearance as ambassador to the United States was designed not only to remind President Reagan of Zaire's strategic value, but also as a propaganda blow to Mobutu's enemies in the American Congress. Some years before, when Nguza had been out of favour in Kinshasa, he had testified to Mobutu's corruption before a Congressional committee.[57] His subsequent appearance as the president's representative to Washington was a clear sign that Mobutu was stronger than any of the opposition forces that challenged him. Thus, in a typically adroit piece of diplomacy Mobutu had delivered a warning to his enemies and an equally timely reminder of his value to his friends just before issuing his challenge to the IMF.

It is notable that around this period Mobutu was very active in his role of guarantor of western interests throughout Africa. Zaire resumed its participation in the OAU, after having walked out when the Saharan Democratic Arab Republic was recognized, only to revive the idea of an all-black forum, arguing that this proposal was not aimed against anybody (an assertion that might be treated with some scepticism by Libya).[58] Mobutu also followed the French lead in sending 350 troops to Togo to help put down the attempted coup of September 1986 against President Eyedama.[59] He also took the opportunity to draw media attention to Zaire's role in the Chadian conflict during a visit to Hissan Habré in the wake of the recapture of the strategic town of Oudi-Doum by Habré's Fant forces in March 1987. Mobutu complained that the western media invariably focused on the assistance rendered to Chad by western forces, whereas Zairean assistance, he said, 'has contributed immensely to the victories won by the Fant over the enemy'. This assistance had involved training 2,000 Chadian commandos at the Kotakoli centre in Zaire and provision of Zairean pilots for Chadian military aircraft. According to Mobutu 26 Zaireans were killed in the Chadian conflict.[60]

Perhaps the most crucial card in Mobutu's hand is his role in helping to siphon American arms to UNITA forces in Angola. This operation involves the old Kamina airbase situated near the Angolan border. News began to emerge in early 1987 to the effect that the Belgian-built airbase was being used as a crucial staging post in the supply of arms to UNITA. Apparently, shipments of American arms, including machine guns and rocket launchers, are transported from

America to Zaire in cases marked 'machine parts' by the privately owned St Lucia Airways, which is based in the Caribbean island of St Lucia. It has been reported that cargo planes belonging to St Lucia Airways have been observed landing at Ndjili Airport in Kinshasa during the night. Either the plane will be carrying arms, or it will pick up arms and supplies brought in by American military C130s and C141s. Having refuelled and taken on any cargo that may await it, the plane will fly on to Kamina where the arms are unloaded by UNITA men under the guard of American soldiers. In August 1987 it was reported that the previous few months had seen an average of three flights a week.

The Americans are anxious to maintain the security of this operation and the Zaireans have taken extraordinary pains to assist them. No Zairean personnel take direct part in the transfer of weaponry, which is run by black Americans masquerading as Africans. When news of the operation broke, the CIA decided it had to vet all journalists who wished to visit Zaire in order to protect Kamina's security. As a result, all foreign journalists who wish to visit Zaire must have their visa applications cleared by the American embassy in Kinshasa. Zairean consulates abroad that have difficulties in determining how to deal with journalists waiting to visit Zaire have to refer their queries to the US embassy rather than to their own government. Western diplomats have expressed concern about the safety of journalists since soldiers guarding the Kamina airbase have order to fire at intruders on sight.

Mobutu is clearly aware of the importance of the Kamina airbase as a bargaining chip. In a visit of December 1986 he asked the American administration to rehabilitate the base and to make an immediate commitment of US$20 million for this purpose. The value placed on the base by the Reagan administration is signified by the fact that the Americans were already considering asking Mobutu for base rights at Kamina. It has even been suggested that Pentagon strategists advocated that Kamina be used as a refuelling stop for American bombers during the April 1986 raid on Libya in the event of Britain refusing to co-operate with their venture into 'Rambo politics'. Evidently, the Kamina airbase is of considerable strategic importance to the USA.[61]

By co-operating with the Americans over Kamina, it would appear that Mobutu has been able to win concessions in the economic sphere. During the same visit that Mobutu encouraged the Americans to take over Kamina, President Reagan referred to him as 'one of my oldest and closest friends in Africa', sympathized over Zaire's 'heavy debt burden' and promised that Washington would do its best 'to ease the way' in negotiations with the Fund. A senior official in the US administration was also quoted to the effect that the IMF should give Zaire 'room to manoeuvre' to boost its growth rates and that the US would support Zaire at international bodies.[62] Mobutu had pulled off his old trick of exploiting his strategic value to his western guarantors in order to maximize his autonomy in the economic sphere.

It would appear that the US administration fulfilled its promise to ease Zaire's path with the Fund. Indeed, they caused a senior official of the IMF to resign in protest. Mr C. David Finch, the head of the Fund's exchange and trade relations department, told the IMF's board that his resignation had been prompted by American use of undue pressure to induce the Fund to reduce the conditionalities on loans to Zaire and Egypt.[63]

The first results of America's efforts were felt during the internecine negotiations for Zaire's 1987 budget. Initially the government placed the deficit for the year at Z8,000 million, and then revised the figure down to Z3,839 million. However, negotiations with the IMF established that Zaire could have a deficit of Z6,000 million and so the government promptly went to work boosting capital spending and remuneration. A US government source was quoted as saying that the 'IMF met Zaire halfway on the wage increase issue' by allowing 'small' increases in pay, including public sector wage rises of 20 per cent from June 1987, on top of the 40 per cent rise of May 1986. Zaire has also finalized a new agreement with the Fund to replace the April 1986 standby arrangement that was abrogated when Mobutu announced his limits on debt service. The new agreement is worth about US$126 million, part of which may be in the form of a lump sum compensation for declining export receipts attributable to falling copper and cobalt prices. For his part, Mobutu has apparently abandoned his version of creeping default and opted for the continuation of the flotation of the zaire.

Clearly, Mobutu has won some concessions from the Fund, though the full extent of them will only become clear over time. Whilst the IMF has had to compromise some of its principles it has at least managed to end the Zairean rebellion before it effectively began and to steer Mobutu back on to an approximation of the path of free-market virtue. As has been the case with all the preceding stabilization programmes, the real losers are likely to be the people of Zaire, who will have to pay the higher taxes and the higher petroleum prices that have been agreed with the Fund in order to try and lower the budget deficit.[64]

CONCLUSION

In answer to the questions posed at the beginning of this case study, we have to note that Zaire's debt is to a substantial degree the result of corruption and mismanagement, although the role of structural factors such as declining commodity prices should not be under-emphasized. The kleptocratic nature of the Mobutu regime is central to any explanation of Zaire's relations with the IMF. Prior to 1982, the Zairean 'aristocracy' gulled the Fund at every turn, abusing the terms of every stabilization programme that they agreed. It was only when the country's economic situation grew irretrievably desperate that Mobutu made his peace with the IMF. Even so, there is evidence to suggest that Mobutu implemented IMF conditionality in such a way that the perquisites of his 'aristocracy' were protected at the expense of the wellbeing of the lower strata of Zairean society. It would seem that his external guarantors were content to back him in this strategy by supplying the repressive apparatus necessary to quell any resultant popular discontent. When Mobutu found this strategy to be unsafe he reverted to his original tactic of trading on his strategic value to induce the USA to win him economic concessions from the Fund. This strategy appears to have been successful.

5

Ghana: indebtedness, recovery, and the IMF, 1977-87

by Jeffrey Haynes

INTRODUCTION

Between the early 1970s and the early 1980s the economy of Ghana regressed to the verge of collapse. There was a persistent heavy rise in price levels of goods and a slowing down in the growth rate of per capita incomes. Negative growth rates were registered for several years. From the early 1970s living standards of the average Ghanaian plummeted. One of the outcomes of the deteriorating economic conditions was political instability: between 1966-81 five military coups jolted Ghana.

While Ghana's economic degeneration had multiple causes, including generally fairly poor terms of trade during most of 1970-87, there is little doubt that over-ambitious attempts to build a large public sector on a narrow, poorly supported agrarian base (cocoa, timber) was a major cause of the country's problems. Most political leaders, whether civilian or military, believed that economic growth and their own political survival required the state to develop jobs, industries, and public welfare services. Governments could then use public funds, both to develop political support, as well as for personal financial gain. This broad, enduring programme led to increasingly large budget deficits and high domestic credit expansion, the major contributors to the inflation of the 1970s and early 1980s. The unwillingness of successive governments to adjust to external shocks that increased real costs (e.g. the 1973-4 and 1979-80 oil price rises) meant that the currency became highly over-valued.

Starting in April 1983, the Provisional National Defence Council (PNDC) government undertook a number of major reform measures aimed at producing a resumption of economic growth. By May 1987, Ghana's currency, the cedi

(₵) had been devalued fifty-seven-fold: from ₵2.75 to ₵158 to the United States dollar (US$). Cocoa producer prices were increased and prices of many commodities 'decontrolled', while interest rates were raised. Wages and salaries, however, did not rise sufficiently to cover the vastly increased prices. A key component of Ghana's economic adjustment programme was that the country received an infusion of foreign capital from the International Monetary Fund (IMF) and the World Bank, so that the adjustment would generate economic growth. This inevitably produced an acceleration in Ghana's international indebtedness, from US$1,115.6 million in 1982 to US$2,400 million in 1985 (see Table 5.1). This chapter looks at the causes for Ghana's growing international indebtedness from the mid-1970s and seeks to identify reasons for this accretion of debt. The PNDC's economic policies and approach to the international financial agencies, such as the IMF and World Bank, form the second part of the chapter.

ECONOMIC DECLINE AND GROWING INDEBTEDNESS: 1977-83

It is difficult to quantify precisely the decline in living standards in Ghana from the 1960s, partly because of the paucity of economic statistics between 1977 and the mid-1980s, and partly because of the difficulty of assessing living standards where the populace is not totally dependent on the market economy. However, a general picture seems to emerge of an across-the-board rise in living standards in the 1950s, stagnation in the early 1960s, followed by a decline which became precipitous in the 1970s. By the end of the decade economic regression was reflected in many areas. Output in all sectors was abysmally low, while food production had not kept pace with the estimated 2.5-3 per cent per annum population increase. Cocoa production, traditionally the mainstay of the economy and accounting for an average two-thirds of export earnings, was approximately half of what it had been fifteen years earlier, down from 572,000 tons in 1964-5 to 288,000 tons in 1978-9. Gold mining was performing at a similar level; production in most manufacturing industries represented only a marginal utilization of capacity (20-25 per cent was common), while the formerly important timber sector was at a virtual standstill. Economic decline had eroded Ghana's once

Table 5.1 Macroeconomic indicators for Ghana

	1982	1983	1984	1985	1986 (est.)
GDP (₵ bn)	90.06	215.2	276.0	-	-
Real GDP growth (%)	-7.2	0.7	7.6	6.1	5.3
Consumer price inflation (%)	22.3	122.9	39.7	10.3	23.8
Population (million)	11.69	11.99	12.29	12.61	12.94
Exports fob[a] (US$m)	873	439.6	571	630	773
Imports cif[a] (US$m)	705	500	591	740	-
Current account (US$m)	-109	-174	-61	-166	-
Reserves minus gold (US$m)	138.9	144.8	301.6	478.5	379.7
External foreign debt disbursed (US$m)	1,115.6	1,141	1,122	2,400	1,800
Debt service ratio[b] (%)		50.3	45.6	62.9	63.6
Cocoa production[c] ('000 tons)	179	158	195	205	230
Exchange rate (av.) ₵ per US$	2.75	3.45	35.3	54.1	89.2[d]

Sources: Economist Intelligence Unit, Country Report: Ghana, Sierra Leone, Liberia, 1 (London, The Economist, February 1987) p.2; West Africa, (2 March 1987), p. 404

a Converted at annual average exchange rate
b Government of Ghana estimates, including IMF and arrears reduction
c Crop year beginning in calendar year
d January-November

impressive economic and social infrastructure; education, health, transport, and communication sectors had almost disintegrated. The combined effect of all this was that the standard of living and quality of life of Ghana's people had declined to pre-independence levels, the result of a tragic deterioration of the economy.[1] Since 1970, per capita income declined by 30 per cent, import volumes fell to one-third of their previous levels, real export earnings declined by over half as exports declined from 21 per cent to 4 per cent of gross domestic product (GDP), while government revenue covered only 35 per cent of total expenditure; the remaining 65 per cent was paid for by domestic and international funds, resulting in a heavy indebtedness.[2]

It is this background context which must be borne in mind in any discussion of Ghana's foreign indebtedness. The difficult economic conditions, however, cannot appropriately be attributed to a single regime or development strategy. Instead they arose from structural and policy-based factors. Ghana, like most African countries, is caught in a situation where efforts to achieve economic growth are complicated by a global economy beyond its control. To lay the entire responsibility for a declining standard of living and falling GDP upon the operation of that global economy is convenient, for it shifts blame for economic difficulties away from governmental decisions to an externalized 'invisible hand'. However, a balanced view of Ghana's economic decline and accompanying international indebtedness, must take into account the external limitations that the international economic system places on state action, before any discussion of the issues of domestic policy failure and mismanagement can be taken up.

As Dos Santos argues, economies such as Ghana's, with their historic structural links with Western Europe and former colonial masters, find concrete expression in lasting trade, investment, and financial ties.[3] A recession in the west, for example, as in the early 1980s, is reflected in a decline in the demand for Ghana's exports, a situation aggravated by a heavy debt-servicing burden (i.e. the amount of interest and repayments on outstanding debt paid annually), and adverse commodity terms of trade (i.e. the ratio of export to import prices). Further, oil imports alone account for approximately half of total export earnings on average. As a result Ghana found itself severely constrained by this combination of factors; the result was a reduction in total foreign exchange at a time of steep energy prices and rising costs for machinery, chemicals, and other manufactured goods and raw materials.

Although an important factor, however, the workings of the international economic system cannot be held solely responsible for Ghana's economic decline. While this acted to condition and limit domestic economic choice, a severe decline in agricultural and industrial output, contributing at least as much to general economic decline, must be laid at the door of inefficient and inappropriate public policies and general bureaucratic mismanagement.

A heavy responsibility for Ghana's diminished aggregate productivity and balance of payments crises in the 1970s is borne by the military regime of General I.K. Acheampong (1972-8) and the succeeding government headed by General F. Akuffo (1978-9).[4] Although drought affected the country during the second half of the decade, these military juntas remain responsible for the considerable fiscal and administrative mismanagement that occurred. Acheampong's fiscal policies led to an expansion of public demand which was not met by increasing output in the domestic economy. The consequence was rapidly escalating inflation rates (over 100 per cent per annum from 1977), gross imbalance in the external trading accounts, a steep rise in net credit to the government from internal banking sources to finance the budget deficits (₵81 million/US$284 million in 1977), sharp increases in unplanned government expenditure, a jump in the money supply from an average ₵281 million/US$102 million in 1971 to ₵1,761 million/US$640 million in 1977, and worsening foreign exchange reserves.[5] Government expenditures increased more rapidly than revenues; the result was to print more and more money to cover deficits. By 1978 the economic situation had deteriorated seriously; high inflation, widespread shortages, and extensive unemployment became features of the Ghanaian economy. Compounding this mismanagement, a number of highly placed government officials and senior military officers were engaged in an apparent frenzy of corruption - misusing import licences, awarding contracts to girlfriends and other favourites, and taking dubious loans.[6]

THE ARMED FORCES REVOLUTIONARY COUNCIL: A REACTION TO ECONOMIC REGRESSION, JUNE-SEPTEMBER 1979

It was against this background of shortages, inflation and unemployment that Ghana's foreign indebtedness rose from US$895 million in 1975 to US$1,429 million in 1979. In the latter year, international financial institutions began to refuse Ghana further credit as arrears of payments on short-term loans amounted to some ₵1,190 million/US$432 million. In the following year (1980) total short-term debt rose to US$358.4 million, of which the most important element was arrears on current payments, accounting for 62 per cent (US$221 million) of this type of debt. Medium-term debts were US$336 million, consisting of pre-1966 suppliers' credits (i.e. credits advanced by foreign suppliers of goods and services) rescheduled under the Rome Agreement of 1974.[7] Long-term debts amounted to US$662 million. External debt thus amounted to US$1,356.4 million, with a debt service ratio estimated officially at between 5 and 6 per cent of total exports of goods and services. During the decade external medium- and long-term debts grew at an average yearly rate of 11 per cent.[8]

The composition of the external debt from 1970 showed a major increase in the proportion of debt owed to official creditors. The share of this official or public debt increased from 54 per cent in 1970 to 72 per cent in 1979. The bulk of this increase came from a rapidly growing debt to the International Development Association, the World Bank's 'soft-loan' affiliate, and the World Bank itself; by 1982 some 36 per cent of all external debt was of this type. Private indebtedness, made up almost entirely of suppliers' credits and accrued during 1964-6, declined from 46 per cent of total debt in 1970 to only 15 per cent in 1982.[9]

Growing indebtedness was reflected in the increasingly difficult economic conditions experienced by many Ghanaians. In particular soaring prices led to widespread governmental unpopularity. In June 1979 a coup led by the lower ranks of the armed forces succeeded in ousting the incumbent military regime, which had itself removed Acheampong's 1972-8 regime the previous July. Following a four-month 'housecleaning' (i.e. the institution of a moralistic, at times violent, attempt to 'purge' corrupt elements who were held to be accountable for the 1970s' economic debacle), this regime, the Armed Forces Revolutionary Council (AFRC), handed over power to an elected civilian regime.[10] The AFRC, in power from June to September 1979 and led by Flight-Lieutenant Jerry Rawlings, embarked on a series of economically populist measures which displayed both idealism and an apparent lack of understanding of the medium-term consequences in about equal measure. Rawlings' AFRC was deeply offended by the corrupt practices of senior military officers and state bureaucrats and moved swiftly to deal with the more obvious exploiters. High-ranking military men were stripped of their assets and imprisoned, while former heads of state Acheampong and Akuffo, along with six other senior officers, were executed; alleged hoarders of consumer goods had their stocks confiscated and sold at state-controlled prices by soldiers, while the predominantly female market traders who charged more than the prices set by law were publicly flogged and their heads shaved. Accra's central Makola Number One Market was destroyed by soldiers using dynamite. Ghanaian businessmen charged with making illegal deals were seized. The Cocoa Marketing Board (the state body which bought cocoa from the cocoa farmers and sold it on the world market) was reorganized, and the Ministry of Cocoa Affairs and a number of senior officials were investigated and the former restructured because of the discovery of widespread corruption and illegal deals.[11]

In furtherance of the 'housecleaning', the AFRC imposed price controls which, by means of the gun, were enforced by the army and police. This was immensely popular with many people, as it meant that for the first time in many years citizens could afford to buy goods previously selling at prices beyond most individuals' reach if they were available at all. However, the exercise in price control enforcement led to a rapid depletion in stocks of goods which were not replaced. In sum the economic consequences of the AFRC, although making a contribution to the acceptance of frugality in public life, were largely transient (in the case of the transfer of wealth from traders to consumers via the selling of goods at cheap prices) or largely self-defeating (given the effects of price controls and forced selling of 'hoarded' goods on productive and distributive activity).[12] While the AFRC exhorted people to take part in the so-called 'moral revolution', it was naive of it to overlook the erosion of norms of behaviour through economically rational responses to the economic decline (such as the hoarding of goods in a period of high inflation, and the selling of goods above the meaningless controlled prices). The incoming civilian government thus inherited a difficult legacy from the AFRC's populist intervention which did nothing to ameliorate the structural failings of the economy. Rawlings made it clear, however, that if economic conditions did not speedily improve the new civilian government could expect to be removed by the military.[13]

The incoming president, Dr Hilla Limann, stated on coming to power, that the economy was in 'a shambles' and 'bankrupt'.[14] Economic indicators pointed to a likely continuation of hardships for Ghana's people: consumer goods were in short supply, reflected in an inflation rate in 1980 of 116 per cent per annum; production and imports were at low levels; foreign currency reserves were negligible; and crude oil prices rapidly rising. By 1981 foreign loans to Ghana had ceased, owing to the government's inability to service its debts. As a result of these factors economic conditions did not improve for the mass of the people. The almost inevitable coup followed, with Rawlings returning to power on 31 December 1981.[15]

THE PROVISIONAL NATIONAL DEFENCE COUNCIL AND ECONOMIC DEVELOPMENT, 1982-7

Rawlings' 'second coming' was widely perceived as revolutionary in character and populist in its aspirations. Nineteen eighty-two began with slogans about the desirability of 'people's power' and the negative aspects of 'neo-colonialism', with the new regime, the Provisional National Defence Council (PNDC), appearing particularly hostile to financial institutions such as the IMF and World Bank. The problems of the economy, it was proclaimed, were closely linked to its 'neo-colonialist' structure, implying covert control of the economy by foreign businesses. The PNDC appeared most unlikely at this stage to seek an IMF financial package, implying currency devaluation, major reductions in public spending, and price rises of goods and services. The Rawlings regime rejected the expected conditions put forward by the IMF for the provision of external funding, with a major reason for this rejection relating to the conditions set by the latter for granting loans. Dr Obed Asamoah, Secretary (minister) for Foreign Affairs, made this clear when he said that, 'The government was unwilling to accept the massive devaluation of the cedi which the Fund was going to recommend'.[16] Devaluation on this scale would have triggered, the government believed, sharp consumer price increases and necessitated substantial reductions in social welfare programmes. Instead, the PNDC preferred to emulate former President Nkrumah in the early 1960s, who had refused an IMF loan on the Fund's terms. Accra radio recalled Nkrumah's 'courage' in rejecting the pressures to devalue the cedi, and added that since then the country's leaders had 'spinelessly yielded to IMF pressures'; the 'result had been the spate of massive devaluations of the cedi after 1967 ... in 1971, ... and by the SMC (i.e. Acheampong's regime) seven years later'. Further, the official commentary stressed:

> In the atmosphere of corruption ... during all those periods of devaluation, the loans failed to make any improvement in the living standards of our people ... Many of the loans found their way into the pockets of politicians and other officials ... (T)he present revolution has set its face against these evils, ... and only when they are eliminated will the economy become strong, only then will we be able to tell whether the cedi is overvalued or not. Until then, all talk of devaluation must cease.[17]

It is clear from this that the PNDC appeared to believe that the major problem of the economy centred on the question of the morality of senior officials and bureaucrats. It did not seem to occur to the government that in a situation of economic decline, where wages and salaries were unable to meet daily expenditures, people in suitable positions would be tempted to use any contacts or influence they might have in order to increase their incomes. This 'moral' approach to the economy put much more stress on affordable prices and the availability of goods than on tackling the structural problems of the economy: the over-reliance on imports, and the low level of production of foodstuffs, of exports such as cocoa, gold and timber, and of manufactures. During 1982, government attempts to improve the economic situation revolved around attempted 'bootstrap' stabilization programmes. Real cocoa prices were raised by reducing the payment-lag to growers from nine months to one month - which was a critical shift, given the near 100 per cent rate of inflation. Attempts at improving transport, external balance, and fiscal balance, were unsuccessful owing to the state of infrastructure and the low levels of import capacity. Attempts to reverse public sector decline were ineffective for the same reasons, and also because government wages and salaries were so low as to preclude a normal workload or to enforce anti-corruption measures. Measures to improve social relations by price controls and productive efficiency by diktat were ineffectual. In addition, the maintenance of an exchange rate of ₵2.75 to the US dollar, against a rate of 30 to 40 on the black market, meant that many economic transactions were conducted at the black-market rate.[18]

The structural change in morality, which now stressed the deleterious effects of corruption and exploitation, did nothing to enhance production in a climate of import-starvation, while the government's anti-imperialist rhetoric led to a distinct coolness on the part of potential external sources of finance. By late 1982, however, the PNDC had come to the conclusion that 'bootstrap' stabilization - let alone recovery - was impossible; as a result serious, yet initially tentative, contracts were made with the IMF and the World Bank towards an externally supported programme. In April 1983, the Economic Recovery Programme (ERP) was launched, which was virtually a standard IMF 'package'.

On the face of it, it is remarkable that an IMF loan was sought, following the early PNDC pronouncements, which had been notable for their attacks on transnational corporations and international financial institutions. However, the diverse make-up of the original PNDC in 1982 led to a considerable ideological divergence of opinion, which had been masked in the early days of the 'revolution' by the anti-imperialist tirades. Different factions were represented as follows: a retired senior army officer and a priest were the focal points for the middle classes; the radical nature of the PNDC was exemplified by the inclusion of representatives of the urban discontented such as workers, rank-and-file soldiers, and revolutionaries. Significantly, Rawlings was not the creature of either broad faction. Instead he appeared the pragmatist, unwilling to accept policy directions which stemmed from ideological dogmatism. In this respect, Rawlings was unwilling to accept the policy suggestions of the PNDC 'left', which centred on the best means of changing the 'neo-colonial' economy through a combination of self-reliance and financial inputs from the 'progressive' countries - and particularly from the USSR, Libya, and North Korea.[19] To the PNDC 'right' this was anathema. The right felt that aid should be sought from all sources, particularly the west; and, if necessary a deflationary IMF-style 'package' should be instituted to improve the economy in the medium-term.[20]

The organized left was a product of the 1979 AFRC period, from which a number of socialist-oriented groups had evolved. These included the June 4 Movement, the People's Revolutionary League of Ghana, the New Democratic Movement, and the Kwame Nkrumah Revolutionary Guards. These groups and micro-parties (the largest, the Kwame Nkrumah Revolutionary Guards, had a membership estimated at 2,000)[21] were more or less explicitly revolutionary socialist parties which wished to galvanize Ghana towards a path which would involve the destruction of a state system controlled by recurring actors: party political government based in the middle classes and the military elite. The revolutionary groups were predominantly student organizations, which were joined by small groups of intellectuals and workers.[22]

The leaders of these groups (including PNDC member Chris Bukari Atim) had helped to mould Rawlings' world-view during his time out of power between 1979 and 1981.[23] When the 31 December coup took place they clustered in and around the PNDC, and these 'progressives' (as they called themselves) were initially predominant in the post-coup period. Although differences existed between them, there had developed a shared theory as to the causes of Ghana's decline which was a mixture of dependency theory's core-periphery analysis, anti-westernism and Kwame Nkrumah's theory of neo-colonialism, which he had evolved and published fifteen years earlier.[24] They felt that the post-31 December period should begin economically with a partial withdrawal from the capitalist world economic system. The problem of the economy and its management was one of neocolonialism, which had constituted a block on development. Rawlings claimed that, 'Ghana's engagement in the international capitalist system has contributed in no small measure towards the country's present predicament'.[25] Specifically the main source of the people's impoverishment lay in the alleged repatriation of huge profits by transnational corporations (TNCs); the depredations of corrupt leaders were conditioned by this structure: a critical precondition for revolution lay in

Ghana's disengagement from it.

An opposing view was held by the right in and around the PNDC, including Council members, Brigadier Nunoo-Mensah and Reverend Damuah. They posited that, in Geoffrey Kay's well-worn dictum, a lack of exploitation rather than its excess had caused Ghana's underdevelopment.[26] It was argued that since Nkrumah's anti-western policies in the early 1960s, foreign capital had been retreating from Ghana rather than increasing its alleged stranglehold, and that this above all else had caused a severe decline. In addition successive governments had had to resort to over-taxing Ghana's cocoa farmers who had voted with their feet by moving into untaxed food production, smuggling cocoa to Ghana's francophone neighbours (Ivory Coast, Togo) where prices were higher, or both. The best way to lessen the effects of smuggling and increase the tax-take for the government was to increase the producer price of cocoa; in this way less of that commodity would be diverted into boosting Ivory Coast's and Togo's cocoa production and more into helping Ghana's economic recovery. Politically nothing wrong was seen with the legacy bequeathed by colonialism; it was considered that party politics was a modernizing influence in helping to break down regressive tribal factors. Internationally it was imperative to make friends with everyone, regardless of ideology.[27]

Initially it appeared that Rawlings was prepared to endorse the left's economic policy; attempts were made to enforce price controls and to reduce urban rents. These measures failed to turn round the economy, however, and in combination with Ghana's 'progressive' allies' failure to promise useful amounts of financial aid, Rawlings and his closest advisers became convinced of the necessity, as well as the desirability, of seeking external aid through the confines of an IMF/World Bank-supported programme. Rawlings became increasingly impatient with the left's inability to produce a realistic alternative to the 'IMF option'; two coup attempts in October and November 1982, partly as a result of the announced decision to call on the IMF and World Bank, in which there was allegedly leftist involvement, led to the latter's virtual exclusion from policy-making circles and the exile in Europe or neighbouring West African countries of many of their leaders.[28]

In December 1982, it was announced that an Economic Recovery Programme (ERP) was to be put into practice from the following April's Budget. The 1983-6 ERP was basically an orthodox IMF policy prescription. The programme was based on an initial 'shock' treatment, particularly in respect of changes in the exchange rate, and supported by increases in real resource flows over the 1983-6 period.

The main elements of the ERP included a massive and sustained devaluation, changes in fiscal and monetary policy, increases in the prices paid to cocoa farmers, a general economic liberalization, and measures to control inflation.[29] The first step was reform of the exchange rate. From ₵2.75 to ₵30 to the US dollar in 1983, was followed by rapid downward moves to ₵50 to the dollar in 1984. In 1985, for reasons which are not clear, but which were probably related to the amount of public hostility which the PNDC was receiving from most sections of the urban population - including the bureaucratic and managerial professionals and workers - the trend slowed down, with the rate reaching only ₵60 to the dollar. This was followed in January 1986 by the movement of the cedi to 90 to the dollar. In late 1986 the cedi was 'floated' against other currencies, except for some essential imports, including petroleum products, which the government wished to keep as low as possible in price for internal political purposes. The rate for these imports was maintained at ₵90 to the US dollar. In February 1987, however, the 'first window' rate was abolished; henceforth the value of the currency would be set by the price which would-be importers were willing to pay. This was an attempt to retain for the state some of the money which was being lost to the black market. By April 1987, the prevailing exchange rate for the cedi was in the region of ₵156=US$1, which was near to the black-market rate against the dollar. Thus in four years the cedi had been devalued from ₵2.75 to the dollar to ₵156; a cumulative fifty-seven-fold reduction in its nominal value.

Fiscal policy called for reductions in the government borrowing requirement, initially largely by expenditure cuts; monetary policy was designed to hold domestic credit formation below 20 per cent, largely by reducing government borrowing, and to achieve positive real interest rates so as to raise domestic savings: by 1985 interest rates had reached 20 per cent, while officially inflation was only 10 per cent.

Producer cocoa prices were to be raised rapidly in real terms. At least implicitly it was assumed that this would be consistent with raising net government revenue from cocoa, because domestic prices and Cocoa Board costs would grow less rapidly than cedi receipts would be boosted by devaluation.

Liberalization included ending almost all price controls (which were nearly totally ineffective) and all ceiling agricultural purchase prices. Retail prices of consumer goods and taxes on a range of public services were increased. Public sector spending was to be curtailed in order to bring down the budget deficit and to cut the wage bill of the enormous public sector; at the same time the PNDC announced its intention of selling off or reorganizing the numerous parastatals, many of which had been loss-makers for several years. At the same time inflation was to be reduced from the 50-120 per cent rates which had characterized the late 1970s and early 1980s. This was seen as possible, even in the light of massive devaluations, because for most transactions, especially at the retail level, prices were related to the black-market exchange rate, not the wholly artificial official one.

The Economic Recovery Programme depended for its success on attracting external financial support in order to import the raw materials and equipment necessary to fuel the export sector. In August 1983, the programme was allotted US$377 million from the IMF in standby and compensatory financial facilities for 1983-4. Following the IMF lead, US$800 million was pledged by bilateral and multi-lateral sources for the 1984-6 period.[30]

ECONOMIC RECOVERY: 1983-6

Despite the Provisional National Defence Council's initial hostility to the international financial institutions, by 1983 it was clear that it had opted for the IMF/World Bank road in preference to the more autarchic policy measures of the left. However, as stated above, the economic programme was not defined by ideological dogmatism or by undue pressure from the IMF/World Bank. What dictated the putting into operation of a deflationary Economic Recovery Programme was the realization that, under the circumstances, Ghana had nowhere else to turn for economic relief. By 1982 Ghana's disbursed debts amounted to US$1,115.6 million, with debt servicing totalling some US$65 million per annum. Of the total, US$949.4 million was owed to official creditors (i.e. US$402.3 million to multilateral lenders such as the World Bank and its soft loan affiliate, the International Development Association; US$547.1 million to bilateral creditors), and US$166.3 million in suppliers' credits.[31] This amounted to some US$93 for each of Ghana's twelve million people.

It would be incorrect to assume that the PNDC was forced into this type of programme. Dr Kwesi Botchwey, PNDC Secretary for Finance and Economic Planning, declared that: 'The harsh economic conditions which face us today, should leave us all in no doubt whatsoever that... we have reached a make or break point where we must either apply the most effective and necessary cure or suffer unavoidable disaster'. He ended by asserting that, 'There is simply no middle ground'.[32] Most of the conditions stipulated by the IMF such as price reforms, production and export incentives and fiscal policy reforms, 'constituted the heart of the recovery programme... and reinforced our own initiative', the government claimed.[33] Despite these claims, however, there was a widespread belief in Ghana that the economic recovery programme had been imposed on the PNDC against its will. However, it appears that the latter had become genuinely convinced that an IMF-style programme was the most likely to provide benefits in the long-term to Ghana's people. The revolutionary rhetoric of 1982 had masked the internal divisions in the PNDC. While it had initially appeared that the powerful Rawlings was in agreement with the leftist elements in the regime regarding the end-result of the revolutionary process (i.e. socialism), once the leftist elements had been ousted in late 1982 and the economy showed no signs of improving, the way was clear for an eventual reconciliation with the IMF.

The PNDC had inherited an apparently insurmountable series of hurdles in the form of international indebtedness, hyper-inflation, low productivity and falling exports. During 1982 exports showed no improvement: cocoa and other exports could not be brought to the country's ports because of poor road conditions and the state of the country's railway, while during the year Ghana's terms of trade dropped by 31 per cent. On top of this a series of natural disasters exacerbated the crisis. These included the expulsion of over one million Ghanaians from Nigeria in January 1983, and an enduring drought and resulting bush fires, which destroyed thousands of hectares of cash and food crops.[34]

It appears, then, that Ghana had very few, if any, realistic alternatives to the adoption of stringent IMF-supported measures to address the situation of economic decline. In reality, the cedi's devaluation and the price rises outlined in the 1983 Budget represented a point of coincidence between the genuine needs of the Ghanaian economy, as increasingly understood by Botchwey and Rawlings, and the type of policy measures which the IMF/World Bank required as a condition for loans. The first condition for carrying out the economic programme was adequate finance, with which to increase industrial output and agricultural production, and most importantly, to rehabilitate the transport infrastructure. These constituted the immediate necessities. Given the failure of the Eastern European socialist bloc countries and Libya to offer financial aid on a significant scale, the PNDC returned to Ghana's traditional sources of capital in the west and in turn accepted the desirability of export-led growth, or at least recovery. In order to attract funds from both bilateral and multilateral donors, it was necessary for Ghana to gain the 'IMF seal of approval', in the form of initial loans as a sign that the PNDC government was worthy of international support despite its earlier outbursts directed against the west.

A further dimension of the rapprochement between Ghana and the west was in the context of the latter's strategic and political interests and the IMF's credibility in the Third World. There was a desire in some European and North American governments that Ghana should not be forced into a closer relationship with the USSR and its Third World representative, Cuba, along with Libya - just as Angola, Ethiopia, and Mozambique had been a decade earlier. In addition, the IMF's credibility needed boosting after charges that it was indifferent to the plight of economies which had declined as precipitously as Ghana's had in the 1970s. Clearly there was much at stake for both the PNDC and the IMF in making the necessary changes to the economy in the medium-term, which under any foreseeable programme the latter would support would probably entail taking drastic actions which would certainly create widespread societal displeasure.[35]

When the 1983 Budget was announced, hostile reaction to it centred on the large increases in the prices of many commodities (with some items tripling in price),[36] relative to the much lower wage rises allowed. Large anti-

PNDC rallies took place in the capital, Accra, and in the provincial city of Kumasi. Chief among these were student demonstrations which led to the closing of the country's three universities. The Ghana Trades Union Congress condemned the ₵25 minimum daily wage (less than one US dollar) as 'inappropriate' in the light of the 'excessively high rates of (price) increases', while the professional middle class and the Church used the occasion of the budget to call for the PNDC to stand down to make way for an elected government.[37]

Nineteen eighty-three was a very bad year for the PNDC government and the people of Ghana. A coup attempt in June (the most serious of the more than twenty that the country suffered between 1982 and 1987), the effects of the April budget, and shortages of food (mostly due to the effects of drought), led to an increasingly desperate situation, which was exacerbated by the very high inflation rate of 125 per cent per annum.[38] High prices for petroleum and kerosene (the latter extensively used for lighting in the rural areas where electricity is virtually absent) added to the anti-PNDC feeling, and appeared to support the contention of PNDC critics that the Council was responsible for the economic crisis, did not care for the welfare of the people, and was only intent on pleasing the IMF and World Bank. Such was the continuing economic crisis that the PNDC was forced to review the 1983 budget, announced in April, six months later in October. The regime had planned to spend some ₵24 billion (US$800 million), of which 47 per cent was to come from taxes on international trade and other transactions (₵1 billion; US$366 million). Due to the low volume of both imports and exports (see Table 5.1), this amount did not materialize. Because the increased minimum wage and the rapidly expanding costs of goods and services were creating higher government expenditure, the regime made attempts to reduce both recurrent and capital expenditure. Increased revenue was also gained by raising the prices of cigarettes, beer, and petroleum products. Loans bagan to flow in July 1983, although with a very low disbursement rate, and directed at rehabilitating the export sectors and the transport infrastructure; the effects, however, were not immediately apparent. By the end of 1983, the PNDC's economic and political fortunes were at a very low ebb.[39]

Signals from the PNDC, such as pressing on with the economic recovery programme despite widespread disaffection from students, workers, the middle class, and the Christian church, led to the successful conclusion of a donors' conference organized by the World Bank in Paris in late November 1983. The government was able to gain pledges from the several western states and international lending organizations present for US$156 million in loans to be disbursed during 1984, in order to pursue the ERP initiatives, and to secure tentative agreement for similar levels in 1985-6, provided that the policy initiatives begun in the 1983 budget were continued and the balance of payments deficit brought down to around US$150 million.[40]

Despite the PNDC's success in establishing good relations with the west and the resumption of foreign loans, it still faced the problem of how to restore production levels without sacrificing the pursuit of social justice, which had been an important element in support for the regime during 1982. Finance Secretary Botchwey recognized this problem and admitted in February 1984, that efforts intended 'to alleviate the rigours of the IMF programme (had) collapsed completely'.[41] It was clear that the programme was proving to be harsh relative to the living standards of many Ghanaians. The minimum daily wage of ₵25, when set against the government-run Central Bureau of Statistics' estimate of ₵300, was obviously entirely inappropriate in terms of a worker's ability to feed, clothe, and house him- or herself and family. Whilst it was clear that the PNDC was not able to finance wage rises of this magnitude (another ₵73 billion/US$2.43 billion would have been necessary per annum),[42] the regime reacted to criticisms of this nature by accusing those who demanded wage rises of being 'enemies of the revolution', rather than making clear the reasons why it could not afford to pay.

The 1984 budget continued the IMF measures and attempted to restrain inflation, rationalize prices, and expand exports. The PNDC, aware of its still fragile position, did not explain clearly to the Ghanaian people that a central part of the ERP involved drastically cutting government expenditure on public-sector employment. This could have been done either (and preferably) by large-scale redundancies, or by allowing real wages to fall so drastically that there would be wholesale voluntary resignations from government employment. Generally speaking, the latter strategy was adopted in 1984, with a shift towards the former policy of redundancies in subsequent years as the government began to feel more self-confident.

In contrast to internal disaffection, the external donors, led by the IMF, were very pleased with Ghana's performance. The country was 'on target ... and meeting all the performance criteria' required by the Fund. If the PNDC 'maintained the momentum in the handling of the economy and if the climatic conditions changed for the better, the economy should begin to improve'.[43] During 1984 the economy began to recover, although this was at least in part due more to good rainfall, which boosted food and export crop output, than to the effect of the ERP. After years of decline GDP rose by 7.6 per cent, although this was almost entirely accounted for by increases in agricultural output. Industrial production showed no improvement, while the performance of the export sector was mixed; cocoa's monetary value was higher than in 1983 owing to better world prices although output did not significantly increase (up from 158,000 tons in 1983 to 175,000 tons in 1984). On the other hand, the value of two of Ghana's other important export commodities, gold and diamonds, fell, even though production was higher, because of lower international prices. Food prices were 25 per cent lower in 1984 than 1983, which reflected the improving weather conditions.

As living conditions showed some signs of improvement, the government felt able to resume its policy of removing subsidies and controlled prices from consumer goods, a policy which had begun in 1983. During 1984, all but 17 commodity prices were deregulated, a clear indication that the PNDC aimed at the establishment of a liberal market economy, particularly since the 17 items were allowed to find their own price levels without government intervention. The World Bank representative in Ghana praised the continuing policies on prices as being an additional 'bold step in the right direction ... the key for the revival of the country's economy and development', and applauded the raising of cocoa producer prices as being conducive to the development of the rural areas.[44] In the 1984 budget, the cocoa producer price was raised from ₵20,000 to ₵30,000 a ton (US$600, following the further devaluation of the cedi in 1984 to ₵50=US$1).

The raising of the producer price of cocoa was a key element in the PNDC's strategy of export-led growth. It was hoped that the estimated 50,000 tons of cocoa that were smuggled into the neighbouring states of Ivory Coast and Togo, where prices were higher, paid in the internationally convertible Communauté Française Africaine (CFA) currency, and consumer goods freely available, would instead be sold to the Cocoa Board. In this way it was assumed that net government revenue from cocoa would increase in line with the cedi's devaluation. While Cocoa Board purchases of cocoa did increase over the first stage of the ERP (1983-5), from 158,000 tons to 205,000 tons, over the same period the world price of cocoa fell. At the same time timber exports recovered from US$12.3 million to US$30 million, which was made possible by programme loans made under the ERP, combined with the price incentives given by devaluation. The same can be said of the halt in gold output decline (from 8,601 grams in 1983 to 10,583 grams in 1985).[45]

These results led to a glowing report from the IMF/World Bank: the ERP had led to 'sustained improvements in economic policies and performance'. Following GDP growth in 1984 of 7.6 per cent, 1985 saw a further 6.1 per cent improvement; in the latter year the budget deficit was contained at 2 per cent of GDP, inflation fell from 125 per cent in 1983 to 10 per cent, positive real interest rates of 20 per cent were attained, and most subsidies and price controls were removed.[46]

A three-year medium-term programme for 1986-8, known as the Structural Adjustment Programme (SAP), was launched in mid-1986. The short-term goal of stabilization gave way to attempts to 'improve living standards on the basis of increased production and the efficient provision of basic social services'. SAP required a very large commitment of external loans (see Table 5.1) to achieve its target of 5 per cent annual growth in GDP and 1.5 per cent increase in per capita incomes. The Ghana government estimated that new aid requirements of US$550 million were needed in both 1987 and 1988 in addition to the US$600 million secured for 1986.

Despite optimistic economic pointers, Finance Secretary Botchwey announced in August 1986 that the economy was in 'deep crisis'.[47] Part of the problem was due to insufficient internal revenue generation and a shortfall in expected export earnings. Both these features were a direct result of the ERP, which led to a reduction in wages and salaries and lower than expected taxes on international trade and hence less government revenue, and the exclusive reliance on export-led growth; in the context of falling world prices, this did not bring in the expected amount of foreign exchange despite the increases in output achieved across the board. The problem cycle, however, was completed by the less-than-outstanding disbursement of Ghana's loans; this rate fell from 34 per cent in 1984 to a mere 21 per cent in 1985.[48] Both the PNDC and the IMF stressed that aid would be most effective if given in the form of quickly disbursed 'programme support' (food and commodity assistance), instead of 'project aid' which was slower to be disbursed. More than half of new commitments in 1985, however, were project aid compared with only 20 per cent in 1984. Clearly what was perceived as being best for Ghana by the government and the IMF was not most desirable for bilateral donors. Not only was disbursed aid inadequate for recovery, but it was directed towards the areas which would be expected to generate more advantages for businesses from the donor countries in terms of orders for equipment and services.

In line with the expectations of the PNDC and the IMF/World Bank, external loans outstanding at the end of 1985 amounted to US$2,400 million, made up of US$655 million owed to the IMF, US$136 million to other multilateral creditors including the World Bank, US$966 million to bilateral donors, US$442 million owed to western banks, and with arrears on payments amounting to US$200 million. Debt service ratio, including repurchases to the IMF and arrears, amounted to 63 per cent of export proceeds in 1985, 63.6 per cent in 1986, and a projected 63 per cent in 1987, falling slightly to 61.9 per cent in 1988.[49] These very high debt service ratios came about partly at least because of the collapse of world commodity prices during the 1980s. As far as export earnings were concerned, the PNDC had been led to believe by the World Bank that it would increase its foreign exchange earnings by expanding output; yet cocoa alone registered a 40 per cent fall in price in 1986 compared to the previous year. Nineteen eighty-seven was no better as prices continued to drift downwards; the medium-term signs were gloomy: predictions were that prices would continue to fall, perhaps for the rest of the 1980s.[50]

In the light of these sombre portents, how wise was the PNDC to embrace wholeheartedly the 'IMF option'? To pose the question, however, is to imply that the PNDC <u>had</u> a realistic alternative to the path it took. Given the failure of alternative sources of finance and the apparent implausibility of the left's self-reliant strategy, which Finance Secretary Botchwey considered would have taken

Ghana 'back to the Stone Age', the regime had little choice but to adopt a programme which the international financial institutions and bilateral donors would deem worthy of support. As we have seen, the PNDC adopted the Economic Recovery Programme in order to reverse the economic decline, and the Structural Adjustment Programme in order to restart economic growth which was predicated upon an increase in exports. Improved rural living conditions were desirable for both humane reasons and for more pragmatic political reasons. It was clearly understood by Rawlings and his advisers that living conditions in the countryside were almost uniformly more awful than in the towns owing to an absence of clean water, electricity, and hospitals. For more pragmatic political reasons it was necessary to stimulate a support-base, given the hostility directed at the PNDC from its erstwhile urban supporters.[51]

THE SAP AND URBAN DISCONTENT

The reaction of urban workers was generally hostile to the Structural Adjustment Programme (SAP). The announcement of a further 32,000 labour redundancies in 1985-6, in addition to the more than 25,000 effected in 1984-5, had the result of increasing worker and Trades Union Congress resentment at the PNDC's policies. While redundancies were necessary in the context of reducing public sector expenditure, it was considered by many workers that the PNDC should not make employees redundant without the existence of a realistic programme to redeploy them. This was absent. In early 1986, the explosive nature of this question was demonstrated by an incident at the Hall of the Trade Unions (TUC headquarters) in Accra. Following the arrest of several union leaders because of their vocal opposition to the redundancies, an estimated one thousand police with armoured cars surrounded the TUC Hall to control a crowd of workers which had gathered to register their displeasure.[52] Similarly, an issue over workers' allowances generated further friction between workers and the PNDC In April 1986, the TUC threatened a general strike when the government attempted to withdraw one of the estimated 105 workers' allowances which it had previously increased in value. The government attempted to withdraw the allowance when it became clear that the new rates would add approximately US$50 million to the budget, which could not be supported. When faced with the ensuing uproar, the government backpedalled and rescinded the decision to withdraw the increased allowances, although it was not apparent that it had discovered a replacement strategy to reduce its wages bill by the required ₵4-5 billion (US$50 million, following January 1986 devaluation to ₵90=US$1) necessary to remain within spending limits for 1986.[53]

By mid-1986 it was clear that the IMF and World Bank were displeased with the PNDC's handling of the question of pay and allowance levels. The former began to express publicly their disquiet at the inability of the PNDC to keep governmental budgets within agreed parameters. At the same time Ghana's repayment burden was set to remain increasingly burdensome until at least 1990. Amortization of debts rescheduled under the Rome agreement of 1974 began in 1983 on expiry of a ten-year grace period. Arrears of short-term debt payments were to be settled at the rate of US$60 million per annum. Also adding weight were oil import debts and other short- to medium-term credits to be serviced. Debt servicing came to US$72 million in 1986. It was estimated to total US$187 million in 1987 and US$246 million the following year, 1988. In addition loans from the IMF were to be repaid during 1987-9. In sum this meant that over half Ghana's export proceeds would go to service debts until the end of the 1980s. Finance Secretary Kwesi Botchwey admitted in May 1986 that Ghana could not do without a medium-term IMF programme, 'given the kind of repurchases (repayments to the IMF) which are staring us in the face'.[54]

Disagreement with the IMF over minimum wage increases delayed presentation of the 1987 budget scheduled for early January. This highlighted the major problems which the government faced as it tried to weigh the tangible economic benefits of satisfying the Fund against the potential social and political costs of the measures it was compelled by the latter to introduce. In February 1987 a Ghanaian delegation led by Finance Secretary Botchwey held talks with the IMF and the World Bank in Washington over an estimated US$150 million structural adjustment loan and three-year extended fund facility (necessary for the SAP), and a performance review of an October 1986 US$67 million one-year standby agreement with the IMF.[55]

The 1987 budget was finally presented in late February 1987. It abolished the two-tier exchange rate introduced the previous September, and raised the daily minimum wage by 24 per cent, from ₵90 to ₵112. The new rate was in line with the inflation rate officially estimated in 1986 of 23 per cent, and IMF guidelines. The trade unions, however, argued that inflation was effectively much higher than the official estimate. In early 1987 they pressed for a minimum wage of ₵150, which would have maintained the traditional parity with the dollar. In contrast to former years, and especially 1983, however, the union anger was subdued and did not lead to demonstrations, petitions, or threatened strikes.[56]

The streamlining of the exchange rate meant that essential imports, such as oil products and drugs, and official debt servicing and cocoa exports, all formerly subject to the 'first window' rate of ₵90, would henceforward be measured at the single higher rate arrived at in the weekly foreign exchange auction in Accra, which the regime took pains to control by releasing only certain amounts of US dollars. In May 1987 the cedi reached an exchange rate of ₵158 to the dollar. While this was still below the parallel rate of ₵180 to the dollar, it demonstrated that the PNDC was sincere about reaching a cedi/dollar rate which reflected the real exchange comparability of the two currencies.

CONCLUSION

The Structural Adjustment Programme was predicated upon a continuance of the export-led structural adjustment, dependent upon aid flows from the west and government policies to keep public expenditure as low as possible in order to maintain economic growth and to repay debts already incurred. However, the experience of 1983-6 was not without its worrying side. Ghana vainly strove to rehabilitate the economy during this period with inadequate and inappropriate foreign assistance whilst attempting at the same time to contain urban discontent as people's aspirations fell short of practical possibilities. As we have seen, stagnating living standards of urban workers led in the 1983-7 period to protests directed against the PNDC and its 'partners in economic progress', the IMF and World Bank. The regime lost much of its initial post-coup popularity, at least in the urban areas, and was perceived as having 'sold out' to the west without benefits accruing to the city dwellers.

However, despite this urban condemnation, it would be incorrect to assume that the PNDC was an IMF 'stooge'. By 1987, Ghana was suffering from 'adjustment fatigue'; the loans had failed to bring an improvement in living standards that many people had expected: for this the PNDC was, somewhat unjustly, blamed. The initial optimism of 1984's recovery had evaporated, while the desire (rather than the expectation) for short-term financial gains was understandably rising after more than five years of austerity, while the ability of the PNDC to avoid damaging conflicts with, for example, labour, appeared to be waning. At the same time many Ghanaians, especially in the rural areas, perceived themselves to be better off than in 1981, and incomparably so than during the nadir of 1983. In the countryside there was a significant number of locally designed and financed community projects, including the provision of wells, dams, schools, and health clinics, which had an undoubted impact on public service provision, and which implied, by the evidence of voluntary financial contributions from residents of the areas involved, that the incomes of the latter were by and large above subsistence levels.[57]

While this 'self-help' was laudable, the continuation of 5-6 per cent growth - with rising rates of government recurring spending and of domestic spending to GDP and an estimated 2.5-3 per cent population increase - was unlikely to allow much increase in *per capita* consumption. While much better than the 1974-83 period, growth of only 1 per cent or less a year is unlikely to be consistent with social stability. Even the expected growth rates, however, are not assured. Much depends on no new period of drought before the end of the 1980s and a major and sustained increase in food production. Furthermore the necessary foreign loans and export earnings levels are by no means assured. The late 1980s were marked by a shortfall of over 25 per cent of the necessary resource transfers; by this reckoning the only way to gain the needed income was by 100 per cent redrawing on IMF repurchases (repayments). While export quantity projections were probably attainable, it remained doubtful that the value of Ghana's exports would reach the levels planned by the PNDC and the IMF in the light of falling commodity prices in the 1980s and, by some accounts, into the 1990s. Cocoa fell on the world market between 1983 and 1987, a trend that may well continue, especially if Ghana's production increases to the projected 300,000 tonnes per annum, and if Malaysia's explosive rise in output continues (up from 24,000 tonnes in 1979 to more than 100,000 tonnes in 1986, with a projected production level of 200,000 tonnes for 1990).[58] In 1986 the export value shortfall was by and large covered by the world fall in petroleum prices, but the prospects for another similar windfall in the future do not seem bright.

With the unpredictability and volatile nature of recent falls in commodity prices, Ghana's recovery remains highly dependent on donor support. Yet, without a doubt, the Economic Recovery Programme must be rated a considerable, if qualified, success. Stabilization was achieved (even with falling prices for Ghana's exports) and the first steps towards recovery taken. The Structural Adjustment Programme (1986-8), however, suffers from several major problems, as the economy moves into the recovery phase. Principal among these is the government's relationship with the IMF. If the regime adopts the politically more acceptable option of allowing increased short-term consumption through the means of wage rises over and above the inflation rate, this would no doubt threaten future credit. This would be an unfortunate development, as debt service and interest charges were scheduled to total over US$200 million a year in the short term.[59] Second, despite the apparently sincere desire of the PNDC to alleviate the unsatisfactory living standards of many of its people, it was forced on several occasions by the Fund to reduce its development budget; in 1986, political pressures forced current spending up and IMF conditionality caused overall spending ceilings to fall. The possibility of the development spending being the 'sacrificial lamb' in the future remains high.

To western governments and financial institutions such as the IMF and World Bank, Ghana is the 'success story' of West Africa. The paradox is that the PNDC government is doing all the 'right' things at immense political cost, yet failing to produce a speedy economic recovery, although stabilization has been achieved. However, if the IMF and World Bank cannot settle Ghana's short-term financial needs, particularly to give some relief from the rigours of debt-servicing, it appears likely that internal discontent will trigger a successful coup which will bring both the PNDC and its fragile economic stabilization/recovery programme crashing down. This would not be in the long-term interests of Ghana or the IMF/World Bank; for the former because the

PNDC government probably represents the best option at the present time in terms of effectiveness, bearing in mind the former regimes' failures to take the necessary economic steps that the Rawlings-led regime has undertaken; for the World Bank because much of their joint credibility in Sub-Saharan Africa rests on Ghana's continued recovery. Ghana remains a prime example of how tenuous economic stabilization and recovery can be within the confines of a restricted primary-product dependent economy, using deflationary policies and a high level of foreign financing to develop.

6

Sierra Leone: debt and the fiscal crisis of the state

Sierra Leone has seldom caught the attention of international commentators or the world press. It has not been devastated by the drought which affected several African countries including Ethiopia, Sudan, and others in the Sahellian region. Neither has it achieved the strategic or international political influence and significance of states such as Algeria, Angola, Egypt, Kenya, Nigeria, Zambia, and Zimbabwe. While it has had its share of political violence, this has been on a much lower scale than in Chad, Equatorial Guinea, Mozambique and Uganda. And looking back to the 1950s and 1960s, it was not led to independence by the charismatic persona of a Kwame Nkrumah, who hoped to achieve the rapid transformation of Ghana to a modern industrial economy and society; or by a romantic such as Julius Nyerere, who hoped to turn Tanzanian peasants into citizens of modern communes.[1]

There was nothing extraordinary or of apparent intrinsic interest in the pragmatic and, as it became increasingly clear, politically expedient approach to nation-building and economic development taken by its post-colonial leaders. But at independence in 1961, there was every expectation that a country with a population of just under three million people, occupying an area of about 72,000 square kilometres (about the size of Austria or Scotland), endowed with considerable agricultural potential, fairly sizeable deposits of gems and industrial diamonds, bauxite, rutile (or titanium dioxide), plus more modest deposits of iron ore and gold, and a small but well-established educated middle class, would find a formula to enable it to diversify its economy and continually raise living standards. Indeed, a very common saying among Sierra Leoneans of all social statuses and classes as they ruefully contemplate the unfilfilment of this expectation is 'Sierra Leone has no reason to be poor.'[2]

These optimistic expectations of independence were also shared with other African and developing countries although post-colonial inheritances, endowments, and specific circumstances differed from country to country. A number of Latin American and Asian states, appropriately labelled Newly Industrializing Countries (NICs), did manage to find a formula for high growth rates and economic diversification during the three decades since 1960. And several African countries including Botswana, Cameroon, Ivory Coast, Kenya, Malawi, Mauritius, Morocco, and Tunisia have managed to achieve impressive levels of economic growth and modest diversification. By contrast, Sierra Leone's performance in these respects has been dismal. Along with several other Sub-Saharan African (SSA) countries, it was clear by the end of the 1970s that Sierra Leone had little capacity to break away from its role of exporting primary resources. In many of these countries, moreover, incomes fell throughout the 1970s and it is thought possible that incomes per head in the late 1980s might be lower than in 1960.[3]

Consideration of the Sierra Leone case raises several issues which are general problems and affect other African countries that have also experienced economic decline. Amongst these are the debilitating effect on development of personalized or neopatrimonial rule and policies; the structural difficulties of a commodity exports economy; and the multiple consequences of urban bias, institutional, and infrastructural decay. Our understanding of these and other well-known themes in contemporary discourse on Africa's predicament can be enhanced by consideration of some specific aspects of the Sierra Leone case.

The common difficulties that Sierra Leone shares with other SSA countries include the features of a commodity-export economy; inappropriate development policies, inconsistent economic or development management; personal rule, political stagnation, and institutional decay. But specifically, Sierra Leone's economic decline has taken place within the context of relative political stability. This is all the more remarkable given the turmoil - as measured at least by the incidence of military coups - that accompanied decline in other African countries including Burkina Faso, Ghana, and Nigeria. And although the circumstances are different, political stability and economic decline is a feature that Sierra Leone shares with Tanzania (where, as in the former, there has even been a peaceful transfer of power from one leader to another); and to a lesser extent with Zambia (where there was an unsuccessful coup attempt in August 1986 and, at other times, sporadic urban-based riots) and with Zaire (where guerrillas have intensified their challenge to the authority of the Mobutu regime in Shaba province).

By the usual measurements of performance, Sierra Leone's economic position has deteriorated since the early 1970s. As studies of the origins and character of economic decline by Kamara, Johnson, and Funna make clear, variables such as real growth of GDP, overall balance of payments, the rate of inflation, investment, savings, debt and public expenditure deficits have consistently displayed worrisome trends.[4] These trends and the explanations offered for them are not unfamiliar in Sub-Saharan Africa although the strength of emphasis on explanatory factors, prescriptive action, and underlying theoretical assumptions vary among analysts. External and internal causes can be identified. The former includes deteriorating terms of trade, the impact of the oil-shocks of 1973-4 and 1979-80, and 'soft' commodity and mineral markets; as well as internal policies (or lack thereof) on public expenditure and investments, prices, credit, exchange rate, debt management, and ineffective controls on diamond smuggling and the thriving underground or black-market economy.

The implications of these factors are again very familiar in SSA. Sierra Leone is one of the poorest countries in the African region and one of the poorest in the world, with a GNP per capita of US$310 in 1984 and an average life expectancy at birth of 38 years. Available data on income and life changes distribution also suggest that Sierra Leone is an extremely unequal society. The political context within which economic decline has taken place is also well-known. Politics in Sierra Leone, as in most other African countries, is very much a personalized affair. Personal rule has been analyzed in a number of ways but a useful way of approaching the concept is to suggest that in Sierra Leone it has the features of a neopatrimonial polity - a derivation from Max Weber's notion of patrimonial domination.[5] In the application of the concept to Sierra Leone, politics is an overtly personalized competition for political office, access to which guarantees both formal and informal revenues (or corrupt income). As Medard and from a different theoretical perspective Szeftel[6] have argued, in a context of incipient capitalism the state is a resource in itself. Such political authority there is relies on a process of preferment rather than upon institutional or ideological bases of consent. Hence political legitimacy is fragile and development or economic strategy whether defined as meeting basic needs (e.g. China), import-substitutional industrialization (most of Latin America), or exported growth (north-east Asia) has to give way to control and survival as the main objective and principle governing political behaviour. Arising from this is a political culture in which public office corruption, nepotism, patronage, and the distribution of spoils are part of a process of securing and maintaining political support.

The consequences of this pattern of politics are to be seen in a range of arenas, skewing development efforts and undermining impartial and rational means of resource distribution. Sierra Leone is not unusual in experiencing such consequences. Its immediate neighbours, Liberia and Guinea, for example, have had similar experiences. But the point that personal rule can be associated with relative economic success and progress is one that should be made with emphasis. Not to recognize this is to fall into the deterministic trap of lumping all African states into the same straight-jacket. Ideology and even leadership style of personal rulers accounts for this variance. Thus a number of African countries combine the features of personal rule and progress in some, of the policy areas that were mentioned: for example, Cameroon, Ivory Coast, Malawi, Morocco, and Tanzania; or among non-African countries, South Korea, Mexico, and Thailand. This suggests that personal rulers and other political elites do have some choice (exercised with varying degrees of political ingenuity and resourcefulness) in policy-making and in insulating the bureaucratic process of policy administration from the worst effects of this pattern of governance. In the case of Sierra Leone, institutions of development management have not been insulated from a political culture of laxity toward bureaucratic organization and processes. The result - so common in many African countries - has been institutional decay.

If the basic structure of Sierra Leone's economy was developed under colonial rule, much of the responsibility of its current predicament has to fall on the political elite surrounding post-colonial rulers. It is all the more remarkable, therefore, that decline has been accompanied by relative political stability.

Sierra Leone: debt and the fiscal crisis

When compared to many other African countries, Sierra Leone is remarkable for its political stability and relative lack of fundamental change, disorder, and political violence. President Siaka Stevens was the most dominant political figure, at the pinnacle of the neopatrimonial polity from the late 1960s to 1985. The rules, practices, and customs of this polity and the resort to selective authoritarian measures constrained political activity of an oppositional nature. The adoption of a single-party constitution in 1978 institutionalized this mode of governance. Aside from that of the trade union movement, any protest activity that did emerge into open view was spontaneous and anarchic in character. But the general position was one of political stagnation, acquiescence, and drift.

An ageing figure, President Siaka Stevens announced his imminent retirement from politics in 1985. A conference of the ruling All People's Congress Party was called to rubber-stamp approval of his hand-picked successor, Major-General Joseph Momoh, the former head of the Sierra Leone military, and a nominated member of parliament and cabinet member. Following an election in which he was the only candidate, Momoh took over as president on 28 November 1985 amidst great euphoria about the possibilities of change in a 'new order'. So far there have been few changes in the political composition and direction of the Momoh regime, aside from cabinet reshuffles in 1986 and again in April 1987 following the implication of the vice-president in a plot to assassinate the new president.

The authoritarianism lurking beneath the surface of the neopatrimonial pattern of politics is of a relatively benign kind. There have been few instances of state-organized political violence and very few political deaths. Stevens was no Amin, Bokassa, or Nguema. Although there was dissent, it had little focus, and it did not represent a major challenge to his rule. Organized opposition groups in exile had little effect upon domestic politics. Most significantly, Stevens was able to stage-manage a successful and peaceful transfer of power and he remained a powerful figure behind the scenes as chairman of the party until 1987.

If the political disorder of economic decline in Ghana, Liberia, or Uganda is more readily explainable, the sources of political stability in Sierra Leone can also be identified. An important part of the explanation is the lack of an alternative in the form of a political party or in the form of a radicalized junior officers' cadre in the military such as those that overthrew discredited regimes in Ghana and Burkina Faso. Another part of the explanation has been, Stevens' artfulness in using various strategems - patronage especially - to secure and maintain support. It is an open question as to whether President Momoh has similar Machiavellian instincts.

Sierra Leone is a relatively small African debtor, certainly when compared to the major African debtor states of Sudan and Nigeria and, of course, South Africa. The latest edition of the World Bank's World Debt Tables gives a figure for Sierra Leone's total external debt of US$527.4 million in 1985, considerably smaller than the figure for the neighbouring states of Liberia and Ghana with debts of well over US$1 billion; or Nigeria, whose total external debt is estimated at approximately US$20 billion, with estimates ranging between US$12 billion and US$22 billion.[7] Clearly regimes differ in their level of external indebtedness, but they also differ in a number of other ways.

Recently there have been a number of attempts to classify American debtor countries, according to several distinct criteria. Green and Griffith-Jones provide a typology of indebted African countries, based upon a rough classification of their gross domestic product (GDP).[8] There are three categories of countries: low, lower-middle, and upper-middle levels of output. Examples of low per capita output African economies would include countries such as Burkina Faso, Liberia, Malawi, and Sierra Leone. Sierra Leone is in a sub-category of countries which have high debt service requirements, and are dominated by considerations regarding commercial arrears, export credits, IMF and World Bank credits, and short-term bank credits.[9] Lower-middle income countries, with annual incomes of US$400-US$999 per capita in 1981, are characterized by debt structures which feature commercial arrears in large measure, and a high level of external debt. Green and Griffith-Jones cite the examples of Nigeria, Cameroon, Kenya, Ivory Coast, Ghana, and Zambia in this category of country. There are only two countries in the upper middle-income category, defined as having a 1981 annual per capita income of over US$1,000: Mauritius and Gabon, which have a middle-level of debt servicing which is mostly made up of commercial debts and non-concessional export credits. A similar classificatory scheme is employed by Mathonnat, who places Sierra Leone in the category of relatively moderate indebtedness within the normal range of debt-servicing requirements.[10] Thus Sierra Leone has a comparatively low level of external debt in a low-income economy. It does not have the level of external debt of Nigeria, nor the scale of commercial arrears of Cameroon or Gabon. While the level of Sierra Leone's external debt may be relatively small, its impact has been great, as external agencies such as the IMF and the World Bank have sought to impose policy changes as external indebtedness has grown. Sierra Leone has neither the political and strategic significance nor the size of domestic market of countries such as Sudan or Nigeria, which have used these assets to achieve relatively lenient treatment of their external debt problems.[11]

In analysing the various ways that external debt problems have manifested themselves in Sierra Leone, the chapter will focus upon the following questions: the size and composition of Sierra Leone's external debt, and how it got into debt; the consequences of increasing external indebtedness; and the effectiveness of the policy changes insisted upon by Sierra Leone's external creditors.

ORIGINS OF THE DEBT CRISIS

Sierra Leone's external debt has grown dramatically in the period since 1978. The rapid growth has been due to a number of factors, including the fiscal crisis of the Sierra Leonean state, with declining official export earnings and government revenue, and wasteful and corruptly used government expenditures, in the context of a world recession which has affected most African states.[12] From the late 1970s onwards, the governments of Siaka Stevens, and later Joseph Momoh, have sought to attract several external sources of financial support, have renegotiated and rescheduled external debt, and have become increasingly reliant upon the approval and credit of the IMF. Sierra Leone's latest and probably short-lived stand-by agreement was announced by the IMF in November 1986 and ran into difficulties in 1987. How can the growth of external debt be explained?

Sierra Leone's position in the international economy deteriorated during the 1970s. Economic growth was less than 1.5 per cent between the financial years 1971 and 1979; and considerably worse thereafter. The economic growth rate has declined in every year of the last five (1984-8), except for a small increase of 0.5 per cent in 1985. Slow economic growth in the 1970s was due to the decreasing volume and value of official mineral exports, despite an increase in world diamond prices in the late 1970s. Two million carats of diamonds worth Le50.4 million were produced in the 1970-1 financial year; but the official output had dropped to 834,000 carats worth Le122.9 million by the 1978-9 financial year. Part of the decline in production was due to a depletion of resources, but in addition to official exports, substantial quantities of diamonds, and agricultural products, were also smuggled out of Sierra Leone. A large 'parallel' or black-market economy emerged, based on smuggling by Lebanese entrepreneurs and their political allies. Its size and significance accelerated in the late 1970s and early 1980s. The size of the parallel market was estimated at Le100 million a year in December 1982: it grew as a way of avoiding foreign exchange restrictions.

Declining official exports reduced government revenues, as Sierra Leone's tax system relies heavily on direct taxes. A World Bank study estimated that export and import duties, together with excise taxes, yield more than 70 per cent of government tax revenues.[13] In such circumstances, with rising government expenditures, it was perhaps not surprising that balance of payments problems emerged, and with them a greater burden of international debt. The public debt grew from Le60.4 million in 1972 to Le299.9 million in 1981; and the debt service ratio increased from 10 per cent in 1971 to 22.0 per cent in the early 1980s (see Table 6.1). From the late 1970s, the government of President Siaka Stevens sought to attract any external sources of financial support, and also asked for a renegotiation and rescheduling of external debts. The first rescheduling was in 1977, when the Sierra Leonean government got the agreement of the Paris Club for a rescheduling of US$39 million. A second and third rescheduling occurred in 1980 and 1984 as Sierra Leone's economic position worsened.[14]

External financial support has been sought from many quarters, and this search for funding can be said to explain some of Sierra Leone's more unusual positions, or changes of position, in international relations. The key political figures in the ruling All People's Congress (APC) party - including Stevens and his successor Joseph Momoh - are broadly pro-

Table 6.1 Sierra Leone: external indebtedness

US$m

	1970	1975	1980	1981	1982	1983	1984	1985
TOTAL EXTERNAL DEBT			425.1	446.9	502.4	520.8	432.3	527.4
Long-term debt	60.5	149.4	350.8	350.3	396.2	387.6	328.0	390.0
Public and publicly guaranteed	60.5	149.4	350.8	350.3	396.2	387.6	328.0	390.0
Private non guaranteed	0.0	0.0	0.0	0.0	0.0	0.0	0.0	0.0
Use of IMF credit	0.0	5.8	28.3	55.6	51.2	68.2	74.3	78.4
Short-term debt			46.0	61.0	55.0	65.0	30.0	59.0
PUBLIC AND PUBLICLY GUARANTEED LONG-TERM DEBT								
Debt outstanding, including undisbursed	85.3	187.9	466.7	498.8	513.3	501.2	459.5	513.9
Official creditors	55.8	106.4	324.7	361.0	396.8	398.3	364.1	406.8
Multilateral	18.8	52.8	152.9	203.8	208.5	219.9	231.8	251.9
IBRD	10.8	16.7	13.7	12.5	11.6	10.9	9.7	9.1
IDA	6.5	23.3	34.0	62.1	65.5	83.0	99.6	105.0
Bilateral	36.9	53.6	171.8	157.2	188.4	178.4	132.4	154.9
Private creditors	29.5	81.5	142.1	137.8	116.4	102.9	95.4	107.1
Suppliers	26.3	62.5	118.3	106.3	87.8	76.2	70.7	82.5
Financial markets	3.2	18.9	23.8	31.4	28.7	26.6	24.7	24.6

Table 6.1 continued

US$m

	1970	1975	1980	1981	1982	1983	1984	1985
Debt outstanding and disbursed	60.5	149.4	350.8	350.3	396.2	387.6	328.0	390.0
Official creditors	33.2	78.9	230.2	228.9	281.8	285.0	235.5	286.6
Multilateral	6.3	29.7	93.3	95.2	112.8	117.1	122.0	146.5
IBRD	6.3	11.6	13.4	12.5	11.6	10.9	9.7	9.1
IDA	0.0	10.5	29.1	31.4	37.1	42.5	47.4	58.8
Bilateral	26.9	49.1	136.9	133.7	169.0	167.8	113.6	140.2
Private creditors	27.3	70.5	120.6	121.4	114.5	102.6	92.5	103.4
Suppliers	24.1	57.3	96.8	90.0	87.8	76.2	68.0	79.1
Financial markets	3.2	13.2	23.8	31.4	26.7	26.4	24.5	24.3

Source: World Bank, World Debt Tables, 1986-7 Edition, First Supplement, (1987), p.166

western in their political outlook. Yet in 1982 Sierra Leone ratified the Islamic Conference charter. Sierra Leone has also established diplomatic relations with Iran and Saudi Arabia, and has had loans from the Islamic Development Bank to cover crude oil imports from Saudi Arabia. Economic necessity, rather than a changing ideological disposition, explains these political moves. A similar explanation applied to President Stevens' continued attendance at the annual Franco-African summits.

Sierra Leone's major sources of international credit are more usual ones however. In 1985 the total of public and publicly guaranteed debt, including undisbursed debt, was US$513.9 million with US$406.8 million owed to official creditors and US$107.1 million owed to private creditors. Official credit came from a number of sources including the World Bank, and bilateral sources such as the United States, United Kingdom, West Germany, and The Netherlands. Of the debt owed to private creditors, US$82.5 million was in the form of short-term suppliers credits, often taken out on unfavourable terms. In general, the terms of commercial debts incurred by the Stevens regime have become harsher as its indebtedness has grown.

There have been a number of political effects as a result of the deteriorating economy and growing indebtedness. Popular discontent at rising prices and shortages of basic commodities was fuelled by the public excesses of the OAU (Organization for African Unity) meetings in 1980. One popular expression was: 'OAU for you, IOU for we'. Hoarding and speculation in rice and petrol resulted in a series of protests, expressed most obviously in the general strikes of 1981 and in comment during the 1982 one-party elections, but also in a series of 'anarchic' demonstrations in Freetown in 1982-3, and recently by students, trade unionists, and schoolchildren.

In its response to these expressions of protest, the Stevens regime had increasingly little room to manoeuvre. In order to obtain oil for the refinery in Freetown, scarce foreign exchange, or oil-rich friends, were needed. But the sources of foreign exchange began to dry up in the late 1970s as official export volumes and values declined. The emergence of a vibrant black or parallel economy in the period meant that the fiscal basis of the Sierra Leonean state was progressively undermined. Private credit was available only on an increasingly severe set of conditions, and official sources of credit became both more attractive and more restrictive in policy terms. External creditors - such as the IMF - have sought policy changes as well as prompt repayment of what is owed, and have held up external credit payments when the policy conditionalities have not been adhered to. Increasing external debt led to increasingly severe conditionalities, including a demand for policy changes which affected the somewhat fragile base of the Stevens regime. The demands of external creditors that government expenditures be reduced conflicted with the imperative of a system based upon favouring political supporters within a patron-clientelist political economy.[15]

An example was the case of subsidies, and in particular the pricing and distribution of rice, the staple food. Sierra Leone was relatively self-sufficient in rice until the late 1970s. Rice imports have subsequently grown in size and, with crude oil imports, have used up much scarce foreign exchange. Theft of imported rice arriving in the Freetown docks led to a cut in deliveries under the United States PL480 aid scheme, from 10,000 tonnes in 1983 to 3,400 tonnes during 1984, and rice prices doubled during 1984. Politicians were able to speculate in rice, as they were given the task of distributing it in their constituencies.[16] The availability and cost of rice (and oil products) are very sensitive political issues in Sierra Leone, and in other West African states. It was for political reasons that the Stevens regime resisted, at least initially, IMF pressure to cut subsidies on petrol and rice. As President Stevens said, these are 'dangerous areas'. The IMF 'are asking us to commit political suicide'.[17]

The IMF were able to ask for such policy changes because the Sierra Leonean government had become increasingly reliant on external financial support, especially from the IMF. IMF stabilization programmes have become a regular feature of the economy since 1979, when a one-year balance of payments support arrangement started, attached to some familiar policy conditionalities: reducing government expenditure, imposing financial discipline, and reducing the trade gap.[18] The IMF appears to have been relatively satisfied with the Sierra Leone government's performance under the stand-by arrangement, as it had been with an earlier stabilization programme.[19] Balance of payments support was followed by an extended agreement, which allowed the government to purchase up to the equivalent of SDR 163.8 million (US$200.4 million) over the three years from early 1981. Under the enlarged access scheme of the IMF the agreement was subsequently increased to support worth SDR 186 million (US$230 million). Almost immediately, however, the supported programme ran into trouble, due to the IMF's view that the Sierra Leone government was unable to meet the criteria laid down. The IMF regarded a fall in exports of alluvial diamonds and agricultural products as sufficient to endanger the programme of support. By the end of 1981, the foreign exchange reserves were at a very low level and totalled Le17.4 million (US$14.6 million).[20]

Since 1981 the Sierra Leone government has found it increasingly difficult to obtain IMF support for its programmes. The Sierra Leone government has been unwilling or unable to meet some IMF conditions for further support, objecting to their inflexibility.[21] Four major issues have subsequently been matters of contention between the Sierra Leone government and the IMF. These are, first, what the IMF regarded as an over-valued exchange rate. Second, the question of low returns for agricultural producers, and subsidies for specific commodities. Third, 'financial indiscipline' in government expenditures; and, finally, the effects of the new and unusual foreign exchange system, especially in relation to the influence of the Lebanese and other entrepreneurial groups.

FLOATING OR DROWNING?

It appears that the IMF conditions with respect to Sierra Leone's exchange rate have followed a pattern identified by Payer.[22] The general model of conditionality includes the devaluation of the exchange rate. Sierra Leone has had a series of changes in its foreign exchange formula since 1978 (see Table 6.2). The involvement of the IMF in these changes can be clearly indicated. In November 1978 the leone was 'de-linked' from sterling and tied instead to the SDR, the IMF's national currency. This can be seen as a commitment linked to receiving balance of payments support from the IMF in 1979-80. The 'de-linking' was an effective devaluation of 5 per cent.

In the officially regulated economy, the government instituted a queuing system for foreign exchange - known as the 'pipeline' - which contributed to increased smuggling and the creation of a large parallel economy. In December 1982, as a result, the exchange rate system was modified under

Table 6.2 External support and conditionality

Paris Club reschedulings	
1977	US$39 million
1980	US$37 million
1984	US$50 million
1986-7	- not yet known
IMF support	
1979-80	One-year balance of payments support: Le22 million/US$26 million.
1980	Three-year extended agreement, allowing purchases of US$200.4 million over period from early 1981. Suspended.
1983	Purchase of US$22.3 million under the IMF's compensatory funding facility.
1984	One-year stand-by support programme: US$51.9 million. Suspended.
1986	November: one year stand-by programme, and three-year concessional funding under the Structural Adjustment Facility (SAF).
Devaluations/Changes in Exchange Formulae	
1978	'De-linking' of the leone from sterling; effective devaluation of 5 per cent.
1982	'Two-tier' exchange rate.
1983	Devaluation as part of abandonment of 'two-tier' system; new unified rate of US$1 = Le2.46 established.
1985	Devaluation; change to US$1 = Le6.
1986	June: flotation of the leone. In July, US$1 = Le20.
1987	Continued downward flotation and subsequent government-supported stabilization. In April, US$1 = Le53, stabilizing at US$1 = Le22 in late 1987.

Sources: Various, especially Africa Economic Digest, and the quarterly assessments of the Economist Intelligence Unit (London, The Economist).

the direction of the new Finance Minister Salia Jusu-Sheriff, a former opposition leader, and a one-time possible contender for the succession to President Stevens. A two-tier exchange rate system was established, similar in principle to those adopted by many other Third World governments - such as Uganda and Sri Lanka - with IMF support programmes. The two-tier system was designed to 'stabilize and rejuvenate the economy', Jusu-Sheriff declared.[23] It represented a further devaluation of the leone as well as an (unsuccessful) attempt to reduce the size and significance of the parallel economy. It led, naturally enough, to further support from the IMF, which had approved the scheme in principle. Initially the IMF had suggested an across the board devaluation of 40 per cent, according to a senior Bank of Sierra Leone (central bank) official.[24] In February 1983, Sierra Leone was granted a purchase of SDR 20.7 million (US$22.3 million) under the IMF's compensatory funding facility, to cover a shortfall in diamond export earnings in 1981-2.

By the middle of 1983 it was clear to both Jusu-Sheriff and the IMF that the new exchange rate system was not achieving its objectives. Smuggling was not decreasing; it was flourishing. Jusu-Sheriff himself estimated in June 1983 that about 60 per cent of diamond production, and all gold production, was being smuggled over the borders. Bottlenecks in the supply of foreign exchange were causing major problems. It meant a decline in imports and a fall in GNP. More importantly, however, there were shortages of basic domestic and commercial items, including spare parts, newsprint, and imported foodstuffs. The local brewery stopped production. Many Sierra Leoneans thought that the Lebanese and Afro-Lebanese entrepreneurs were able to manipulate the foreign exchange system.

The two-tier system of exchange rates was unpopular; it became increasingly so as shortages continued. The leone was again devalued in July 1983 when the two-tier system was abandoned, and a new unified rate of US$1 = Le2.46 was established. Negotiations for a further stand-by credit from the IMF had started the month before the devaluation. Agreement was delayed, partly due to the IMF's own problems in securing financial support.

Eventually, in December 1983, a letter of intent was signed by Jusu-Sheriff, agreeing a one-year stand-by support programme for the period January-December 1984. A credit of SDR 50 million (US$51.9 million) was potentially available during the period; but only two drawings of credit were received, and this support programme was suspended.[25] From June 1984 to late 1986, the government was involved in a process of almost continuous negotiation with the IMF to secure further external finance.

In September 1984, Jusu-Sheriff was demoted and moved from the post of Finance Minister to the lesser position of Minister of Development and Economic Planning. Jusu-Sheriff's decision to implement economic policy measures 'approved' by the IMF had contributed to his change in the political hierarchy of the Stevens government. He was also a casualty of the politics of succession; his inability to get further IMF support, even after a series of economic policy changes, and a devaluation, was also a liability. A further devaluation of the leone took place in February 1985, and in June 1986 it was floated. The value of the leone deteriorated from being worth 50p in 1978 sterling values, to being worth just over 1p in April 1987. It fell dramatically in the aftermath of the agreement reached with the IMF in 1986, sinking to a level of US$1 = Le55, before recovering to a government-supported level of US$1 = Le22 in late 1987.

The IMF has been consistent in its recommendations for devaluation or flotation of the leone over the period since 1978. It appears to have sought a large across-the-board devaluation for several years, along with a package of other policy measures. A substantial cumulative devaluation and, later, a flotation of the leone have subsequently taken place.

The Sierra Leone government was relatively easily treated by the IMF in the period immediately after the de-linking of the leone in 1978. A major growth in government expenditure, including the cost of Organization for African Unity meetings, at the time of declining exports, ensured that subsequent Sierra Leone government requests for balance of payments support were to be met with demands for severe conditionalities. As Payer has pointed out, the rationale behind an IMF devaluation conditionality is that devaluation would increase exports.[26] In the case of Sierra Leone, official exports (and imports) have fallen substantially since the 1970s. Export volumes and values reached their lowest recorded levels in 1982-3. Major mineral extractive companies withdrew from production or slowed down production in Sierra Leone in the 1970s and 1980s. Austro-Mineral, previously involved in iron ore production, and BP Minerals/Selection Trust, withdrew or became managers.

The IMF appear to have thought that devaluation, plus other policy measures, would have a major beneficial effect upon the Sierra Leone economy. But the IMF over-estimated the various governments' ability to implement policy changes and, in particular, did not fully appreciate that structural factors in the economy - including smuggling - were deeply embedded, and served vital political interests.

In the period since 1978, devaluation alone has been insufficient. It has to be accompanied by a series of policy measures designed to reduce smuggling and increase government revenue. The government's earning power had been undermined by the emergence of the parallel economy. Its own ministers were involved. Some were made examples of.[27] The Stevens regime was not able to implement effectively a series of policy measures advocated by the IMF, including restrictions upon government expenditure, reducing the size of the cabinet, and an improvement in the efficiency of parastatal organizations. A devaluation was a much easier policy decision to make and implement, given that devaluation is a central bank activity. The progressive deterioration of the international value of the leone has had a series of dramatic effects upon Sierra Leonean economy and polity. Prices of essential commodities have increased, and soared beyond the purchasing power of many in both rural and urban areas. Price inflation of items such as rice, petrol, and kerosene was also a consequence of the IMF-inspired policy measures of reducing state subsidies on consumer items. For example, the consumer price of sugar rose in late 1986 to Le850 for a 112lb bag, compared with the earlier price of Le187; and petrol was officially Le30 a gallon in March 1987, but those with the money needed Le250-300 to buy a gallon in April.[28] By the end of 1986 and early 1987, several outside observers had concluded that Sierra Leone had become a country where many nationals could not afford to live.[29]

The IMF's role in the impoverishment of both urban and rural populaces was central. It sought these policy changes at a time when the regime was undergoing the trials and tribulations of establishing and consolidating the position of the new president Joseph Momoh, who succeeded the ageing Siaka Stevens in November 1985. Despite the fundamental deterioration in the quality of life of many Sierra Leoneans, it is surprising that active protest against the IMF measures has been relatively muted.[30] Economic necessity rather than political expediency was of course the rationale behind the devaluation and flotation. But the expected benefits - and the appreciation of the leone - are likely to be long awaited.

'GETTING THE PRICES RIGHT' (OR WRONG?)

Low returns for agricultural producers and the question of subsidies for rice and petrol have also been a major concern of the IMF. Increasing prices paid to agricultural producers has been a major policy suggestion of IMF negotiators in recent years. In this they are reflecting the view of their fellow Washington institution, the World Bank, and in particular the perspective upon Sub-Saharan Africa found in the Berg Report.[31] Producer prices were raised in March and after the July 1983 budget, for example. In the budget the producer price for coffee was raised by 138 per cent and that for cocoa went up by 108 per cent. Unfortunately, the desired results did not emerge. Despite two increases in the price paid to producers, the volume of purchases recorded by the Sierra Leone Produce Marketing Board actually fell. As the governor of the central bank pointed out, coffee and cocoa purchases almost halved.[32] Subsequent producer price increases have not led to a marked up-turn in official production as yet.

The IMF's conditions in other policy areas have been far more politically sensitive. The cost of rice subsidies was questioned, but in addition the IMF have pressed for a reduction in the subsidy for petrol and other oil products. Finance Minister Jusu-Sheriff claimed in 1983 that the state subsidy for petrol resulted in the lowest consumer price in Africa. He subsequently raised petrol prices by 47 per cent in the 1983 budget. Petrol prices were again raised in January 1985, in 1986, and in 1987. Erratic supplies and price increases have led to hoarding, queueing, political manipulation of distribution, and increased prices (or shorter journeys) on public transport. Petrol supplies are more often available in the capital, than in rural Sierra Leone. Petrol shortages and price increases have led to protests by urban workers and schoolchildren, and have reinforced existing inequalities.

CURBING WASTE

A third area of IMF policy interest was in what was described as 'financial indiscipline' in government operations, both in government departments and in the parastatals. There are again echoes of the Berg Report. The IMF sought to influence the government to cut down expenditure and, especially, to reduce wastage in parastatals such as the produce-marketing and electricity boards. Pricing policies were questioned. The current government response is one of privatization.[33] Government expenditure, though difficult to control, has been reduced. Budget indicators of government expenditure are unreliable, however, as the government uses the mechanism of a supplementary estimate to cover extra expenditure. Cost over-runs are high. This is apparent in both official figures and unofficial assessments. In the 1970s and 1980s, ministries have grown in size as they respond to a pattern of politics based on a form of patron-clientelism.

The IMF's strictures on financial indiscipline have been at least verbally accepted. President Stevens made frequent calls for probity in public life, though the political will of the regime to pursue the implications of such pleas can be questioned. His successor - the ex-head of the Sierra Leone Military, Joseph Momoh, who took over in November 1985, has made similar appeals, in an attempt to establish a 'new order'.[34]

THE POLITICS OF THE PARIAH ENTREPRENEURS

The final area of conflict between the IMF and the Sierra Leone government is somewhat unusual: it concerns a new system for allocating foreign exchange, and especially the role of private companies dominated by Afro-Lebanese and Lebanese entrepreneurs in this system. The IMF's view was that a new foreign exchange committee and diamond mining company usurped the functions of the central bank. The IMF cannot negotiate with what amounts to a private interest group, officials are reported to have argued. Privatization has been taken too far.[35]

The origins of this conflict between the IMF and Sierra Leone can be traced to the formation in October 1983 of a committee to allocate scarce foreign exchange to importers. It included representatives of government, the

Bank of Sierra Leone (central bank), commercial banks, the Chamber of Commerce and the Labour Congress, and manufacturing industry. Jamil Said Mohammed, a leading Afro-Lebanese entrepreneur, was a member. The committee's role was to allocate foreign exchange on the basis of guidelines provided in the annual budget. Official imports were allowed in only after approval by this committee.

In the autumn of 1984, BP Minerals decided to sell its stake in the National Diamond Mining Company, withdrawing from all its operations in Sierra Leone. BP's holding in the diamond mining company was purchased by a private company, the Precious Minerals Marketing Company (PMMC), which was set up a few weeks earlier in August 1984 and whose managing director was Jamil Said Mohammed. Shareholders included the government with 25 per cent, and local Lebanese entrepreneurs. At the same time as the PMMC was established, the foreign exchange committee was reconstituted. President Stevens chaired the foreign exchange committee, which met monthly. In effect, the PMMC, and in particular Mohammed and Stevens, determined the allocation of foreign exchange, and consequently the supply of official imports into Sierra Leone.

These changes resulted in an intermingling of the interests of a private company and the state. Not only did the PMMC have a major role in deciding what was officially imported; the new company was also given the right to retain most of its proceeds from the sale of gold and diamonds overseas. The central bank had, consequently, no effective control over most of the diamond and gold export earnings.[36]

The delay in reaching an agreement with the IMF, and the protracted negotiations from June 1984 onwards, can be attributed in part to conflict over the role of the PMMS, and key individual businessmen, in government decision-making. Autonomy of decision by the PMMC was a major issue until the dissolution of the management early in 1986. PMMC was a product both of ex-President Stevens' close relationships with entrepreneurs in Sierra Leone, and the worsening condition of the economy, leading to a withdrawal by external firms. The IMF's insistence upon propriety in foreign exchange matters was one of the reasons behind the withdrawal of Jamil Said Mohammed from the Sierra Leonean economy.[37] Political change at the presidential level also meant that a challenge to Mohammed's (and other Lebanese entrepreneurs') hegemony was able to emerge. Liat, an Israeli-backed construction and import-export firm with South African links, was encouraged by President Momoh to operate in Sierra Leone. Thus the conflicts of the Middle East were temporarily replicated in Western Africa.[38]

The IMF's attitude towards local entrepreneurs such as Mohammed provides a paradox. The IMF and the World Bank are committed to promoting a private enterprise solution to Africa's current predicament, which involves an emphasis upon free enterprise and a restricted role for the state. Yet the IMF refused to accept some of the foreign exchange conditions insisted upon by the vibrant capitalism of Mohammed and his associates. Free enterprise may be a desired policy choice, but its implications and consequences in terms of the Lebanese entrepreneurial stratum were baulked at.

CONCLUSIONS

From 1978 onwards the Sierra Leone government's room for manoeuvre has progressively narrowed. Initially, in 1978-9, the government was able to draw international credit relatively easily, helped by a high world price for diamonds. An IMF stabilization programme was agreed, and substantial financial support was also secured. The high world price for diamonds disguised the decline in official production of diamonds and other mineral and agricultural products which form the basis of Sierra Leone's economy. Increased smuggling and the development of a 'parallel' economy undercut the revenue base of the state, and led to a fiscal crisis as there was a growing gap between revenues and expenditures. Government expenditure continued to climb, and led to increasing recourse to sources of external credit. Sierra Leone's economic deterioration meant that the pressing need for further external support gave the IMF and other creditors exceptional leverage to insist upon the implementation of specific economic reform proposals. Under the Presidency of Siaka Stevens there was at times resistance to the measures proposed, whereas Momoh since 1986 readily accepted the necessity of pursuing specific policies in return for external assistance. The policy measures implemented in 1986 drastically altered the conditions of Sierra Leonean life.

So far Sierra Leone's substantial economic deterioration has led to escalating price inflation, shortages and hoarding. 'Getting the prices right', several devaluations and a flotation of the leone, privatization, and cuts in subsidies, have not regenerated an economy in fundamental crisis. It may be that economic revival will eventually become a reality, but in the meantime the measures insisted upon by Sierra Leone's external creditors have led to political unrest and disquiet which has undermined the precarious legitimacy of Momoh's 'new order'.

7

External debt and Francophone Africa: the effects of a special relationship

Francophone Africa is different - so many observers say. Unlike the former colonies of the other European powers, the former French dependencies have retained and in some cases enhanced their relationships with the ex-metropolitan power. There is an enduring legacy of colonialism expressed in the notion of a 'Francophone' community, which is seen in concrete terms in military links and a persistent dependent economic relationship. As Sandbrook has expressed it:

> Many a strongman's regime owed thanks to France in the 1960s when it suppressed riots and uprisings. And under the direction of President Giscard d'Estaing there was a fresh spate of interventions in the late seventies.[1]

This tradition of self-interested interventionism has continued in the 1980s, despite a socialist victory in the 1981 French election. President François Mitterand of France responded to a public injunction from US President Ronald Reagan that France should 'assume its historic responsibilties' by intervening in the conflict in Chad in 1983.[2] Many earlier examples of French intervention can be given.[3] The French military presence - seen in military agreements and the location of French troops in six African states - is complemented by enduring economic links.

Though the economic links between France and the Francophone states have weakened in Africa's post-independence period, strong economic relationships survive in a number of areas.[4] The currency of twelve Francophone states - the CFA franc - is linked to the French franc, and to France's benefit as the Francophone countries concerned have to deposit at least 65 per cent of their foreign exchange earnings in the Bank of France. French investment in some Francophone states continues to be high, while large numbers of French citizens are now resident in countries such as Gabon, Senegal, and Ivory Coast. French citizens selling fruit and vegetables in Dakar's markets may be a trivial example of French influence, but it is indicative of a persistent relationship. In addition to economic and military ties, France's relationships with its former dependencies are united by factors relating to the pervasiveness of French culture, language, and political style.

Though there may be 'a certain mystery' as to 'why France gets away with it' - as Golan expresses it - the relationship is stronger than that between other former colonies and their former metropolitan powers.[5]

In this context this chapter examines the linkage between questions of external debt and the special ties between Francophone Africa and France. Twenty African states are usually identified as members of a 'Francophone' group, though the twenty are composed of fifteen former dependencies, two former United Nations territories administered by France, and three former Belgian colonies (see Table 7.1). The new states are diverse in character, ranging from the quasi-marxian military regime in Benin to the conservative autocracy of Houphouet-Boigny in Ivory Coast. Levels of economic development, structure of production, and character and composition of external debt all vary considerably. Some Francophone states - such as Burkina Faso - have low levels of indebtedness; others - such as the Ivory Coast - are heavily indebted, as a consequence of the relatively benign view of their developmental prospects in the 1970s.

The remainder of this chapter concentrates upon the politics of debt in the Ivory Coast, chosen because it is one of the fifteen 'heavily indebted' Third World countries identified in the Baker Plan and also because, as Fieldhouse suggests, 'almost alone among Black African states, Ivory Coast stands in the literature as a story of apparent success after decolonization'.[6]

THE IVORY COAST: MIRACLE OR MIRAGE?

The Ivory Coast is an example of an extremely personal form of rule, epitomized in the central political figure since independence in 1961 of President Felix Houphouet-Boigny.

Table 7.1 Francophone Africa

The following are generally recognized as the 'Francophone African' states:

Former colonies	Mauritania	
	Senegal	
	Mali	
	Guinea	
	Burkina Faso (formerly Upper Volta)	
	Ivory Coast	
	Niger	
	Benin	
	Chad	
	Central African Republic	
	Gabon	
	Congo	
	Madagascar	
	Djibouti	
	Comoros	(15)
French-administered UN territories	Togo	
	Cameroon	(2)
Formerly Belgian-ruled	Zaire	
	Rwanda	
	Burundi	(3)

Aged 81, Houphouet-Boigny is in his sixth term of office as president, with each term lasting five years.

Like Siaka Stevens in Sierra Leone or Mobutu in Zaire, Houphouet-Boigny is at the top of a pinnacle of personal political power in Ivorian life. Though the regimes differ considerably, they can all be classified as examples of neopatrimonial forms of rule, a derivative of Weber's idea of patrimonial domination.[7] One difference is the apparent economic success of Houphouet-Boigny's regime, which had steady growth rates at least until the world economic shocks caused by the OPEC oil-price rises of the 1970s.

Ivorian economic growth is traditionally based upon the

three principal exports of coffee, cocoa, and timber, although some export diversification has taken place. The Ivory Coast is a major world producer of cocoa, and its economic fortunes are therefore intimately linked to world commodity prices. Recent collapses in world coffee and cocoa markets have therefore hit the state's revenues hard, and continued reliance upon fluctuating export prices has led, in part, to an escalation of external debt. Total external debt was US$256 million in 1970; this rose to US$8.3 billion in 1987, making Ivory Coast one of Sub-Saharan Africa's most heavily indebted states. Growing indebtedness led to the imposition of an IMF austerity programme which ran over a six-year period, followed by a suspension of debt payments in mid-1987.

The 1980s thus saw a question mark raised regarding the characterization of the Ivory Coast as an economic miracle. The wider relevance of the Ivorian model for African agricultural development was also questioned, as the country's peasant-based agriculture, its receptive attitude to foreign investment, and its relatively benign form of personal rule had combined to create the high levels of indebtedness. There are important parallels, as well as significant differences, to the Zairean case under Mobutu. Zaire and the Ivory Coast were both favourably regarded by western interests, though there was considerable disquiet at Mobutu's tyrannical and corrupt regime which was seemingly unresponsive or incapable of change. Both were seen as solidly conservative and pro-western in orientation, with each a considerable success story, if success in politics is measured in terms of personal political survival.

The Ivorian case was, however, regarded as a much more benign case of personal rule. The patron-clientelist form of politics implicit in such systems has by all accounts been kept under reasonable control in Houphouet-Boigny's regime. Though there were some excesses,[8] levels of corruption, graft, and maladministration were lower than in the neighbouring states of Liberia and Ghana, or the comparable case of Senegal under Senghor. Whilst apparently more 'neo-colonial' than its neighbours or some other African states, the Ivorian regime was able to record measurable developmental advances, until the entire development path was again questioned in the mid 1980s.[9] An administrative system relatively isolated from the malign aspects of patrimonial rule, and a vigorously free market and open economy approach did not prevent the emergence of such a crisis. We now turn to an outline of the development strategy identified as the Ivorian 'miracle'.

DEVELOPMENT STRATEGY IN THE IVORY COAST

Ivorian development strategy post-independence has been variously categorized. Samir Amin has argued that the colony was in some respects a labour reserve where development had, in effect, not begun by the early 1950s.[10] Since that period, as Amin predicted, there has been considerable economic growth, exploiting the availability of cheap land and labour, and favourable international markets, with growth directed by a stable statist regime which has sought to boost agricultural productivity by price incentives. As Fieldhouse points out, Amin also suggested that that form of development would not continue unabated for ever.[11] Industrial development would be stymied by the small domestic market, and the profits of agricultural surplus would be misused or exported overseas. Economic growth would be slowed, and political tensions would emerge. In terms of debt, the regime would become increasingly indebted as it sought to 'square the circle' of planned statist development based upon a fluctuating world commodity price-based revenue.

Contrary to many impressions of the Ivory Coast as a liberal economic model, the regime is in fact statist and interventionist in character, as well as tied closely to France. Many have identified this French control of, for example, the import-export trade (via trading companies such as SCOA, the Société Commerciale Ouest Africaine) as the essence of neocolonialism.[12]

Though there have been various forms of import-substitution industrialization, usually involving specially created subsidiaries of French companies, the key ingredient of the Ivorian 'miracle' has been a growth in agricultural production. Many figures can be given which indicate the expansion in this area. Cocoa production increased from 94,000 tones in 1960-1 to 240,000 tons in 1974-5, and up to 590,000 tons for 1986-7.[13] Coffee production increased from 178,000 tons to 280,000 tons in the same period, 1960-87. Ivory Coast has become Africa's third largest cotton producer after Egypt and the Sudan, with a record crop of 214,000 tons being produced in 1986-7.[14] Food production has also increased substantially.

The explanations for this expansion in agricultural production are complex. Areas of cultivation have been expanded dramatically, and much of the production is dependent upon a fairly large immigrant labour force. But a significant factor has been the relatively generous producer prices paid by the state marketing board. This can be expressed in a different way: the Ivorian board, the Caisse de Stabilisation, has been less exploitative of its peasant producers than many other marketing boards. Hecht suggests that this generosity should not be exaggerated, but the higher producer prices, coupled with a lack of deterioration in the rural-urban terms of trade, are central factors in explaining this growth.[15]

Since the late 1970s, however, world coffee and cocoa prices have dropped dramatically. Ivorian export dependence upon these prices, and the escalating cost of oil imports, have led to a turn round in the Ivorian regime's financial circumstances. Adverse trade balances have developed, and external debt has grown substantially since 1977. External debt more than doubled in the two years 1977-9, for example, and as with other African states in economic difficulty, the IMF was quickly on the scene. As Loxley points out:

> Since 1981, the Ivory Coast has entered into a three-year Extended Facility with the Fund and three Stand-by Arrangements covering a four-year period (1984-7), receiving balance of payments assistance to the tune of over SDR 733 million. Over the same period, the World Bank has approved three Structural Adjustment loans totalling over US$650 million.[16]

The availability of such levels of credit is an indication of the favourable way in which Boigny's regime was viewed by western interests in the early to mid 1980s. An austerity programme was introduced, but targets were not met. The IMF also insisted upon tariffs and export subsidies which were an indirect way of altering the country's exchange rate. As the Ivory Coast has the CFA franc as a unit of currency this cannot be altered unilaterally as it is tied to the French franc at a fixed rate. Given the IMF's predilection for changing the foreign exchange formula as part of a programme of adjustment, this has proved to be an obstacle.

CURRENT ECONOMIC CRISIS

Though there were initial successes in the adjustment programme, the regime descended into severe economic crisis. This became evident in 1987 with a major collapse in world prices for coffee and cocoa, and increasingly strained relations ensued between the Ivorian government and the IMF. Ivory Coast's economic crisis emerged despite the regime being the first African country to have been given a multi-year debt rescheduling agreement by the Paris Club.[17]

Debt repayments were suspended in May 1987, the first time in twenty-six years of independence. Debt service payments would have been CFA350,000 million, or approximately US$1.15 billion. In some ways this announcement was more dramatic than that of Zaire, which we discuss in chapter 4. Zaire's debt amounted to less than that of the Ivory Coast. Much of the Ivorian debt is commercial debt, contracted at high rates of interest. Of the 1987 debt service, over a third is commercial debt repayable to the London Club of creditors. Total debt service will peak in 1989 at CFA377,000 million (US$1.56 billion), an expected 35 per cent of export earnings.[18]

The Ivorian regime is thus faced with a series of difficult choices. Part of this emerging financial gap between export income and government expenditure has been created by the government's policy of maintaining relatively high producer prices. Lowering producer prices could have adverse effects in terms of future production. In addition it would seem likely that the Ivorian regime will be expected to face another bout of austerity measures insisted upon by the IMF, even though the previous six years of austerity have produced mixed results at best. Further austerity measures will have politically destabilizing results, coming as they do at the time of uncertainty regarding the succession to, and transition from the ageing Houphouet-Boigny. Though the succession debate - a familiar feature in personalist regimes - has declined in importance following a constitutional amendment in 1985 giving a key role to Henri Konan Bedie, the president of the National Assembly, the sensitivity of the issue is likely to continue. The Ivorian regime has the advantage of being able to pass on the costs of austerity to the many migrant workers from neighbouring states, which may help the regime to continue its relatively smooth political evolution. It has also the advantage of being viewed relatively favourably by external creditors, though the evidence would suggest that this is a wasting asset.

There is some dispute about the significance of the May 1987 decision to suspend debt repayments. As West Africa reports:

> Some saw such a move by a hitherto model debtor and exemplary economic manager as a graphic illustration of the economic crises facing governments throughout the continent; others saw it as a political manoeuvre by one of Africa's most esteemed leaders to secure a fairer deal from the west for the continent's governments in distress.[19]

Behaving as Zaire had done, the Boigny regime's suspension of debt repayments was a tactic used by a favoured client to get better terms for further credit. Given the Ivory Coast's centrality as part of the Francophone 'family', and the innate conservatism of Houphouet-Boigny and his regime, it could hardly be otherwise. The Ivory Coast's economic miracle is proving to be transparent - somewhat like a mirage - and too dependent upon exports of agricultural produce. The splendours of the Ivorian capital, Abidjan, are dependent upon fragile agricultural growth in a volatile and unpredictable world market. The consequences have been an escalation of indebtedness and some familiar austerity measures, mediated only by a close and continuing politico-economic linkage with France. In the next section we turn from the Ivorian case to consider the question of the special relationship between France and the Francophone African countries, and consider how the relationship affects the external debt issue.

A SPECIAL RELATIONSHIP?

The Ivory Coast's close links with France are just one facet of a complex set of France/Francophone Africa relations. Some aspects of these relationships have been explored in detail, other are more shadowy.[20] The main elements have been called the pillars of indirect colonialism by Joseph, and can be briefly described.[21]

A first pillar is monetary in character; the linkage between the French franc and the currencies of the former dependencies. Joseph argues that this tied relationship has been to the benefit of France, not only due to the location of the Francophone reserves in the French treasury, as mentioned above, but also due to the impact of the reserves in limiting or reducing France's global deficit. There is clearly a conflict of interest between the Francophone states and France in this respect, though the franc does buttress the weaker Francophone currencies. In respect of debt, the monetary linkage creates problems for externally-suggested adjustment programmes which are predicated upon a devaluation or flotation of the national currency.

A second pillar is the military agreements between the Francophone states and France, and the French military presence in Africa. As Chipman argues, the military linkages have to be understood in relation to France's view of its role in the world: 'The fact that Africa provides a "field of action" for French power is fundamental to French military and therefore political confidence'.[22] Luckham has provided a useful history of France's military interventions (see Table 7.2), but his list of interventions needs updating to include the French operation in Chad, 'Operation Manta', during 1983-4 which involved supporting Hissen Habré's forces against Libyan incursions. It is also worth adding that Luckham's listing does not include far more covert or subtle forms of intervention, often in support of favoured clients. The military agreements between France and the African states were initiated on independence; recent renegotiations of their terms have included provisions for French intervention in the event of domestic or foreign challenges to the governments concerned.[23]

Why does France continue to play this central military role? Partly, as Chipman suggests, for rayonnement (or glory), but also because of the strategic and economic significance of former French Africa.[24] Trade links are still important, especially with the major Francophone states. France's needs for oil, uranium, copper, phosphates and other minerals are also satisfied to a considerable degree from Africa. But the dependence is of course unequal, for, as Staniland suggests, 'Francophone states, in the mid-eighties, were still depending on France for between 40 and 60 per cent of imported goods and services'.[25] France's role in Africa - part gendarme, part businessman - is a factor which will affect the politics of debt in so far as this relates to the Francophone states. But, as we have seen with other African states, political and strategic factors do affect debt

Table 7.2 French military intervention in Tropical Africa

Country	Year	Reason for intervention
Cameroon	1959-64	Counter-revolutionary war
Senegal	1959-60, 1962	Support for President Senghor during dissolution of Mali Federation and attempted coup by Mamadou Dia
Congo	1960, 1962	Suppression of riots
Gabon	1960, 1962	Suppression of riots and uprisings
	1964	Reversal of coup against President M'ba
Chad	1960-3	Suppression of riots and uprisings
	1968-75)	
	1977-80)	War against Frolinat
	1983-4)	War against Goukouni Woddeye
Mauritania	1961	Suppression of riots
	1977-8	Air support against Polisario in former Spanish Sahara
Niger	1973	Prevention of military mutiny/coup
Djibouti	1976-7	Operation against Somali irredentism
Zaire	1977, 1978	Suppression of Shaba rebellions
Central African Republic	1979	Support for coup against Emperor Bokassa I

Source: R. Luckham, 'French militarism in Africa', Review of African Political Economy. 24 (1982), p.61.

issues, although their influence varies depending on the state concerned. In the case of Francophone Africa, some states are clearly more influential than others and this will, naturally, affect the treatment of their debt problems.

Analysts differ as to their judgement of the influence and significance of the twenty Francophone states, and offer divergent classifications. Zartman suggests a 'geopolitical' analysis of the Francophone community, and divides the states into three zones: the Active Zone (from Senegal to Zaire), the Passive Zone (south and east of Zaire), and the Mixed Zone of the Mediterranean and Red Sea shores. The Active Zone includes what are identified as the four core Francophone states of Senegal, Ivory Coast, Cameroon and Gabon.[26] In this identification of the 'core' of Francophone Africa, Zartman shares the assessment of Joseph, though from a very different theoretical position.[27]

We would argue that treatment of debt issues is likely to differ between this identified core, and the rest of the Francophone states. As we have seen in respect of the Ivory Coast, the regime was allowed extraordinarily high levels of lending in the early 1980s, and there does appear to be a degree of tolerance of the regime's albeit temporary incapacity to implement policy conditionalities. Houpouet-Boigny's regime became sufficiently indebted to join the ranks of the Baker initiative's seventeen most indebted Third World states, although the fact that the debt included a substantial proportion of commercial debt indicates that past judgements were clearly favourable as to the regime's developmental potential.

Other core states, like the Ivory Coast, are recipients both of major French investment and an apparently friendly approach towards their debt problems, provided that policy reform accompanies further credit. All the states have French bases on their soil, and military assistance teams operate. It can thus be argued that the patterns and treatment of indebtedness reflect a broader French and wider western perception of the value of individual members of its Francophone African community. The special relationship does exist, and it influences debt politics in much the same way as it influences other aspects of France's relations with its Francophone African clients.

8

Ways out of the debt trap

Most of the states of Africa are caught in a seemingly intractable debt trap. The IMF noted that only fifteen out of forty-four African states had been able to service their debts without falling into arrears, or needing debt relief during 1980-5.[1] The tutelage of the IMF and the World Bank has proven to be an inadequate response to what has emerged as a long-term crisis rather than the short-term liquidity problem that was initially anticipated. As we have seen, the Fund's stabilization programmes are of dubious efficacy in the African context. Austerity often leads to stagnation and lowered living standards, without eliminating the economic waste associated with clientelist polities. Free-market policies and devaluation will have a limited effect in boosting African exports that are faced with a stagnant world economy and fiercely protected European and American markets.

Joan Nelson has described the problems facing African countries trying to undertake adjustment programmes as follows:

> Poorer and less flexible economies, especially those in Sub-Saharan Africa, confront a cruel dilemma with respect to the attempted speed of adjustment. In many cases their economies are not capable of rapid adjustment. A shock approach can indeed 'balance' the budget and trade account, but only by reducing consumption, government services, production, and employment far below any level that could facilitate real adjustment, that is, altered composition and expanded capacity for production. Indeed, a Draconian approach in such economies can impair capacity for real adjustment. But some of these countries lack the

> resources - internal and external - to pursue the more gradual yet purposeful course which offers the best promise. Available resources are so badly out of line with needs that there is no avoiding drastic cuts in imports and domestic spending, whatever the cost to progress towards sustainable adjustment and resumed development. Without more adequate financial assistance, debates about the optimal speed of adjustment have a bitter theoretical flavour for such governments.[2]

This suggests that any attempted solution to Africa's debt crisis must combine a gradualist approach with enhanced supplies of financial aid. In this chapter our aim will be to establish what other elements must be involved in the formulation of any viable solution to the debt crisis. First, we shall examine what has been done in the attempt to solve, or at least alleviate Africa's problems. Thus we shall investigate the efficacy of such initiatives as the Baker and Lawson Plans. Attention will also be paid to the various proposals that have been put forward as potential solutions to the crisis. In this context we shall analyse the programmes advocated by analysts such as Lever and Huhne and by organizations such as the Brandt Commission and the Organization for African Unity (OAU). This examination of what has been done and what might be done to solve Africa's crisis will enable us to draw conclusions about what a comprehensive approach to ending the debt crisis might involve.

WHAT HAS BEEN DONE

Initially, the reaction of the creditor states to the debt crisis was far from generous. The United States under the Reagan presidency was particularly unsympathetic. This was especially significant given that the IMF, the World Bank, and the IDA are all funded to a considerable extent by the USA. The accession of a hardline monetarist president (at least in his views on other countries) to power seemed to stimulate a hardening of attitudes to these institutions. Reagan's White House and the Congress were reluctant to continue supporting them at equivalent levels, or sought to change the rules of their operation.[3] The IMF's enlarged access programme - which allowed countries to obtain up to

150 per cent of their quota - was phased out on American insistence.[4] The IMF had to ration loans in 1983, which affected support for Nigeria and Mali. Support for Sierra Leone, Zaire, Somalia and the Gambia which was in the pipeline was also delayed.[5] The IMF appropriation was held up in Congress in 1983, and the Reagan administration held down its commitment to the seventh replenishment of the IDA so that the Fund totalled only US$9 billion rather than the US$12 billion originally intended.[6]

An apparent change of heart was manifested at the IMF/World Bank meeting in Seoul on 8 October 1985. The meeting adopted a plan proposed by US Treasury Secretary James Baker consisting of the following elements. First, commercial banks were supposed to provide new loans worth US$20 billion to the fifteen largest debtors. Second, the World Bank and the Inter-American Development Bank were to make an extra US$9 billion available over the next three years, again, to the largest debtors. The third major concession was aimed at the poorest developing countries outside the 'fifteen'. It entailed reactivating the IMF Trust Fund for the exclusive use of the poorest states, thus making available some US$3 billion over three years, provided that the recipient states accepted IMF conditionality. This Structural Adjustment Facility (SAF) was the element of the Baker Plan that was of most potential use to Africa. To this can be added the World Bank's 'special facility for Sub-Saharan Africa' (SSA), which was started in 1985 with US$1.2 billion.[7] This is suggestive of a considerable thaw in monetarist attitudes in the west and might be seen as an indication that the creditor nations are becoming aware of Africa's need for substantially enhanced financial inputs.

However, if we compare the amounts likely to flow to SSA under these arrangements with the African debt, which is variously estimated at between US$150-200 billion in 1987, we can see how inadequate this new deal is. We have already seen that Africa's debt service payments exceed fresh financial inflows. The IMF alone received repayments of SDR 1,472 million (US$1,840 million) in 1986, whilst its disbursements in the same year amounted to only SDR 776.8 million (US$970 million). Indeed, it has been calculated that the Fund is owed some US$6 billion by the nations of SSA.[8] It must also be noted that the commercial banks were most reluctant to supply the US$6 billion in new loans during 1986-7, which was to be their initial contribution to the

Baker Plan. By September 1986 less than US$2 billion of this amount had been forthcoming.[9] The World Bank has pointed out that developing countries as a whole paid much more in interest than they received in net new commercial lending during 1986, despite reduced interest rates. It estimated that 'negative net transfers on account of long-term loans were possibly of the order of US$29 billion in 1986 and were once again concentrated on the HICs' (highly indebted countries).[10] Clearly, these arrangements do not even represent a palliative for Africa's ills. They will certainly not provide the environment in which Africa can undertake the structural adjustments needed to achieve sufficient economic growth to service its debts and resume its development. This is particularly the case given that the Baker package envisaged no modification of the IMF/Berg conditions for aid. African governments were still to be presented with demands for Draconian austerity programmes and large devaluations even as they struggled to service their debts.

A number of other initiatives have been taken by creditor states and institutions, including such innovations as multi-year rescheduling agreements (MYRAs) and debt-equity swaps. Under the terms of a MYRA, a debtor state will be given much longer to meet its obligations than under a conventional one-year rescheduling agreement. The average original maturity of MYRAs for middle-income countries has been twelve and a half years, as compared with seven years for prior reschedulings. The rationale underlying these arrangements is that they eliminate the insecurity associated with the need for yearly rescheduling negotiations and give debtor states a chance to readjust and to eliminate the payment difficulties that led to debt servicing problems. Naturally, IMF approval is a prerequisite before any state can be accorded the benefit of a MYRA. Unfortunately, the Paris Club seems loath to agree MYRAs irrespective of whether or not a debtor state has the Fund's approval. The only African states to have received this benefit at time of writing are Congo, Ivory Coast, and Nigeria. Neither of the first two agreements covers interest and it might be suggested that the arrangements for principal are less than generous. The percentage of principal rescheduled declines for each successive year of both agreements. Nigeria also found that it was unable to win the terms it had hoped for with its London Club creditors willing to reschedule only a fraction of the amount it asked for and charging stiff negotiation fees into the bargain.

However, those states that have to renegotiate their repayments yearly are in an even worse position. States such as Zaire, Togo, Senegal, and Madagascar have had to negotiate successive agreements of one to one and a half years' length throughout the last decade. Zaire has had no less than eight agreements since 1975, whilst the other above-mentioned states have had five each. The ineffectiveness of this arrangement is revealed by the fact that the Paris Club has been obliged to give relief on previously rescheduled debt to the Central African Republic, Madagascar, Zaire, and Zambia. In the Zairean case relief on debts that have been rescheduled on successive occasions is now greater than that on the original maturities.[11] Clearly, yearly reschedulings are a completely inadequate response to the difficulties of many African states. They do not allow sufficient time for the adjustments needed to enable heavily indebted states to meet even their deferred repayments and consequently debts simply accumulate with each rescheduling. Despite this situation the Paris Club has proven most unwilling to have recourse to MYRAs and has not given generous terms to those states that have obtained such an agreement.

As it has become clearer that many Third World states will not be in a position to service their debts in the foreseeable future, many commercial banks have made provisions against bad debts. The first to do so was the largest American bank, Citicorp, which made provision against non-payment of US$2.5 billion by Latin American states in May 1987. Effectively, it was acknowledging that a quarter of its Latin American debts, amounting to US$15 billion, were unlikely to be paid. Another US bank, Manufacturers Hanover, followed suit, taking precautions against non-payment of US$1.7 billion. The Bank of England encouraged British banks to join this trend and National Westminster Bank increased its bad debt provisions by 30 per cent of total debts owed to it (i.e. £828 million out of a total of £2.8 billion). The Midland Bank also made provision against non-payment of nearly one billion pounds out of total Third World debts of £4.26 billion.[12] Many analysts have greeted these measures as a turning point in the debt crisis, arguing that they signify that the commercial banks have accepted the fact that large proportions of the debt will never be repaid. However, it is questionable as to how far these provisions will benefit Africa, given that most of the debts that they deal with are those of the hugely indebted Latin American states. In any case, it has to be noted that these debts have not actually been written off. The banks have not relieved debtor states of their formal obligations to pay their debts, but have simply made provision against non-payment. This is a far cry from the debt 'forgiveness' advocated by certain commentators.

However, this proliferation of bad debt provisions reflects a growing awareness among the banks that much of the debt is unlikely to be paid, which may give an impetus to debt conversion schemes. Such schemes have tended to fall into one of two categories. They may involve the exchange of foreign currency debt for domestic currency debt, or foreign debt may be traded for local currency to be invested in the debtor state. An investor can buy the debt at a discount from the creditor bank and can then negotiate with the debtor state to exchange the debt for local currency. The discounts at which debts are available vary with the debtor state. The obligations of the major Latin American debtors have been sold at discounts of 20-40 per cent, whilst the debts of many African states have been traded at discounts of as much as 70-90 per cent (for example, Zambian debt was being sold at a discount of 80 per cent as at May 1987). All the parties to such transactions benefit to some degree. The bank has reduced its exposure to risky debts. The investor has acquired an asset in the debtor state at a better rate of exchange than the official rate. The debtor state itself has got rid of an obligation that had to be paid off in foreign exchange and gained some foreign investment. Unfortunately, the World Bank has pointed out that there are some disadvantages to such schemes. The provision of domestic currency to finance them may fuel inflation. If the government decides to avoid this by paying investors in marketable government bonds, interest rates may rise, increasing the budgetary costs of domestic debt. Furthermore, where the discount offered on the debt is large (as in many African cases), domestic investors may be tempted to buy it, purchasing the foreign exchange they need on the parallel market, and then selling the debt to the state for its face value in local currency, thus emerging with what will often be a substantial profit. Such practices will tend to equalize the discount offered on the official exchange rate by both the debt conversion schemes and the parallel market.[13] Nevertheless, such schemes offer debtor states an opportunity to dispose of some of the onerous obligations that have held back their development. It might also be argued that the rising interest rates, which are thought to be associated with the issue of government bonds, are a fairly small price to pay to be rid of debts that drain off the foreign exchange so badly needed by most Third World states. Clearly, debt conversion schemes are an innovation to be welcomed.

We must remember, however, that such schemes do not as yet represent anything remotely approaching a comprehensive solution to the debt crisis. In early 1987 the World Bank estimated that total sales for debt conversion had amounted to no more than US$5 billion out of a total of US$30 billion owed to the commercial banks. It noted that most US banks were rather wary of the prospect of the growth of a secondary market for debt, since it might reduce the value of all the Third World loans held by them. Consequently, they wanted to restrain the growth of such a market.[14] However, this was prior to the actions of Citicorp and Manufacturers Hanover in expanding their bad debt provisions. Such measures clearly signify an increasing awareness of the probability that the debts will never be paid off at their face value, which may have the effect of persuading the banks to cut some of their losses by means of entering into debt conversion schemes where they have not already done so. Such a prospect might go some of the way to providing much needed relief for Third World debtors, but such relief may be provided only at a cost. Having had their fingers so badly burned, it is unlikely that the commercial banks would be willing to lend to the Third World for the foreseeable future and African dependence on aid for capital inputs would be further reinforced.

In fact there is some evidence to suggest that the creditor states and institutions have begun to understand the necessity for a co-ordinated initiative to deal specifically with the debt crisis in low-income countries and particularly in Africa. The speech given by Barber Conable, the President of the World Bank, at the annual meeting of the Bank and the Fund in September 1987, reflected this concern:

> Africa's courageous reform efforts are being hampered in many cases by a shortage of financial resources exacerbated by a severe burden of debt. Urgent, determined, and co-ordinated action is needed, as the Venice Economic Summit (of the Group of Seven in July

> 1987) recognized, to relieve the debt-distressed low-income countries and to mobilize the additional resources essential to economic recovery.

Given this apparent blessing by the Group of Seven, the Fund and the Bank began to formulate another initiative to help the 'debt-distressed low-income' category of states, particularly those of Africa. However, it would appear that they got off to a bad start, largely due to bureaucratic rivalries between the two organizations. Although they produced a jointly backed initiative, each institution lobbied for adoption of that part of the plan that favoured its own interests rather than pressing for acceptance of the whole plan. Conable explained the initiative in the following terms:

> For the group of about fifteen highly indebted low-income African countries undertaking adjustment programmes, the objective is to mobilize at least US$1.5 billion in additional external resources each year in 1988-90. This would permit a modest growth of two per cent per capita annually in GDP, some growth in consumption, and the maintenance of debt service ratios at manageable levels of about twenty-five per cent in these countries.
>
> The key components of this programme are:
>
> 1) concessional debt relief in the Paris Club, including lowered interest rates and extended grace periods and maturities as well as continued conversion of loans to grants;
>
> 2) increased flows from IDA [International Development Association], together with expanded co-financing from other donors and speedier disbursement in support of adjustment operations; and
>
> 3) support for the enlargement of the Structural Adjustment Facility as proposed by the managing director of the Fund.[15]

The Fund, under Managing Director Michel Camdessus, tended to emphasize the latter element of the plan, proposing that the Structural Adjustment Facility be trebled to SDR 9 billion (US$11.4 billion). It also proposed to modify its conditionality to give recipient states more time to undertake economic adjustment.[16] The Bank, however, argued that centre stage should be occupied by its soft loans affiliate, IDA. The eighth replenishment of IDA was set at a regular budget of US$11.5 billion, with supplementary contributions bringing it up to US$12.4 billion, for the three years beginning at July 1987. Half of this is to be allotted to Africa, bringing IDA's contribution to the continent up to US$2 billion a year as compared with US$1.6 billion per annum under IDA 7. However, the Bank also hopes that IDA will gain another US$200-300 million a year for Africa in lump-sum contributions from the industrialized states. It also hopes to mobilize substantial funding through co-financing.

One senior World Bank official explained that co-financing has proven to be 'a terrific breakthrough in terms of getting more money for Africa', the reason being that it 'is more attractive to the donor countries because they can continue to claim direct credit for the money'. Indeed, when the Bank's Special Facility for Africa was created in 1985, about US$700 million was obtained in co-financing from states such as the US and the UK in addition to IDA and facility credits. However, at previous press briefings Conable had admitted that co-financing has not produced as much additional funding as had been hoped for. Nevertheless, the Bank has argued that on this occasion it hopes to raise an additional US$300-500 million a year. Furthermore, it has suggested that this idea is likely to be preferable to the donor states rather than the Fund's proposal of trebling the SAF, for the aforementioned reason that co-financing redounds directly to their credit. The final element of the Bank's proposals consists of a hoped-for US$300-400 million in interest rate relief from the Paris Club.[17]

It might be argued that the waters have been further muddied by the advent on the scene of the Lawson Plan, named after its principal backer, British Chancellor Nigel Lawson. This proposal consists of three elements, these being continuation of the process of converting old aid loans into grants; lengthening repayment periods from the current norm of ten years to fifteen or twenty years for rescheduled loans, with grace periods of up to ten years; and a reduction of interest rates on official debt.[18] It has been suggested that under the latter proposal Paris Club loans would carry concessional interest rates three per cent below market rates, which in itself would save the fifteen most indebted African states some US$350 million a year.[19] However, it must also be remembered that Chancellor Lawson has expressed his concern at the weak conditions demanded in recent IMF stabilization programmes. He has been quoted to the effect that:

> Some of the new programmes have very little prospect of bringing about the amount of adjustment needed in the countries in question. This is not in the interests of debtors themselves, nor of the Fund; and we must all work together to reverse this trend. I trust that the Fund management will always insist on adequate adjustment measures in its programmes - and I include here supply-side improvement. The Fund Board should support only programmes of this kind. And the creditors of the Paris Club should not reschedule a country's debt repayments without firm assurances that the appropriate policies are in place.[20]

This runs directly counter to Camdessus' proposal to modify IMF conditionality, at least to the extent of allowing more time for adjustment. The Fund's new position is born of a surfeit of evidence to the effect that 'getting the prices right' is not sufficient to bring about economic recovery in Africa. The Lawson position would seem to suggest that the Fund should revert to the 'shock' treatment criticized by Nelson.

There was considerable doubt as to how many of these proposals would actually be adopted, given the unfavourable economic situation. Even before the stock market crash of October 1987, US opinion was becoming increasingly concerned with the massive deficit and how it might be reduced. Congress and the Reagan administration have fought each other to a standstill over which items in the federal budget to cut. Concomitant to these developments there has been a growing antipathy to aid, never the most popular of causes with the American public. Conservative politicians criticized the Bank and the Fund as promoting socialist development abroad. Given this context and the divisions between the Bank, the Fund, and the British as to which proposals should be adopted the prospects for their adoption seemed bleak.

In fact more progress has been made than might have been expected. The Bank lobbied Washington hard for an increase in its funding and Conable evidently used his connections to good effect, for Baker reversed the Reagan administration's opposition to such a measure. On 23 September 1987, he announced that Washington would back a capital increase for the Bank of between US$40 billion and US$80 billion. This is welcome to Africa since it means that some US$3 billion per annum will be available from 1988 rather than the US$2.1 billion that SSA received in 1986.[21] However, Washington would not approve the proposed trebling of the Structural Adjustment Facility. Anxiety over the deficit made it inevitable that funding would not be available for both the Fund and the Bank. Baker suggested that Camdessus should approach those countries with a chronic surplus, such as West Germany and Japan, for increased funding; after intense lobbying the IMF has won promises from twenty industrial states of support for the expansion of the SAF to US$11.4 billion.[22] Unfortunately, some of these gains may be in jeopardy. Although Baker has promised the Reagan administration's backing for the eighth replenishment of IDA and the Bank's capital increase, there must be severe doubts as to whether an independent Congress bent on budgetary cuts will allow both these allocations to go through in full. Furthermore, Lawson's valuable proposal of concessional interest rates appears to have fallen by the wayside. The USA and West Germany oppose this on the grounds that it might set a precedent for negotiations with the large Latin American debtors. The British argue that a 'ring fence' can be set up around the poorest fifteen states and that, in any case, this concession is inevitable given the inability of these states to meet their growing obligations.[23]

Support for this contention comes from confidential documents drawn up by the Bank, which raise doubts about the prospects for raising the additional US$1.5 billion a year (not forgetting the US$1.4 billion minimum rescheduling) that Conable saw as necessary to enable the fourteen poorest African states to meet their debt repayments and maintain a modest level of growth during 1988-90. Apparently, the Bank fears that the industrial states will be unwilling to provide these sums. Given that it has estimated that the needs of these states will rise to about US$5 billion a year in the 1990s, the longer-term prospects are indeed bleak. The Bank is afraid that without more aid, African efforts to adjust their economies will be bogged down due to lack of political will to proceed. According to one Bank official, 'Managed, coherent, and internationally supported adjustment is on trial in Africa' and 'If it fails, we will see a much more chaotic and wrenching kind' of adjustment.[24] This raises the question of what the debtor states might be able to do to alleviate if not resolve their difficulties in the all too likely event that the creditor states fail to provide adequate resources to assist them in this aim. We shall turn our attention to this issue in the next section.

WHAT MIGHT BE DONE?

The central fear of the creditor nations is that the debtor states might take matters into their own hands and initiate action that would be deleterious to creditor interests. In particular, they fear the possibility of a major default. This line of action may begin to seem ever more feasible to the debtor states for as long as the situation pertains where they are expected to pay more in debt servicing than they receive in new capital. Indeed, this is the line of action that has been recommended by Fidel Castro since 1985. Castro argues that the initiative lies with the debtor states and has been quoted as saying: 'It is a unique opportunity for Third World countries. For the first time in history, we have the opportunity to take the initiative since we have been paying until now and we must simply say: we won't pay.'[25] Castro builds what appears to be a fairly convincing case for default, arguing that it is neither economically, or politically feasible to pay the debt, since the economic rigours involved in paying would lead to political collapse. He also suggests that it is immoral to expect the Third World to pay the debt, because:

> Most of the money that was loaned left the country and returned to the industrialized countries; a substantial part was stolen and embezzled; another part was spent on arms; another was wasted away; and perhaps a part was employed in the infrastructure or some useful social investment.

To bolster his moral case, Castro also invokes the legacy of imperialism and metropolitan exploitation of the Third World, proclaiming - 'it's they who are the debtors and we are the creditors'.[26] Certainly, it is hard to deny the truth of Castro's observations on the politico-economic infeasibility of paying the debt and there is considerable evidence as to the exploitative nature of imperialism. In the absence of any determined effort on the part of the creditor states to render genuine and sufficient assistance to the Third World in overcoming the debt crisis Castro's line of thought may begin to seem very persuasive. Certainly, it has been suggested that debtor states could use the threat of default to coerce their creditors into taking a more conciliatory line, given that any large-scale default could cause severe economic problems in the north.

Although such arguments may have some validity for the larger debtors, such as Brazil, Argentina, and Mexico, it is questionable whether either an actual default, or its threat, would produce any benefits for Africa. Whilst Africa's debt is large in relation to the continent's GDP it is small in relation to world debt (some 13 per cent of total non-oil developing country debt in 1983). Even the higher estimates of SSA's total debt suggest that it is barely larger than that of one of the larger Latin American debtors. Certainly, it is not sufficiently large to constitute an effective threat to the northern creditor economies. Under these circumstances it seems likely that any African default would hurt the country, or countries, taking such action more than their creditors, since a default would almost certainly provoke retaliatory action from the north.

For any African default to be effective it would have to be carried out in concert with similar action by one, and preferably more, of the large Latin American debtors. However, various obstacles stand in the path of such collaborative action. It would be difficult to maintain unity between such a large number of diverse states, and the developed north would have ample opportunity for divide and rule tactics. O'Donnell has illustrated this point with reference to the Brazilian announcement of February 1987 that it was suspending all payments of interest on its foreign debt. He notes that within two months of this ultimatum, Finance Minister Funaro was forced to resign and Brazil began to move back towards 'normal' relations with its creditors despite the fact that it was in a weak negotiating position. O'Donnell analyses this apparent failure in terms of game theory, arguing that Brazil was in a situation of 'prisoner's dilemma'. He points out that the object of the game for the creditors is to maintain their unanimity and to prevent the debtors achieving any substantial level of co-operation against them. This can be achieved by levying sanctions against any debtor state that challenges them whilst attempting to buy off that state's allies with side payments. These were the tactics used against Brazil. The creditors withdrew US$60 million of credit and refused Brazil's request for a sixty-day renewal of its short-term commercial lines of credit. Simultaneously, they began to offer other major debtors, such as Mexico, Argentina, Chile, and the Phillipines, far better terms than had been on the negotiating table prior to the Brazilian ultimatum. Not surprisingly, these states played 'prisoner's dilemma' and took the side payments, leaving Brazil in the position of the 'sucker'. The Brazilians faced the likelihood that if they continued their militant stance they would be confronted with ever more severe sanctions, without any compensatory assistance from their erstwhile allies. In the final analysis there was no viable option to capitulation.[27] The success of the creditors in dividing and ruling the largest debtor states in the world indicates the almost insuperable problems that stand in the path of initiating effective co-operative action amongst the nations of one continent. This suggests that the prospects for co-operation, or the creation of a debtor's cartel involving both SSA and Latin America, are effectively insignificant.

It might be argued that if debtor states continue having to pay more in debt service than they receive in new finance they may be driven to the conclusion that the costs of default, including any possible creditor retaliation, are outweighed by the benefits. However, this is to ignore the fact that many Third World regimes are highly dependent on northern military aid to stay in power. One has only to cite the Shaba Wars in which the Belgians, the French, and the Americans intervened to shore up the Mobutu regime (not to mention the frequent interventions of the French across SSA in support of their clients). Where this dependence does not take the form of direct reliance on foreign troops, it will often take the form of training, or the supply of military hardware. Such regimes are most unlikely to default, thus cutting their links with their external guarantors, however severe their debt problems may become. They are more likely to opt to continue their present process of decline, in which the general populace have to resort to the survival strategies (e.g. smuggling and other informal activities) examined in the case studies.

However, such states could still explore the option that Kaletsky has termed 'conciliatory default'. This consists of a partial default, such as the 10 per cent limit put on interest payments by Peru in 1985. Such actions have a number of advantages over a comprehensive default. First, they limit repayments to a manageable level. Second, they are less likely to be construed as a threat by the creditors since they do not signify any hard and fast refusal to pay the debt. Consequently, they are less likely to provoke the severe sanctions that would probably be the result of a complete default. Instead, they may be seen as a signal for a renegotiation of the terms for payment of the debt. It is worth noting that a number of African states have undertaken 'conciliatory defaults', including Nigeria, Zaire, Ivory Coast and Zambia. At time of writing this tactic would seem to have paid some dividends for Zaire and, to an extent, Nigeria. It will be remembered that Zaire managed to win a modification of the terms being offered to it by the IMF, whilst Nigeria managed to obtain some new money and a rescheduling from the London Club. However, it might be argued that these cases show the inherent limits of this tactic. Although Nigeria gained benefits it has to be remembered that the terms it had to accept were far from generous and that the IMF complained that this new aid was inadequate to meet the government's minimal financing need. In other words, 'conciliatory default' did not lead to any solution of Nigeria's debt crisis, or even to its substantial alleviation. We may also note that these two nations are amongst the larger African debtors and (certainly in the case of Zaire) have some strategic value for the creditor states. The importance of these factors is reflected in the differential treatment accorded to African states by the creditor nations. Zaire received successive reschedulings of its debt and funding from the IMF throughout the late 1970s and the early 1980s, despite President Mobutu's apparent inability to abide by the Fund's conditionality, whereas less influential states, such as Sierra Leone, were treated comparatively severely. This suggests that the effectiveness of the 'conciliatory default' tactic will be largely dependent on how much economic/strategic leverage a debtor state can mobilize against its creditors. Even where a state can muster such influence it is unlikely that it will be able to win sufficient concessions to change its economic position substantially.

Another device that has been used by many Third World states to conserve their foreign exchange holdings is countertrade, otherwise known as barter trade. As we have seen, Nigeria had some success with this technique. Whilst the Babangida administration found that care had to be taken to ensure that full value was received, it concluded that barter trade was a useful way of obtaining essential imports without depleting scarce reserves of foreign exchange. However, the World Bank and the IMF have made their disapproval of such transactions known in the strongest terms, complaining that they complicate the monitoring and control of a debtor's foreign exchange holdings and they interfere with the workings of the free market. It would seem then that Third World states are to be deprived of a potentially useful way of alleviating foreign exchange constraints at least partly because it interferes with their creditors' book-keeping.

Having seen that countertrade and varying forms of complete, or partial default seem to offer little hope for any substantial improvement in SSA's economic situation, we might ask what other options have been proposed to solve the debt crisis. A number of initiatives have emerged from Africa itself. One of the first was the Lagos Plan, which many have seen as the African answer to the Berg Report. Indeed, its emphasis was quite different to that favoured by the World Bank. Ravenhill provides a devastating critique of the Lagos Plan of Action (LPA), noting that although it is supposedly premissed on a philosophy of self-reliant development, it constantly reiterates demands for 'a massive and appropriate contribution by the developed countries to the development of Africa'. Rather than providing a strategy for development in the form of a detailed set of policy proposals and costing estimates for achieving its projected goals it resembles, says Ravenhill, 'a mammoth shopping list - with no ranking of the various desired objectives, no price tag, and no conception of the possible trade-offs between one sector and another.' He notes that it recommends that the 1980s should be given over to development of agriculture, agro-industry, socio-economic infrastructure, ending unemployment, underemployment and mass poverty, and satisfying basic needs. How all this is to be done in the space of a decade is not elaborated upon. Ravenhill also points out that one obvious reason why the LPA is more palatable to African leaders than the Berg Report is that it does not mention any of their own policy shortcomings, which have played a part in causing the debt crisis. Consequently, there is no mention of the difficult policy reforms that the World Bank and the IMF regard as essential to any strategy to promote African development, such as the adjustment of over-valued exchange rates and fiscal reform. Certainly, there is no mention of the need to eliminate urban bias, or to control clientelism and associated misallocation and misappropriation of funds. One can sympathize with Ravenhill's conclusion that:

> By placing excessive blame on external/historical factors, and in expecting massive external contributions to assist the realization of its goals, the plan is in danger of diverting governments' attention away from the need for radical domestic economic reform.

Whilst a central element of our argument is that a substantial increase in aid to Africa is essential, the evidence gathered in our case studies indicates that this must be accompanied by wide-ranging domestic economic and political reforms. As Ravenhill points out, these are completely absent from the Lagos Plan.[28]

This cannot be said of Africa's Priority Programme of Economic Recovery 1986-90 (APPER), which was adopted by the OAU in 1985 and then by the United Nations in 1986. Certainly, the APPER makes demands on the north. Its total cost has been put at US$128.1 billion, US57 billion of which is to be spent directly on agriculture, with another US$60 billion allocated to indirect support of the rural sector, through such measures as provision of infrastructure and price support for farmers. The African states have pledged to raise US82.5 billion of this through mobilization of domestic resources, but they also hoped to obtain another US$9 billion a year in external support.[29] However, the APPER does not premiss Africa's recovery solely on demands for aid. A report by the UN Secretary General comments:

> The African countries reaffirmed their primary responsibility for the development of their own continent. To underscore that promise, they committed themselves to the implementation of a sharply-focused, practical, and operational set of activities, priorities, and policies in accordance with APPER; they determined to pursue vigorously appropriate policy reforms; and they undertook to fully mobilize domestic resources for the successful implementation of the UN-PAAERD (United Nations Programme of Action for African Economic Recovery and Development).[30]

The same report notes that by 1987, twenty-eight states had begun to introduce policy reforms. These included many of the measures advocated by the Fund and the World Bank, such as liberalization of markets and investment codes, reduction of subsidies, public sector cuts, increased price incentives for the rural sector, and improvement of distribution networks. Whilst we might welcome the latter measures, the report bears out our findings that austerity policies entail 'severe social cost' and have been 'pressed forward in the face of formidable political risks'.[31]

It is a rather bitter irony that this belated acceptance by African leaders of a measure of responsibility for the continent's fate should have led them to accept a package of measures which cause severe problems and are of dubious relevance to the fundamental need for a thoroughgoing reform of the clientelist state. A more cynical view is that many states may have found themselves in the situation of Zaire in 1983, when Mobutu realised that he would have to go along with the demands of the IMF and the World Bank in order to maintain access to the external funds he needed to finance his patronage circuits. Whatever the reason for African acquiescence to external demands for austerity, it has not borne fruit in the form of an enhanced inflow of resources. As noted above, the APPER requires external inputs of some US$9 billion a year. To this we can add an annual US$14.6 billion to meet Africa's debt service requirements, giving a total of some US$23.7 billion (in 1985 prices) a year needed to finance both APPER and SSA's debt repayments. The UN report notes:

> According to the Development Assistance Committee of OECD, total net resource flows to Africa in 1985 are estimated to have been about US$16 billion, of which some two thirds or US$11 billion were allocated to Sub-Saharan Africa. For the Sub-Saharan region, total net resource flows show a trend decline of five per cent in real terms between 1980 and 1985. For 1986 the figure is estimated at about US$18 billion, which amounts to a decrease in real terms from the 1985 level, when deflated with the dollar-GDP-deflator for major OECD countries.[32]

If we bear in mind that, according to the United Nations Economic Commission for Africa, Africa lost US$19 billion of export receipts in 1986 alone due to falling commodity prices and the decline of the dollar we can see that SSA has minimal hopes of achieving a sufficient financial input to get the APPER off the ground.[33] Given the continuation of stagnant markets and the collapse of the dollar in the wake of the world stock market crash of 1987, these trends must be expected to have worsened during 1987.

A number of commentators within the creditor states have attempted to grapple with these apparently insoluble problems and have put forward various answers. Common factors in most of them are the need for a massive transfer of funds to the debtor states and the desirability of reforming the IMF and the World Bank. This was the approach favoured in the second report produced by the commission headed for the former West German Chancellor, Willy Brandt. The second Brandt Report (of 1983) was produced in an even bleaker international context than that addressed by the first report in 1980. The debt crisis was a new factor in the decline of the international economy and the 1983 report attempted to formulate a solution based on a substantial increase of resources for the IMF and IDA; an increase in the time allowed for repayment of IMF transfers; modification of IMF conditionality to give greater emphasis on maintaining output and employment and equalizing income distribution rather than austerity; and changes in IMF voting procedures to give Third World states a greater voice in the running of the Fund. The Arusha Initiative strikes a similar note, demanding in particular a modification of the Fund's emphasis on free market policies, in order to make allowance for those nations with large public sectors and developments plan premissed on an interventionist state. (The Initiative orginated at a North-South conference held at Arusha in Tanzania in 1980, which resulted in a call for a new monetary order.)[34] To these we may add President Mitterand's proposal of a 'Third World Marshall Plan', which would entail raising loans and grants equivalent to the value of between 0.5 per cent and 1 per cent of the western industrial states' GNP. The difficulty with these plans, like that of the APPER, is that it is unlikely that sufficient resources will be mobilized by the north.

Lever and Huhne add some more elements to the pool of proposals with their plan. They suggest that the banks might be given a new incentive to invest in the Third World in the form of a guarantee analogous to the export credit guarantee schemes operating in many northern states. Under this arrangement organizations such as the Export-Import Bank in the USA and the Export Credit Guarantee Department in the UK would insure commercial bank loans to the Third World against default. This guarantee would be contingent on the banks gradually writing down existing debts. Thus, the existing debt burden could be reduced, whilst new money would be encouraged to flow into the debtor states. Lever and Huhne argue that the allocation and utilization of this funding could be supervised by the IMF. They also advocate changes in the nature of IMF conditionality to 'foster the growth of investment and living standards'.[35]

Indeed, the possibility of reforming Fund conditionality to maintain productivity and improve income distribution has proven attractive to a number of analysts. Korner et al. stress this issue, arguing that a reorientation of IMF stabilization programmes need not even involve changes in the rules governing conditionality.[36] They note that whilst Article 9 of the New Guidelines for the Use of Fund Resources in the Credit Tranches states that performance criteria should normally take the form of macro-economic variables, it also allows for the introduction of further criteria in pursuit of the goals of the IMF agreement. These include 'the promotion and maintenance of a high level of employment and real income' and the 'development of the production potential of all members'. Korner et al. advocate the incorporation of basic needs criteria into IMF conditionality, suggesting that government performance could be assessed according to whether or not it boosted employment, increased agricultural production, enhanced state efficiency, and reduced mismanagement and corruption.

Certainly, if such criteria could be introduced into IMF programmes they might go a long way towards controlling the clientelist tendencies endemic in most African polities, whilst eliminating the most damaging effects of the austerity policies that are currently at the core of most of the Fund's agreements. However, the difficulties involved in designing such conditionality should not be underestimated and there is always a danger that once the Fund has overseen a state's recovery and departed, leaders may revert to clientelist patterns of rulership.

Korner et al. introduce another element into the debate by suggesting that those states with a trade surplus should fund the IMF Compensatory Financing Facility (CFF) to give aid to the deficit states. Where a state has suffered a loss of export receipts due to circumstances beyond its control, such as a decline in the market, protectionist policies, high interest rates, or natural disaster, it would be entitled to aid from the CFF. This entitlement would gradually decline over a period as the claimant nation either recovered, or adjusted to the new market conditions. An alternative to using the CFF for this purpose would be to extend the EEC's Stabex facility to cover all Third World exporters.[36] (The Stabilization of Export Receipts Fund, or Stabex, is designed to compensate Third World - and specifically ACP states -for any decline in their export receipts caused by adverse conditions in the world market for their goods.) Such an innovation would be of vital importance to SSA given the severe losses it has suffered due to a combination of stagnating markets for its products and northern protectionism.

Clearly, there is a large pool of ideas as to how the debt crisis may be solved, or at least alleviated. Although there are many areas of disagreement it would seem that a degree of consensus is emerging as to which amongst these ideas may be practicable. There is clear agreement that a large transfer of resources from north to south is necessary, although there is somewhat less consensus about how large it should be. The Bank and the Fund are just as aware as the African states that increased aid is essential, although they are pessimistic about raising sufficient amounts. Equally, there is agreement that the austerity policies that have been promoted in Africa by the Fund and the Bank should be made less Draconian.

At time of writing it has been announced that the Fund intends to allow more time for adjustment, but it is not known whether it will adopt any of the other changes that have been mooted, such as conditions designed to attain growth, higher employment, and greater social equity. There are also powerful forces in the creditor states that favour a gradual writing down of debt and the introduction of concessional interest rates, as evidenced by the Lawson Plan. The African states for their part have conceded that their plight is partly due to their own policy errors and that politico-economic reforms are essential, although there must be doubts as to how far many governments can (or will wish to) go in eliminating the clientelist networks that underwrite their power. Perhaps the most contentious issue concerns the falling export receipts suffered by African states as a result of declining markets for their products and northern protectionism. Whereas commentators such as Berg argue that African states will simply have to fight for what markets they can get, Korner et al. argue that the surplus states should compensate them through the medium of the CFF, or Stabex. One may discern the elements of a solution to the debt crisis from these ideas. We shall attempt to assemble a coherent set of recommendations as to what should be done about SSA's debt crisis on this basis.

WHAT SHOULD BE DONE?

We propose that if any plan is to have a realistic hope of solving the debt crisis in Africa it must be based on decisive action by both creditors and debtors. Such action would involve four essential elements. First, it must entail the gradual writing down of debt. Commercial banks might be encouraged to do this by the means suggested by Lever and Huhne, that is by the offer of a guarantee of their future loans which is conditional on their writing off a certain amount of debt over a specific period. Debt-equity swaps could also play a useful part in helping indebted states to discharge their responsibilities. It will be noted that a large preponderance of African debt is owed either to national governments, or to multilateral institutions rather than to banks. This could prove to be an advantage to SSA, given that certain nations, including Canada and the UK, have begun the process of writing off at least some of the debts owed to them. We have also seen that the major international institutions have seemingly adopted a more sympathetic attitude to Africa's plight and may be willing at least to consider more generous terms of rescheduling. As we have seen, the concessional interest rates that are recommended in the Lawson Plan could have a considerable impact in alleviating the high debt-service ratios faced by many African states. They might also consider the possibility of adopting a variant on the debt-equity swaps known as debt-development swaps. These would work in exactly the same way as debt-equity swaps, but donor states and institutions would be purchasing debts to set up development projects in the debtor states.

The second element of any plan to help Africa must of necessity involve a substantial input of fresh resources in the form of aid and investment. There are many and variant estimates of how much new funding will be necessary. As we noted above, the APPER demands total expenditure of US$128.1 billion, including external inputs of US$23.7 billion per year, during 1986-90. Indeed, there has finally been some movement by the western states towards providing enhanced aid in the shape of additional World Bank finance and an enlarged Structural Adjustment Facility. Whilst such financing may not be sufficient to end SSA's debt crisis in itself, it could make a substantial contribution to this aim combined with policies of debt forgiveness, concessional interest rates and debt-development swaps. It might also be hoped that some private investment could be raised by adopting the scheme proposed by Lever and Huhne for guaranteeing new loans to the Third World. However, it has to be remembered that the organization designated to back such guarantees (Lever and Huhne suggest the IMF) will also have to be financed accordingly.

Some analysts would object to the above proposals because they entail a danger of moral hazard inasmuch as they reward Third World states for taking out loans they could not repay. These policies would be unlikely to deter such nations from taking out loans they could not afford in the future. Indeed, clientelist polities might well be reinforced by the new input of resources, a situation which in itself would mean that considerable amounts of the new money would be misallocated, or misappropriated. Such an eventuality might be guarded against by changing the emphasis of IMF conditionality in the way suggested by such analysts as Korner et al. Performance criteria designed to penalize mismanagement and corruption, and to encourage economic growth and a measure of social equity could go some of the way to encouraging the development that has eluded Africa for so long.

However, this is hardly a satisfactory solution given that it premisses African development almost wholly on supervision by external forces. This is objectionable for two reasons. First, many Africans would see it as an unacceptable infringement on their sovereignty. Second, there is the question of what would happen over the longer term, when the main problems of indebtedness had been alleviated and the IMF had departed. Might not many states revert to the clientelist policies that were partly responsible for the debt crisis in the first place? With regard to the first objection, Lever and Huhne amongst others argue that creditors are entitled to set certain conditions to try and ensure repayment of their loans.[37] The present authors would also argue that many African states are democratic only in the most dubious sense and that there is a question mark over the extent to which they can legitimately claim to represent the interests of the majority of their citizens. Indeed, it is the clientelist nature of these states that lies at the base of our second objection, the danger of an eventual reversion to unsound and wasteful policies.

The answer to both these objections lies in reform of the state so that it will represent the interests of the majority of the people rather than sectional, largely urban based clientelist groups. Any democratic reform of the African states must entail the political mobilization of the large mass of rural producers who provide the bulk of the resources that are seized and redistributed by such states. With the advent of the agrarian majority onto the political scene such states would no longer be free to institute urban-biased policies and to allocate resources to narrow interests. They would have little option but to follow economically rational policies to achieve growth in order to distribute the benefits to their greatly enlarged constituencies. Thus, the establishment of legitimate democratic states would obviate the danger of a relapse into patrimonialism after the departure of the IMF.

This is a most problematic proposition given that analysts since Marx have agreed that the peasantry tend to be conservative, diffuse, and disorganized. They are more likely to respond to exploitation by having recourse to individualistic solutions, such as flight to the towns, rather than through political organization. Amilcar Cabral, the leader of the successful peasant-based guerrilla movement in Guinea-Bissau, commented on how difficult it was to get the peasants to fight the fiercely exploitative Portuguese colonial regime in his country.[38] However, there are examples of African farmers organizing to achieve concrete economic goals such as controlling the production and marketing of their crops. The process of economic organization will often lead to an enhanced degree of political participation. Adrian Adams provides an example of such organization in the Senegal River Valley, where a co-operative, the Fédération des Paysans Organisés en Zone Soninke de Bakel, was established. It succeeded in organizing local peasant farmers to produce and market their own crops at an increased profit. Adams recounts how the Fédération came into conflict with the state because it followed a policy of maximizing its members' profits, which did not accord with the interests of the Senegalese polity in following an urban-biased policy of providing cheap food for the towns.[39] The central point to be drawn from this example is that agrarian producers can use co-operatives and other forms of popular organization not only to increase their production, but to improve their ability to negotiate with an often unsympathetic state mechanism that is principally concerned to satisfy its clients in the urban sector and the rural elite. This bears out the conclusion drawn by Bayart in the recent debate on democracy in Africa, when he dismisses macro-political experiments with representative institutions and argues:

> Africa's potential for democracy is more convincingly revealed by the creation of small collectives established and controlled by rural or urban groups (such as local associations) than by parliaments and parties, instruments of the state, of accumulation, and of alienation.[40]

Thus, democratic reform must come about through the grass-roots organization of producers campaigning for concrete aims.

Bayart argues that these 'new political mediations will be evolved by Africans themselves, on their own'.[41] Certainly they must be controlled by Africans, but there is at least one school of thought in the development aid lobby, variously referred to as 'community development' and 'community participation', which insists that aid can and should be used to mobilize the Third World poor (particularly the rural poor) to form such organizations. The aim of 'community development' is to encourage such groups to establish their own developmental goals, actively participate in achieving them, and share the fruits of those achievements equitably. Community workers are supposed to 'conscientize' villages by making them aware of their life situations and challenging them to do something about it. Such 'conscientizers' must avoid becoming group leaders since the object is to mobilize the poor to act for themselves. They should also take account of differentiation within the village in view of the danger that local members of the rural elite will attempt to appropriate the lion's share of any benefit for themselves. Perhaps the most problematic area within 'community development' is the relationship between community and state. The literature puts a stress on decentralization of power, but makes little mention of what course to take if the state will not countenance any cession of its influence.[42] Clearly, state opposition is a very likely response to attempts to organize groups that stand outside its clientelist networks and which are likely to make demands on it for a fairer share of resources (that much is indicated by Adams' Senegalese example)

However, it is only by grass-roots organization of the agrarian producers that clientelism can be broken and the groundings for a democratic and economically rational polity can be laid. As we have seen, it is the rural majority who stand at the base of the patrimonial system in two senses. First, the state appropriates most of its resources from the agrarian sector. Second, it is the rural populace who tend to receive least of the state's resources. By equipping rural producers with the ability to seize their rightful share of political influence it becomes possible to control if not eliminate clientelism by depriving it of its resource base. Furthermore, once the state is made responsible to the majority of producers, it will have a strong incentive to follow economically rational policies rather than the particularistic strategies that are currently evident throughout Africa. Thus, it can be argued that the need to provide adequate returns to farmers for their goods will provide an incentive to increased agricultural production. This will augment state resources by obviating the need for food imports with a consequent saving of foreign exchange and/or by boosting exports, which will enhance state receipts. The resources gained by the state can be used for the public investments deemed necessary for development by analysts as variant as John Sender, of Cambridge University, Sheila Smith, of Sussex University, and those of the World Bank. Simultaneously, the increased returns to the countryside may set in motion a process of accumulation that has the potential for transforming the rural means of production, thereby giving an impetus to agro-industrial production.

Clearly, this is an optimistic scenario that would take not a little time to bring into effect. Perhaps the most immediate doubt as to its viability is whether or not it is realistic to envisage the rural majority imposing their will on the state to any substantial degree. We have noted that rural producers display a minimal level of political organization. Co-operatives such as that examined by Adams and community participation projects are few and far between. Consequently, it may be assumed that they are vulnerable to state opposition, which might even take the form of repression in the more authoritarian polities. However, it must be remembered that rural producers have one very potent weapon in that they can decide whether or not to sell their produce on the official market, thus having a voice in how many resources the state is able to appropriate. Furthermore, the debt crisis has weakened many states' capacity for outreach into the rural hinterland whether to deliver public policy outputs (as demonstrated in previous chapters), or to repress what it may see as rural dissidence. These factors present an opportunity for effective organization in the rural areas.

Evidence as to the potential for such organization has emerged from various contexts. Sandbrook has commented on the Lusaka Squatter and Site and Services Project undertaken in 1974 with the backing of the World Bank, the Zambian government, and the American Friends' Service Committee, a non-governmental organization. He notes that there was a strong emphasis on mobilizing genuine popular participation to achieve the project's ambitious aim of upgrading the houses of 17,000 squatters. Householders had an input into decision-making on a wide range of issues and he concludes that, 'The mobilization of squatters has led to their empowerment within the existing political system'. Sandbrook's only reservation about the project is that its focus on Lusaka has accentuated the existing urban bias in Zambian government policy. This leads him to argue:

> In so far as participatory development projects offer some amelioration of pressing problems and the long-term prospect of empowerment of the poor, the bulk of these projects should be located in the rural areas, where most of the poor reside.[43]

Parfitt has gathered evidence from Sierra Leone which indicates that participatory projects indeed have potential for empowering the rural poor. He points out that the Bo/Pujehun Rural Development Project, financed by the Federal German Republic, created a Community Action Fund for small projects to be identified by local communities in accordance with their own needs. Many communities have made use of this scheme and have participated in the financing and implementation of projects designed to satisfy infrastructural and social needs they have identified themselves. The success of this scheme has influenced other agencies to take up the participatory approach. Parfitt also refers to the People's Participation Project based in Pujehun, in the Southern Province of Sierra Leone, which was implemented by the FAO and financed by the government of The Netherlands. This project focused on eight groups of villages, encouraging local communities to organize themselves. Its activities included provision of literacy classes in the local region of Mende, with a view to improving the ability of villagers to deal with government officials, and creation of a credit scheme so that farmers did not need to have recourse to exploitative usurers and traders. By the end of the project in July 1986 a number of independent farmers' groups had been created, which had identified their own proposed projects and submitted them to the FAO for support.[44] In other words, these groups had attained the capacity to lobby their government and external aid agencies.

Given the clear potential of the participatory approach for bringing about the eventual empowerment of the poor, it may be hoped that agencies with a genuine interest in a democratic and economically healthy Africa (whether they be indigenous to that continent, or based in the western development lobby) will embrace this opportunity to set in motion a genuine process of development. Basic needs-oriented conditionality for IMF and World Bank funding could play a role in mobilizing the rural poor to begin this process. An initial productive step would be for the Bank group to change their emphasis from large-scale integrated agricultural projects to grass-roots participatory projects in which farmers would be encouraged to take control of production and marketing, and to articulate their own demands of the state. Thus, the changes in conditionality recommended by Korner _et al._ could be a stepping stone towards the more ambitious aim of mobilizing African producers to increase the accountability of their hitherto imperfectly democratic states.

However, it has to be noted that there may be powerful forces outside Africa that would be hostile to such a programme. In several cases, metropolitan states are allied to clientelist regimes for strategic purposes and would be loath to see them threatened by the arrival of a politically active and demanding rural majority on the scene. As we have seen, the United States supports the notoriously corrupt regime of President Mobutu because he is assiduous in pursuit of American diplomatic and strategic interests throughout Africa. One might also point to Ethiopia, where the USSR props up the repressive and corrupt Mengistu regime in the teeth of opposition from secessionist movements in the Ethiopian provinces of Eritrea, Tigre, and Oromo. Any attempt to break clientelism in such regimes may have to contend with the imperialism of developed states that have strategic interests in the area.

If these recommendations for debt forgiveness, more aid, and greater democracy in SSA are to be successful in ending the debt crisis, a fourth condition must be present. The stagnant markets that hold back African development must be overcome. Ideally this would entail the adoption of Keynesian growth-oriented strategies by the northern states and the abandonment of the protective measures that are continually on the increase. This would eventually benefit the north as the increased export receipts accruing to southern states would create growing demand for northern industrial goods. Unfortunately, given the current economic climate this seems extremely optimistic. However, the development lobby in the north should attempt to lobby as effectively as possible against measures such as the Multi-Fibre Agreements (MFAs), which protect northern textile markets by imposing quota allocations on imports from Third World producers, and the abolition of the agricultural price-support legislation in the USA. The adverse effects of stagnant markets could also be ameliorated by adoption of the suggestion of Korner *et al.* that the CFF (Compensatory Financing Facility of the IMF), or Stabex be used to compensate Third World states suffering shortfalls in their export receipts due to adverse market conditions. It may be pointed out that the European Community's Stabex fund has been in operation for over a decade and has been of great help to signatory states of the Lomé Conventions, whose primary commodity exports to the Community had declined due to the recession. If this scheme could be extended to cover some of the major commodities exported by the south as a whole to all the developed states it would help to alleviate the worst effects of the debt crisis in much of the Third World.

It is our view then that any viable scheme to solve the debt crisis must be composed of these four elements. First, the creditor states and institutions must gradually write off

Third World debts and give preferential interest rates on rescheduled debts. Second, more resources must be transferred to the Third World, both in the form of aid and private investment. Third, the north must abandon, or at least reduce the protective barriers it has raised against Third World goods. Failing this, Third World states should receive some measure of compensation for their reduced export receipts through some mechanism such as Stabex. All of these measures are contingent on creditor action. We have seen that certain forces within the creditor states and institutions are beginning to realize that debt write-offs and increased aid are desirable. Whilst these groups may not have carried the day as yet their growing influence is a hopeful sign. It will be far more difficult to convince the northern states to abandon protectionism, but effective lobbying might achieve some successes and there is always the possibility of campaigning for aid along the lines of Stabex. Finally, if the greater resources committed to African development under such a scheme are not to be wasted, the clientelist states of Sub-Saharan Africa must be made more accountable to the majority of the people. A move in this direction could be brought about by incorporating basic needs criteria into IMF conditionality and orienting World Bank (and indeed other) aid towards community participation projects, which will begin the task of mobilizing the rural majority. It may well be that this is the most ambitious of our proposals, but in the long term it is perhaps the most essential to African development.

9

Conclusion

In the introduction to this book we stressed the necessity for an analysis of the debt crisis that addresses both the macro- and the micro-levels of this problem. Such an approach is essential due to the fact that the origins of the crisis and obstacles to its solution lie in the interplay between factors arising from both these levels. Developments within the international politico-economic system have combined with various aspects of the operation of many Third World political economies to produce the burgeoning levels of indebtedness that have become so evident throughout Africa. Inevitably, this means that any attempt to provide an adequate analysis of SSA's debt crisis with a view to formulating proposals for its solution is fraught with the following difficulties. First, it means that any attempted solution must be addressed to both the international and the local (e.g. national) levels, rather than towards one or the other. It may be noted that most proposed solutions to the debt crisis tend to emphasize measures at one level, often to the exclusion of the other. Thus, debtor states are prone to argue in terms of the need for enhanced aid flows and a fairer international trading system, whilst donor states and organizations (e.g. the IMF and the USA) tend to emphasize the need for certain policy reforms on the part of Third World states. We would argue that in fact a combination of all the above measures will be necessary to address all aspects of the debt crisis.

Second, the salience of the local level implies that the nature of the problem will vary from one state to the next in accordance with the specific political, social, and economic conditions in each country. A uniform programme of reforms, such as those favoured by the World Bank and the IMF, cannot be simply applied across the board in all debtor stages since the nature of the debt problem will vary in different cases. Third, it must be remembered that the debt crisis is in a constant state of flux. The year of 1987 saw considerable movement on the part of the donor states as to what they saw as an appropriate response to the crisis. The debtor states are also prone to radical policy changes in response to variations in their fortunes. In view of this, the foregoing chapters are probably best seen as a snapshot of a continually changing situation. Nevertheless, we have attempted to provide an examination of the African debt crisis that takes account of the multi-faceted nature of the problem and which is sufficiently malleable to have some degree of relevance for each of its variant manifestations.

We initially argued that the origins of the debt crisis were to be found in the interaction of the following macro- and micro-level factors. The initial contradiction that created the conditions for the crisis originated in the north in the early 1970s. This contradiction consisted of the interplay between an inflationary American fiscal policy and the growing tendency towards recession in northern industry. These factors combined to produce an excess of world liquidity on the world financial markets, a situation that was worsened by the OPEC price hike of 1973. Rising oil prices deepened the recessionary tendencies, whilst flooding the international banks with petrodollars. The banks had to find a profitable outlet for this liquidity and the primary commodity boom that had also been triggered by the oil price rise made the Third World seem like a promising prospect. Consequently a flood of loans was agreed with various Third World states. Relatively few African states benefited from this largesse, but amongst those that received substantial commercial loans were such countries as Nigeria, Ivory Coast, and Zaire. Less favoured African states were finding that they needed to draw on loans from state and multilateral donors in order to pay increased oil prices. This downward spiral towards indebtedness was exacerbated by the second oil shock, which had the following fatal effects. First, it substantially increased the budgetary allocations that oil-importing states had to make to their necessary imports of petroleum. Second, it led to the adoption of monetarism in the north, which caused a contradiction of the market for primaries and a consequent slump in prices, together with a considerable rise in interest rates. Thus, many states were finding that their export receipts were declining just as the costs of importing oil and servicing their debts were rising.

These developments on the macro-level of the international economy were most unfortunately complemented by the micro-level characteristics of many African states. As we have noted most of these states have monocultural economies, a situation that leaves them particularly vulnerable to adverse trends in the market for their products. Both Zambia and Nigeria have suffered from such setbacks and have become increasingly dependent on IMF support in consequence. It might be argued that certain states, such as Nigeria, should have been able to utilize their export receipts and loans to diversify into other profitable activities. However, many African states are characterized by neopatrimonial polities, which are prone to degenerate into spoils systems in which large amounts of public funding are wasted. All too many African states have contributed to their own debt problems by wasting and misappropriating commercial loans and aid.

This account of the origins of Africa's debt crisis enables us to identify the following central factors that must be addressed in any attempt to solve the problem. First, many African states are unable to earn sufficient receipts to pay off their debts. Their situation as monocultural primary commodity producers has made them especially vulnerable to recessionary contractions in their northern markets and to the protective barriers that have been raised against them by the USA and western Europe. Second, clientelist politics leads to the waste of resources and to patterns of urban bias in all too many states. A complicating factor is that the imprint of neopatrimonialism is variant across the continent with some states, such as Zaire and Nigeria (during the Second Republic at least), being characterized by extreme levels of corruption and waste and low levels of public policy output, whilst others, such as Zimbabwe and Ivory Coast, have produced significant public policy output that has benefited not only the urban, but the rural populace. These achievements have been made despite the fact that such states also display clientelist tendencies.

None of the solutions that have been adopted, or advocated so far comes completely to grips with these problems. Insufficient aid and rescheduling have been accorded to the debtor states to make any substantial impact on their balance of payments difficulties. There must even be some doubt about the adequacy of the

IMF/World Bank initiative that emerged from the Venice Summit of the Group of Seven in 1987 (see Chapter 8), welcome though it is. Certainly, most of the creditor states have shown themselves unwilling to take action that would really help the African states and raise their protective barriers against primary commodities. It must also be noted that those commentators who do advocate substantial transfers of resources and a measure at least of free trade fail to deal with the problem of neopatrimonialism. This factor must be resolved if the resources that they propose to put into various African countries are to be utilized productively.

Many would argue that the IMF and the World Bank have attempted to formulate a solution that addresses these variegated problems in the complex of policy recommendations that are to be found in the Berg Report and other of their documents. However, it is our contention that the measures advocated by the Fund and the Bank are inappropriate, and often fatal treatment for indebtedness. The deflationary policies so dear to these organizations may indeed reduce government waste of resources, but the evidence from Zaire and Sierra Leone indicates that they do not necessarily eliminate the clientelist networks that underpin the polity in so many African states. The result tends to be that the symptoms of neopatrimonialism are slightly alleviated, whilst the disease itself remains far from cured and is likely to manifest itself again. Furthermore, spending cuts adversely affect many of the public services that actually are delivered by the state and depress the standard of living for the majority of African people. The other elements of the IMF/World Bank formula tend to have equally unfortunate effects. Devaluation often serves to trigger stagflation by raising import prices and causing depressed agricultural and industrial output due to shortages of necessary imported inputs. Clearly this is not conducive to increased exports. This situation is exacerbated by the insistence of the Fund and the Bank on the imposition of free trade on SSA, whilst they continue to blink at (and in some instances actually connive with) the north's imposition of protective barriers against tropical goods, a stance that is hardly designed to encourage African exports. The inadequacy of the funding transferred to Africa thus far and the apparent anxiety of the Fund and the Bank to reduce public spending whatever the social cost, seem indicative of a rather negative attitude to development. They betray a stance in which the central concern is evidently to maintain the ability of SSA to continue servicing its debts, rather than to create the conditions for economic growth and development.

It has been our concern in this book to try and identify the conditions that will be needed to solve Africa's debt crisis in its various manifestations. Our proposed solution to this problem seeks to address the fundamental problems identified above: first, Africa's inability to earn enough export receipts to pay its debts and achieve some level of development; and second the variable effects of neopatrimonialism. With regard to the first issue we advocate enhanced transfers of aid, increased debt write-offs, and adoption of concessional interest rates. However, these should be complemented by efforts to reflate the international economy and to end protection. Given that northern states are unlikely to embrace such policies in the current recessionary situation we would suggest that the CFF, or Stabex might be extended to give aid to states suffering declining export receipts due to contracting markets for their goods. Naturally, we would also argue that the development lobby should campaign as vigorously as possible for any concessions in reducing protective barriers that can be obtained. It must also be remembered that any resources gained for Africa from such policies may be prone to misallocation or misappropriation if the question of neopatrimonialism is not resolved.

The difficulty in dealing with neopatrimonialism is that its impact is variable from one state to another. The only solution that deals with the multiple aspects of this problem is to seek the full democratization of African states, in the sense of making them accountable to a majority of the people rather than minority clientelist groups. As Bayart points out, in the final instance this objective can only be achieved by the efforts of the African people themselves.

We would point to the aid philosophy of community development as providing a plausible (if far from unproblematic) strategy for mobilization of those currently excluded from the political process. In other words we would advocate the adoption of aid strategies directed to 'empowering' local communities in relation to the state. Such a strategy would not cause a contraction of existing public policy output as IMF/World Bank measures have. However, it would constrain African states to minimize the variant levels of waste of resources currently associated with clientelism as they were faced with growing demands from the populace. The Fund and the Bank could help to create the conditions to 'empower' local communities by incorporating basic needs-orientated criteria into their conditionality and stressing grass-roots participation in Bank projects. This would put a constraint on the state from above to produce services, whilst creating the conditions for pressure from below to maintain and expand those services.

There has been considerable movement on the part of the donor states and institutions as to what they see as an appropriate response to the debt crisis. There is a growing consciousness that demands for Draconian adjustment are not the answer to the problem and there are signs of an emerging consensus which might be receptive to the strategy outlined above. This is evident in the appearance of proposals such as the Lawson Plan and the new World Bank/IMF initiative, which clearly recognize the need for enhanced aid and debt relief. The Fund has also recognized that its conditionality must at least be modified and this may open up the possibility for a debate that might push the IMF in the direction of a greater concern for basic needs. There is also evidence of the growing influence of the community-development school of thought within aid circles. Non-governmental organizations such as Oxfam and War on Want have been using participatory strategies for some years now. The results of their projects have been sufficiently successful to motivate various bilateral donors, such as West Germany, and some multilateral institutions, such as the United Nations Development Programme, and the Food and Agriculture Organization, to experiment with community development. To the extent that such projects succeed in mobilizing African communities to work for their own specific developmental goals, they create the conditions for a degree of political activism in the form of demands that the state play its part in development. All of these developments contain the seeds of a viable strategy for the short-term alleviation and the long-term solution to the debt crisis. It remains to be seen whether or not the international community and the African people themselves will embrace this solution.

Postscript

In the months since the main body of this book was completed there has been a deluge of new proposals on how to deal with the debt crisis and particularly its effects in Africa. These have culminated in the emergence of a new agreement (still in outline form at the time of writing) from the June 1988 Toronto Summit of the Group of Seven major industrial states. In this brief postscript we shall analyse these new developments with a view to assessing their potential for solving, or at least alleviating, the African debt crisis.

It may first be noted that the promises to expand World Bank and IMF economic resources arising from the 1987 Venice Summit (see Chapter 8) have been fulfilled. In December 1987 the IMF established an enhanced structural adjustment facility, which is expected to add some SDR 6 billion (US$7.8 billion) to the existing SDR 3 billion structural adjustment facility. The World Bank has earmarked a larger share (amounting to US$400 million a year) of the eighth replenishment of IDA for low-income, highly-indebted African states. It has also been announced that the repayment terms on new World Bank loans will be softened for low-income states (i.e. with per capita incomes below US$836 in 1986) from July 1988. Any debts contracted after this date will be repaid on an annuity basis with repayments of principal rising as the interest payments decline. In other words, debt service payments will be lower in the earlier stages of the repayment process, thus giving borrowers a breathing space before they have to face their full debt burden. According to the Bank, the annuity system will raise its net disbursements to low-income countries by some US$16 billion over the next twenty years. In addition, the Bank is to raise grace periods on new loans for middle- and upper-income states from four and three years respectively to five years, a measure that should increase Bank disbursements to middle-income countries by some US$3 billion in the early 1990s. The Bank has also won guarantees of co-financing from various bilateral donors, the EEC, and the African Development Bank (AfDB) amounting to US$6.4 billion, which is projected to result in additional financing of US$1 billion a year between 1988-90 for 'debt distressed' Africa. The Paris Club also agreed to allow low-income countries longer rescheduling periods, though only on a case-by-case basis.[1]

Equally significant moves have been made with regard to IMF and World Bank conditionality. Both organizations have been showing a greater awareness of the adverse effects their austerity programmes have been having on the Third World poor. This has been reflected in their backing for Ghana's recently initiated Programme of Action to Mitigate the Social Costs of Adjustment (PAMSCAD). The Programme is premissed on the recognition that large sections of the population have been 'economically paralysed' by the adverse effects structural adjustment has had on employment, social services, and consumer price inflation. Consequently PAMSCAD consists of programmes to promote employment generation, community participation projects, and the satisfaction of basic needs. Ghana has managed to win pledges of aid for the programme amounting to over US$85 million.[2] Not only does this promise to improve social conditions for many Ghanaians, but it also represents a step towards the basic needs-orientated aid that could play a major role in promoting the political mobilization of local communities. Such empowerment of local communities was identified as central to the control of the clientelist policies that have typified Africa and contributed to the debt crisis (see Chapter 8). If PAMSCAD is successful, it could become a model for social adjustment programmes across the continent. It could prove most attractive to governments seeking to defuse social tensions, whilst simultaneously forcing them to adopt more accountable procedures of policy making and implementation. However, PAMSCAD will face critical tests over 1988 due to continuing public sector retrenchment and inflation caused by agricultural production shortfalls and the continuing decline of the cedi. Even more problematic is the decline in the world cocoa price, which has caused balance of payments shortfalls. Clearly, PAMSCAD does not represent an answer to the latter problem.[3]

Indeed, the efforts of the creditor states and institutions have been put into perspective by the UN report of February 1988 entitled 'Financing African Recovery', and popularly known as the Wass Report because it was produced by a study group headed by Sir Douglas Wass, formerly a senior UK Treasury official. The Wass Report points out that previous reschedulings have merely contributed to the emergence of an unmanageable debt servicing burden amounting to an annual average of 40 per cent of Africa's gross official export earnings. This has resulted in a situation where there will be a shortfall of US$2 billion in needed funding each year after taking into account the US$3 billion that should be supplied from the promised increases in Bank, IMF, and AfDB funding. In addition to recommending that the funding be found to fill this gap, the Wass Report suggests that the official commitments of the larger African debtors, such as Ivory Coast, should be rescheduled with low interest rates and that commercial bank debt should be converted into securities in appropriate cases.[4] To these proposals we may add the scheme put forward by the Nordic states to set up a western financed fund that would subsidize the interest rates on some US$300 million of arrears owed by about fifteen African states on World Bank loans. The Bank's reaction to this scheme has been lukewarm since it is opposed to debt relief on its own loans.[5]

Perhaps the most widely discussed of the recent proposals is that put forward by the AfDB and Warburgs, the British merchant bank. The essence of the plan is to convert bad debts into securities to be paid over the long term. In the first instance, it was suggested that the plan be implemented in Zaire. Some US$5 billion of Zairean debt was to be converted into tradable securities with a maturity of 20-25 years, carrying 4 per cent annual interest. This element of the plan would have cost Zaire some US$200 million over the life of the scheme. Zaire would also have made annual payments into a sinking fund at a total cost of US$100 million throughout the scheme. The principal was to be repaid from this fund when the securities reached maturity. Implementation of this plan would have reduced Zaire's debt service ratio from an average of 18.4 per cent during 1981-7 to a more manageable 12.1 per cent between 1988-95.[6]

The AfDB-Warburgs plan has been welcomed in various quarters as an important initiative, winning the support of Canada and plaudits from the British Government, whose Lawson Plan it somewhat resembles. However, objections to the scheme were quick to emerge, many of them focusing on the fact that the main beneficiary was to be the kleptocratic state of Zaire. Thus, it was argued that there was a danger of moral hazard since the plan would reward states for economic mismanagement, a criticism that many observers might see as apposite given the Zairean context.

This led the AfDB and Warburgs to suggest that the scheme could just as well be implemented in Madagascar. However, this proposed changed siting of the plan has not disposed of the main criticisms levelled by creditor states such as West Germany, France, Japan, and the USA. A central criticism has been the scheme's apparent lack of conditionality, a serious oversight in the eyes of those creditors that believe in the necessity of economic restructuring of the type imposed by the IMF. It has also argued that there is nothing to stop the debtor nation defaulting. The French government is thought to be opposed to the scheme due to fears that it will reduce the influence of the Paris Club amongst African debtor states. However, the creditors' main objection is that any scheme to securitize a particular nation's debts will spark off a series of similar demands, a fear that has been reinforced by Brazil's recent approach to Warburgs for help in designing a securitization scheme for its US$113 billion debts. It seemed clear that the major creditors were unwilling to consider any remotely radical approach to the debt crisis.[7]

This general impression seemed to be borne out by the IMF-World Bank meeting of April 1988, where there was an evident reluctance to show any leniency to African states in case it led to increased demands from Latin America.[8] However, in the weeks before the Toronto Summit in June 1988 there was an apparent transformation in the attitudes of main creditors. First, the USA gave way on its opposition to interest rate cuts, with Treasury Secretary Baker announcing that creditors could consider the Lawson Plan for lower interest rates, or alternatively they might extend debt maturities. Whilst it has been suggested that Baker's actual intention was to discredit the AfDB-Warburgs securitization plan, it must also be noted that the USA's abandonment of its opposition to concessional interest rates seemed a radical step.[9] The Germans also made conciliatory moves, announcing discussions to write off DM2.2 billion (£700 million) of African debts. The French put forward a plan for discussion at the Summit consisting of three options, one of which was an immediate cancellation of one-third of the official debt owed by some twenty of the poorest nations. The other options entailed rescheduling the debts at market rates over 25 years, or rescheduling over 15 years at preferential rates. These moves raised considerable optimism for the agreement of a new initiative to deal with African debt.[10]

In the event, the initiative agreed at the Toronto Summit is clearly derived from the French proposals in that it consists of three alternatives, including partial debt write-offs, longer rescheduling periods at market rates, and concessional interest rates. In addition, Japan announced a US$1 billion debt relief package for low-income Africa, which consists of a waiver on all capital and interest payments on US$5.5 billion of debt owed by seventeen states. However, any enthusiasm at the outcome of the conference has to take into account the fact that the USA made it clear that the only option it would be willing to consider was that of longer rescheduling periods. The USA opposes debt forgiveness because it believes such measures would set a bad precedent and it has its own budgetary difficulties.[11] This raises the possibility that other creditors will refrain from adopting debt write-offs and concessional interest rates in the attempt to retain some degree of parity in their collective efforts to deal with the debt crisis. It must also be noted that the plan is only expected to cover a maximum of US$40 billion out of total African debt of US$200 billion.[12] Whilst the Toronto initiative is a welcome step forward, it hardly represents a solution to Africa's debt crisis.

One notable gap in the creditors' strategy for dealing with the debt crisis is the absence of any agreement to boost demand for the debtor states' primary goods. As we have seen, intensive efforts to alleviate Ghana's debt problems may well falter in the face of declining commodity markets. According to the Overseas Development Institute (ODI), the fall in demand for primary goods is attributable to two main factors, the first being the move by OECD economies away from industrial production into services, and the second being protectionism. The significance of the former factor may be gauged by noting that the UK share of manufacturing in GDP fell from 33 per cent in 1965 to 25 per cent in 1985. Arguably, the growth of protectionism is even more influential in depressing the market. The ODI has observed that between 1970-85 the EEC made the transition from being a major importer of grains (18 million tonnes in 1970) to being an exporter (16 million tonnes in 1985) due to its protectionist policies.[13] At the World Food Conference in Iowa, a US official noted that Third World states were losing their agricultural markets to the industrialized states due to the ability of the latter to pay farm subsidies which encourage surplus production. The export of this surplus is then subsidized to the extent that Third World produce cannot compete. As a result the share of the industrialized states in world agricultural exports has increased from 42 per cent in the early 1960s to 63 per cent by 1988.[14] Clearly, such policies undermine the capacity of African states to service their debts and finance some level of development. Any solution of the debt crisis must be contingent on the developed states agreeing to refrain from protecting their markets and dumping their excess produce on the world market. The prospects for such an agreement currently seem less than hopeful with the USA deciding to reduce its cereals set-aside programme, which will result in another 10-12 million tonnes of cereals coming onto the world markets according to the EEC.[15] The Toronto Summit evidently preferred to defer any decisions on the problematic question of agriculture until the meeting of the GATT in December 1988.[16] One can only hope that the industrialized states will begin to move towards an appreciation of the need to retreat from the trends of protectionism and over-production that are currently beggaring the Third World. As the ODI has pointed out: 'Can it be in the interests of the industrial countries not to reform a system which starves LDCs of the foreign exchange they would use to buy their exports?'[17]

Certain trends have emerged in the first few months of 1988 which are promising, including the commitment by creditor states and institutions to put more money into Africa and the introduction of PAMSCAD in Ghana. However, the Wass Report points out that this funding may still prove inadequate, and, as yet, there is little sign of a reversal of protectionist policies. The African debt crisis is still some way from being solved.

Notes and references

INTRODUCTION

1. OECD, External Debt of Developing Countries: 1983 Survey, (Geneva, OECD, 1984), pp.48-9.
2. K. Hallberg, 'International debt 1985: origins and issues for the future', in M.P. Claudon (ed.), World Debt Crisis: International Lending on Trial, (Cambridge, Mass, Ballinger Publishing Co, 1986), especially p.9.
3. J.K. Nyerere, 'An address', in Development and Change, 17:3, (July 1986), p. 389.
4. This line of argument tends to be favoured by agencies such as the World Bank and the IMF and is emphasized in many of their publications, such as: the Bank's Accelerated Development in Sub-Saharan Africa (the Berg Report), (Washington DC, World Bank, 1982); and the IMF's World Economic Outlook: April 1986, (Washington DC, International Monetary Fund, 1986).
5. P. Nunnenkamp, The International Debt Crisis of the Third World: Causes and Consequences for the World Economy, (Sussex, Wheatsheaf Books, 1986), especially ch.7.
6. P. Korner, G. Maass, T. Siebold and R. Tetzlaff, The IMF and the Debt Crisis: a Guide to the Third World's Dilemmas, (London, Zed Books, 1986), especially ch.1.
7. See R.H. Jackson and C.G. Rosberg, Personal Rule in Black Africa: Prince, Autocrat, Prophet, Tyrant, (California, University of California Press, 1982); and R. Sandbrook with J. Barker, The Politics of Africa's Economic Stagnation, (Cambridge, Cambridge University Press, 1985).
8. B. Sutcliffe, Hard Times, (London, Pluto Press, 1983), pp. 43-4.
9. H. Lever and C. Huhne, Debt and Danger: the World Financial Crisis, (Harmondsworth, Penguin, 1985), p.44.
10. R.P. DeWitt and J.F. Petras, 'Political economy of international debt: the dynamics of financial capital', in J.D. Aronson (ed.), Debt and the Less Developed Countries, (Boulder, Colorado, Westview Press, 1979), p.20.
11. Nunnenkamp, International Debt Crisis of the Third

World, p.96.
12. Lever and Huhne, Debt and Danger, pp.53-4.
13. A. Lipietz, 'How monetarism has choked Third World industrialization', New Left Review, 145, (May-June 1984), p.77.
14. K. Krumm, The External Debt of Sub-Saharan Africa: Origins, Magnitude, and Implications for Action, (Washington DC, World Bank Staff Working Papers, 1985), pp.7-8.
15. Lever and Huhne, Debt and Danger, p.59.
16. Krumm, External Debt of Sub-Saharan Africa, p.8.
17. N.S. Makgetla, 'Theoretical and practical implications of IMF conditionality in Zambia', The Journal of Modern African Studies, 24:3, (1986), pp.395-6.
18. Lipietz, 'How monetarism has choked Third World industrialization', p.81.
19. Economist Intelligence Unit, Multinational Business Quarterly, 4, (1986), pp.17-19.
20. Multinational Business Quarterly, 4, p.17.
21. Ibid, pp.17-18.

1 THE NATURE OF AFRICAN DEBT

1. Save the Children Fund, 'Dealing with debt' (Save the Children Fund, 1987).
2. N. Lawson, speech to the Interim Committee of the IMF, 9 April 1987. (HM Treasury, 1987).
3. R.J. Pelosky, 'The World Bank and the Baker initiative', Multinational Business, 4, (1986).
4. S. Griffith-Jones and O. Sunkel, Debt and Development Crises in Latin America (Oxford, Clarendon Press, 1986).
5. Africa Economic Digest, (28 September 1985).
6. R.H. Green and S. Griffith-Jones, 'Sub-Saharan Africa's debt crisis', Third World Affairs, 1986 (London, Third World Foundation, 1985).
7. 'African debt', Oxford Analytica Daily Brief, (7 January 1988).
8. Africa Recovery, 4 (December 1987).
9. Report of the UN Secretary-General, 'Progress in the implementation of the UN programme of action for African economic recovery and development, 1986-90' (United Nations, 1987).
10. A billion, is a thousand million, and a trillion is a

thousand billion. The total debt of the 109 developing countries was US$ 1,190 billion in 1987, according to the World Bank's World Debt Tables, 1987-8.

11. World Bank, Towards Sustained Development in Sub-Saharan Africa (Washington DC, World Bank, 1984), p.1.
12. B. Sutcliffe, 'Africa and the world economic crisis' (paper for the Review of African Political Economy Conference on 'The World Recession and the Crisis in Africa', University of Keele, September 1984), section 10.
13. G.K. Helleiner, 'The IMF and Africa in the 1980s', Canadian Journal of African Studies, 17:1, (1983), pp.17, 19.
14. Africa Economic Digest (4 May 1984), p.2.
15. Sutcliffe, 'Africa and the world economic crisis', section 13.
16. R.E. Wood, 'The debt crisis and north-south relations', Third World Quarterly, 6:3, (July 1983), p.705.
17. 'Banking and insurance special report', Africa Economic Digest, (7 September 1984), p.6.
18. Helleiner, 'The IMF and Africa in the 1980s'.
19. K. Krum, The External Debt of Sub-Saharan Africa: Origins, Magnitude, and Implications for Action (Washington DC, World Bank Staff Working Papers 741, 1985), p.24.

2 THE POLITICS OF EXTERNAL POLICY DIRECTION

1. World Bank, World Development Report 1985, (Washington DC, World Bank, 1985), p.27.
2. J. Nyerere, 'No to IMF meddling', (1980), quoted in T. Hayter and C. Watson, Aid: Rhetoric and Reality, (London, Pluto Press, 1985), pp.50-1.
3. Hayter and Watson, Aid: Rhetoric and Reality, pp.112-24.
4. G.K. Helleiner, 'The IMF and Africa in the 1980s', Canadian Journal of African Studies, 17: 1, (1983), p.23.
5. South, 46, (August 1984), p.15.
6. See C. Payer, The Debt Trap: the IMF and the Third World, (Harmondsworth, Penguin, 1974), ch.2; and 'The IMF in the 1980s: what has it learned; what have we learned about it?', in Third World Affairs 1985, Third World Foundation, pp.1-9.
7. For further details see D. Seddon, 'A winter of

discontent: economic policy and social unrest in Tunisia and Morocco', (paper for the 1984 Keele Review of African Political Economy Conference).
8. E.A. Brett, 'The world's view of the IMF', in Latin America Bureau, The Poverty Brokers: the IMF and Latin America, (London, Latin America Bureau, 1983), p.41.
9. J.B. Zulu and S.M. Nsouli, 'Adjustment programmes in Africa', Finance and Development, 21:1, (March 1984), pp.6-7.
10. The World Bank, Accelerated Development in Sub-Saharan Africa (the Berg Report), (Washington DC, World Bank, 1982), p.4.
11. World Bank, Berg Report, p.5.
12. J. Sender and S. Smith, 'What's right with the Berg Report and what's left of its critics?', Capital and Class, 24, (winter 1985).
13. R.H. Bates, Markets and States in Tropical Africa: the Political Basis of Agricultural Policies, (Berkeley and Los Angeles, University of California Press, 1981).
14. M. Bienefield, 'Analyzing the politics of African state policy: some thoughts on Robert Bates work', IDS Bulletin, 17:1, (January 1986), pp.5-11.
15. For information on Mozambique see G. Walt and A. Melamed, Mozambique: Towards a People's Health Service, (London, Zed Press, 1984); and J. Hanlon, Mozambique: the Revolution under Fire, (London, Zed Press, 1984) ch.8.
16. R. Davies and D. Saunders, 'Stabilization policies and the effect on child health in Zimbabwe', Review of African Political Economy, 38, (April 1987).
17. R. Chambers, The Crisis of Africa's Rural Poor: Perceptions and Priorities, (Brighton, IDS Publications, February 1985), pp.13-14.
18. Quoted in West Africa, 21 September 1987, p.1833.
19. 'Exchange rate policies in developing countries', ODI Briefing Paper, 2, (June 1985).
20. S.P. Schatz, 'Laissez-faireism for Africa?', The Journal of Modern African Studies, 25:1, (1987), pp.135-6.
21. Schatz, 'Laissez-faireism for Africa?', p.133.
22. J. Sender and S. Smith, The Development of Capitalism in Africa, (London, Methuen, 1986), p.77.
23. Ibid, p.124.
24. Ibid, p.71.
25. C. Charney, 'Political power in the neo-colonial African

states', Review of African Political Economy, 38, (April 1987), p.50.
26. Africa Economic Digest, (13 December 1986), p.15.
27. Ibid, (17 January 1987), p.2.
28. World Bank, Berg Report, p.23.
29. Sender and Smith, 'What's right with the Berg Report?' p.131.
30. Sender and Smith, Development of Capitalism in Africa, p.120.
31. E. Berg, 'The World Bank's strategy', in J. Ravenhill (ed.), Africa in Economic Crisis, (London, Macmillan, 1985), pp.54-5.
32. R. Gulhati, S. Bose and V. Atukorala, 'Exchange rate policies in Africa: how valid is the scepticism?', Development and Change, 17:3, (July 1986), p.413.
33. J. Loxley, 'The Berg Report and the model of accumulation in Sub-Saharan Africa', Review of African Political Economy, 27:8, (1983), p.200.
34. A Sudanese Economist, 'Sudan: a policy of increasing denationalization of national wealth', Review of African Political Economy, 26, (1983).
35. C. Colclough, 'Competing paradigms in the debate about agricultural pricing policy', IDS Bulletin, 16:3, (July 1985).
36. Gulhati et al., 'Exchange Rate Policies in Africa', pp.406-7.
37. Ibid, p.410.
38. Schatz, 'Laissez-faireism for Africa?', p.134.
39. Sender and Smith, Development of Capitalism in Africa, pp.122-3.
40. H. Lever and C. Huhne, Debt and Danger: the World Financial Crisis, (Harmondsworth, Penguin, 1985), p.86; Lever and Huhne express considerable reservations as to whether even this amount of growth would be adequate to enable Third World debtors to meet their commitments.
41. Schatz, 'Laissez-faireism for Africa?', p.132.
42. World Bank, World Debt Tables: External Debt of Developing Countries, 1986-7, (Washington DC, World Bank, February 1987), pp.12-13.
43. South, 83, (September 1987), p.13.
44. Africa Economic Digest, (1 May 1987), p.8. It is an ironic comment on the Bank's capacity for selective amnesia that the recommendation in its earlier report for Zambia to diversify into coffee is transformed into

an accusation that Zambia is contributing to over-production in the later report.
45. West Africa, (2 November 1987), pp.2148-9.
46. For an analysis of protectionism see World Bank, World Development Report 1987, (Washington DC, World Bank, 1987), ch.8; for further details of the Lomé Convention see T.W. Parfitt, 'The Lomé Convention and the new international order', Review of African Political Economy, 21, (1981).
47. Africa Confidential, 28:15, (22 July 1987), p.4.
48. South, 83, pp.9-10.

3 NIGERIA: THE CIRCUITOUS PATH TO STABILIZATION?

1. Financial Times, (25 February 1986).
2. Africa Economic Digest, (11 January 1986), p.2.
3. West Africa, (12 January 1987), p.80.
4. West Africa, (28 October 1985), p.2255.
5. Herbert Ekwe-Ekwe, 'The Nigerian plight: Shagari to Buhari', Third World Quarterly, 7:3, (July 1985), p.624.
6. Douglas Rimmer, 'The over-valued currency and over-administered economy of Nigeria', African Affairs, 84: 336, (July 1985), p.445.
7. Ekwe-Ekwe, 'Nigerian plight', p.615.
8. Toyin Falola and Julius Ihonrbere, The Rise and Fall of Nigeria's Second Republic, 1979-84 (London, Zed Press, 1985), p.108.
9. See R. Hall's Report in New African, (January 1986), pp.43-4.
10. See Gavin Williams, State and Society in Nigeria (Nigeria, Afrografica, 1980); and Tom Forrest, 'The political economy of civil rule and the economic crisis in Nigeria, 1979-84', Review of African Political Economy, 35, (May 1986).
11. Ekwe-Ekwe, 'Nigerian plight' especially p.619; and Shehu Othman, 'Classes, crises and coup: the demise of Shagari's policy', African Affairs, 83:333, (October 1984).
12. West Africa, (21 October 1985), p.2204.
13. Forrest, 'Political economy of the crisis in Nigeria', p.5.
14. Rimmer, 'The over-valued currency of Nigeria', p.436.
15. Financial Times, (25 February 1985).
16. Africa Research Bulletin - Economic Series, (31

October 1985), p.7920.
17. African Business, (January 1986), p.42.
18. Christopher Colclough, 'Competing paradigms in the debate about agricultural pricing policy', IDS Bulletin 16:3, (July 1985).
19. Martin Godfrey, 'Trade and exchange rate policy in Sub-Saharan Africa', IDS Bulletin, 16:3, (July 1985).
20. West Africa, (28 October 1985), p.2253.
21. Financial Times, (25 February 1985).
22. ARB - Economic Series, (31 December 1985).
23. West Africa (23 December 1985), p.2678.
24. John Ohiorhenuan, 'Brandt, Berg and militarization in Nigeria', IDS Bulletin, 16:4, (October 1985), pp.58-60.
25. West Africa, (23-30 December 1985), p.2678.
26. Ibid.
27. Financial Times, (25 February 1985).
28. ARB - Economic Series, (31 August 1985), p.7843.
29. Africa Economic Digest, (11 January 1986), p.11.
30. New African, (October 1985), p.12.
31. Larry Diamond, 'Nigerian update', Foreign Affairs, (winter 1985-6), pp.330-1.
32. ARB - Economic Series (31 October 1985), p.7920, and (30 November 1985), pp.7956-7.
33. West Africa, (29 September 1986), pp.2032-40.
34. West Africa, (8 December 1986), p.2550.
35. West Africa, (2 November 1987), pp.2158-9.
36. West Africa, (24 November 1986), p.2443.
37. West African Hotline (12 January 1987), p.1.
38. African Business, (March 1987), p.60.
39. Economist Intelligence Unit, Country Report: Nigeria, 2, (London, The Economist, 1987), p.19.
40. Financial Times, (8 April 1987); and Africa Confidential, 29:1, (8 January 1988), pp.1-2.
41. West Africa, (6 October 1986), p.1089, and (23 February 1987), p.359.
42. African Business, (March 1987), p.54.
43. West African Hotline, (12 January 1987), p.1.
44. West Africa, (12 January 1987), p.48.
45. Ibid.
46. Economist Intelligence Unit, Country Report: Nigeria, 2 (1987), p.14.
47. Ibid, pp.18-19.
48. West African Hotline, (1 January 1987), p.3.
49. West Africa, (28 September 1987), p.1901.
50. Economist Intelligence Unit, Nigeria: the Dilemmas

Ahead - a Political Risk Analysis, Special Report 1072 by S. Wright, (London, The Economist, 1986), p.35.
51. West Africa, (6 January 1986).
52. Africa Confidential, (8 January 1988), pp.1-2.
53. Africa Confidential, (29 January 1987).
54. The Observer, (5 July 1987).
55. Richard Hall, Africa Confidential, (16 December 1987), pp.3-4.
56. New African, (January 1986), p.43.
57. Economist Intelligence Unit, Nigeria: the Dilemmas Ahead, p.41.
58. ARB - Economic Series, (31 December 1985).
59. West Africa, (31 January 1986).
60. West Africa, (20 October 1986), p.2197, and (8 December 1986), p.2545.
61. West African Hotline (1 April 1987), p.2.
62. Financial Times, (15 January 1988).
63. Economist Intelligence Unit, Country Report: Nigeria, 2, (1987), p.23; and West African Hotline, (16 May 1987), p.3.
64. West African Hotline, (16 May 1987), p.1.
65. Ibid, (1 May 1987), p.1.

4 ZAIRE: DEBT IN AN ABSOLUTIST KLEPTOCRACY

1. Economist Intelligence Unit, Country Profile 1986-7: Zaire, Rwanda, Burundi, 1, (London, The Economist, 1987), p.9.
2. A. Wood, 'The funding of the permanent crisis: a study of IMF intervention in Zaire', in J. Caballero, G. Nott, A. Wood and M. Lajo, International Monetary Fund Policies in the Third World: Case Studies of Turkey, Zaire, and Peru (University of East Anglia Development Studies Occasional Paper, 1981), p.2.
3. African Economic Digest, (22 March 1986), p.5.
4. African Business, (May 1986), p.29.
5. World Bank, World Debt Tables: External Debt of Developing Countries, 1986-7 (Washington DC, World Bank, February 1987), p.195.
6. C. Young and T. Turner, The Rise and Decline of the Zairean State, (Wisconsin, University of Wisconsin Press, 1985), ch.10, pp.276-325.
7. Wood, 'Funding of the permanent crisis'.
8. Young and Turner, Rise and Decline of the Zairean

State, pp.296-8.
9. Economist Intelligence Unit, Quarterly Economic Review of Zaire, Rwanda, Burundi, 3, (1984), p.14.
10. D. Delamaide, Debt Shock, (London, Weidenfeld and Nicholson, 1984), p.60.
11. T. Callaghy, 'External actors and the relative autonomy of the political aristocracy in Zaire', Journal of Commonwealth and Comparative Politics, 21:3, (1983), p.69.
12. T. Callaghy, The State-Society Struggle: Zaire in Comparative Perspective (New York, Columbia University Press, 1984), especially ch.4.
13. Young and Turner, Rise and Decline, ch.11, pp.326-62.
14. African Business, (September 1984), p.47.
15. P. Korner et al., The IMF and the Debt Crisis: a Guide to the Third World's Dilemmas, (London, Zed Books, 1986), p.101.
16. P. Korner, G. Maass, T. Siebold and R. Tetzlaff, The IMF and the Debt Crisis: a Guide to the Third World's Dilemmas (London, Zed Books, 1986), p.100.
17. T. Callaghy, 'Africa's debt crisis', Journal of International Affairs, 38:1, (summer 1984), p.67.
18. Wood, 'Funding of the permanent crisis', p.11.
19. Quoted by T. Callaghy, 'External actors and the relative autonomy of the poltical aristocracy', p.75.
20. Delamaide, Debt Shock, p.60.
21. Keesings Contemporary Archives, (5 November 1982), p.31793.
22. Callaghy, 'Africa's debt crisis', p.68.
23. Delamaide, Debt Shock, pp.57-8.
24. Callaghy, 'Africa's debt crisis, p.66.
25. Young and Turner, Rise and Decline, pp.255-8.
26. Ibid, p.387.
27. Africa Research Bulletin, Political Series, 23:7, (15 August 1986), p.8140.
28. Young and Turner, Rise and Decline, pp.387-8.
29. Keesings Contemporary Archives, 30, (May 1984), p.32840; and African Business, (September 1984), p.47.
30. Africa Research Bulletin, Economic Series, (April 1985), p.7689; and Economist Intelligence Unit, Zaire to the 1990s: Will Retrenchment Work?, Special Report 227 by Gregory Kronsten, (London, The Economist, 1986), p.25.
31. Financial Times, Survey of Zaire, (9 July 1985), pp.1-2.
32. Economist Intelligence Unit, Zaire to the 1990s, p.17

and pp.27-9.

33. Details from Africa Economist Digest, (24 May 1986), p.32 and (21 June 1986), p.35; Africa Research Bulletin, (30 June 1985), p.7771; Economist Intelligence Unit, Quarterly Economic Review of Zaire, Rwanda and Burundi, 2, (1985), pp.10-11 and 3, (1985), p.11 and 4, (1985), p.6; Zaire to the 1990s, p.54; and Financial Times, Survey of Zaire, pp.1-3.
34. Economist Intelligence Unit, Zaire to the 1990s, p.29.
35. Callaghy, 'Africa's debt crisis', p.72.
36. African Business, (May 1986), p.29.
37. Financial Times, Survey of Zaire, p.8.
38. Economist Intelligence Unit, Quarterly Economic Review of Zaire, Rwanda and Burundi, 3, (1985), p.5; and Zaire to the 1990s, ch.4 and p.52.
39. Financial Times, Survey of Zaire, pp.1-3; Africa Economic Digest, (15 March 1986), p.14; and Economist Intelligence Unit, Zaire to the 1990s, p.57.
40. Economist Intelligence Unit, Zaire to the 1990s, p.31 and p.58.
41. Callaghy, 'Africa's debt crisis', p.72.
42. Economist Intelligence Unit, Zaire to the 1990s, p.39; Kronsten's calculation was to take the budget head for salaries in 1985 at Z6,000 million and divide it by the 1983 figure of 387,000 employees in the public sector. Given that the latter figure is most likely to be unreliable it can be seen that this calculation must be treated with the utmost caution.
43. African Business, (September 1984), p.47.
44. Economist Intelligence Unit, Quarterly Economic Review of Zaire, Rwanda, Burundi, 3, (1984), p.12.
45. Economist Intelligence Unit, Zaire to the 1990s, p.34.
46. J. MacGaffey, 'Fending-for-Yourself: the Organization of the Second Economy in Zaire', in Nzongola-Ntalaja (ed.), The Crisis in Zaire: Myths and Realities, (New Jersey, Africa World Press, 1986), pp.144-5.
47. New African, (December 1985).
48. African Business, (April 1985), p.17.
49. Africa Confidential, 27: 19, (17 September 1986), p.6.
50. New African, (May 1985), p.45.
51. New African, (December 1985).
52. At an informal meeting of the Friends of Zaire in Brussels during 10-11 March 1986, Kengo was quoted as saying that 'a durable and socially acceptable recovery cannot be undertaken without financial assistance from

our partners': Africa Economic Digest, (15 March 1986), p.14.
53. African Business, (October 1986), p.34.
54. African Research Bulletin, (30 November 1986), pp.8440-2; Economist Intelligence Unit, Country Report: Zaire, Rwanda, Burundi, 4, (1986), pp.11-12; and West Africa, (5 January 1987), p.17.
55. Africa Research Bulletin, (30 November 1986), p.8441.
56. Economist Intelligence Unit, Country Report: Zaire, 4, (1986), p.10.
57. Africa Confidential, (17 September 1986), pp.6-7.
58. Africa Research Bulletin, (15 August 1986), p.8140.
59. West Africa, (6 October 1986), p.2135.
60. Africa Research Bulletin, (15 May 1987), pp.8468-9.
61. Details of the Kamina affair are taken from Africa Confidential, 28: 16, (5 August 1987), pp.3-4; and Africa Research Bulletin, (15 April 1987), pp.8451-2.
62. West Africa, (5 January 1987), p.17; and Economist Intelligence Unit, Country Report: Zaire, Rwanda, Burundi, 1, (1987), p.11.
63. West Africa, (30 March 1987), p.625.
64. Africa Research Bulletin, (30 April 1987), pp.8626-7.

5 GHANA: INDEBTEDNESS, RECOVERY, AND THE IMF 1977–87

1. R. Price, 'Neo-colonialism and Ghana's economic decline: a critical assessment', Canadian Journal of African Studies, 18: 1, (1984), pp.164-5.
2. World Bank, Ghana, Policies and Programme for Adjustment (Washington DC, World Bank, 1983), p.xvi.
3. Y. Dos Santos, 'The structure of dependence', in C. Wilber (ed.), 'The Political Economy of Development and Underdevelopment' (New York, Random House, 1973), p.109.
4. See N. Chazan, An Anatomy of Ghanaian Politics: Managing Political Recession, 1969-82 (Boulder, Colorado, Westview, 1983), ch.8; D. Rothchild, 'Military regime performance: an appraisal of the Ghana experience, 1972-8', Comparative Politics, 12: 4, (1980), pp.459-79.
5. D. Rothchild and E. Gyimah-Boadi, 'Ghana's economic decline and development strategies', in J. Ravenhill (ed.), Africa in Economic Crisis (London, Macmillan,

1986), pp.263-4.
6. E. Hutchful, 'A tale of two regimes: imperialism, the military and class in Ghana', Review of African Political Economy, 14 (January-April 1979), p.51.
7. J. Odell, 'The politics of debt relief: official creditors and Brazil, Ghana and Chile', in J. Aronson (ed.), Debt and the Less Developed Countries (Boulder, Colorado, Westview, 1979), pp.253-83.
8. Survey of Ghana, Africa, 160, (December 1984), p.75.
9. World Bank, Ghana, Policies and Programme for Adjustment, p.15.
10. See B. Okeke, 4 June: a Revolution Betrayed (Enugu, Nigeria, Ikenga, 1982); J. Pieterse, 'Rawlings and the 1979 revolt in Ghana', Race and Class, xxiii: 4, (1982), pp.251-73.
11. Okeke, 4 June, p.69.
12. A Correspondent, 'The economic consequences of Rawlings', in The Legon Observer, 11: 12, (16 November 1979), pp.284-7.
13. See, for example, Rawlings' handover speech to the incoming president, Dr Hilla Limann on 24 September 1979; reproduced in Okeke, 4 June, pp.160-3.
14. West Africa, (24-31 December 1979), p.2379.
15. See Rothchild and Gyimah-Boadi, 'Ghana's economic decline', p.265.
16. West Africa, (8 March 1982), p.682.
17. Ibid, (15 March 1982), p.750.
18. See J. Ahiakpor, 'The success and failure of dependency theory: the case of Ghana', in International Organization, 39: 3, (summer 1985), pp.186-90.
19. See Z. Yeebo, 'How the IMF tamed a "Leftist" Apostle', Africa Events, 1: I, (January 1985), pp.17-19.
20. West Africa, (12 July 1982), p.1843.
21. D. Ray, Ghana: Politics, Economics, and Society, (London, Pinter, 1986), p.57.
22. See J. Haynes, 'From "revolution" to "pragmatism" in Ghana', Politics, 7: 2 (October 1987), pp.22-7.
23. Ahiakpor, 'Dependency theory', p.184.
24. See K. Nkrumah, Neocolonialism: the last stage of imperialism (New York, International Publishers, 1965).
25. Ghana News, 12: 2, (Washington DC, February 1983), p.8.
26. G. Kay, Development and Underdevelopment: a Marxist Analysis (London, Macmillan, 1975), p.x.
27. West Africa, (25 January 1982), p.225; (12 July 1982),

p.1843.
28. See Z. Yeebo, 'How the IMF tamed a "Leftist" Apostle'.
29. Republic of Ghana, Summary of PNDC's Budget Statement and Economic Policy for 1983 (Accra, Provisional National Defence Council, 1983), passim.
30. Survey of Ghana, Africa, pp.74-5.
31. Ibid.
32. Republic of Ghana, Summary of PNDC's Budget Statement, (1983), p.1.
33. Ibid, p.27.
34. See L. Brydon, 'Ghanaian responses to the Nigerian expulsions of 1983', African Affairs, 84: 336 (1985), pp.561-85.
35. C. Duodu, 'The IMF's test-tube baby', South, (January 1984).
36. This was only the case, however, for those with access to goods at state-controlled prices. This strata included those with contacts in the government bureaucracy. For others the price rises were less than threefold because they were already paying black-market rates for commodities; see R. Jeffries, 'Rawlings and the political economy of underdevelopment in Ghana', African Affairs, 81: 324, pp.4-22.
37. Y. Asante, 'The meaning of June 19', People's Daily Graphic, (Accra, 19 June 1984), (1982), pp.3 and 7.
38. The Pioneer (Kumasi, 20 June 1983), p.1; The Echo (Accra, 26 June 1983), p.1.
39. Ghana Commercial Bank, Quarterly Economic Review, 6: 1-4, (January-December 1983), pp.1-3.
40. Ibid, p.3.
41. West Africa, (26 March 1984), p.654.
42. This figure was presented in the Ghanaian Times (Accra, 14 January 1984), pp.1 and 3: 'A government expenditure on salaries, subventions and pensions of ₵73,074 billion would be necessary to pay a daily minimum wage of ₵300'.
43. Ghanaian Times, (18 February 1984), p.8.
44. People's Daily Graphic, (3 March 1984), pp.1, 4 and 5.
45. West Africa, (20 January 1986), p.10.
46. Home Front (published by Information Section of Ghana High Commission, London), 5: 1, p.10.
47. West Africa, (25 August 1986), p.1763.
48. Ibid, (4 August 1986), p.1624.
49. Yao Graham, 'Export-led recovery', West Africa, (13 January 1986), p.72.

50. West Africa, (25 August 1986), p.1763.
51. Interview by Jeffrey Haynes with Dr I.K. Adjei-Marfo, PNDC Secretary for Agriculture, Accra, Ghana, (8 September 1985); Ministry of Rural Development and Co-operatives, The Rural Manifesto: Policies, Plans and Strategies of the Ministry of Rural Development and Co-operatives to Effect Accelerated Rural Development in Ghana (Accra, Ministry of Rural Development and Co-operatives, April 1984).
52. Africa Events, 2: 2, (February 1986), p.15.
53. West Africa, (21 April 1986), pp.812-13.
54. Financial Times, (20 May 1986), p.20.
55. Ibid, (23 February 1987), p.3.
56. West Africa, (2 March 1987), pp.404-5; (3 April 1987), pp.701-2.
57. Interviews in Ghana, (June-October 1985); E. Rado, 'Notes towards a political economy of Ghana today', African Affairs, 85: 341, (1986), pp.563-72.
58. Gill and Duffus, Cocoa Market Report, 317, (March 1985), p.5.
59. West Africa, (12 January 1987), p.64.

6 SIERRA LEONE: DEBT AND THE FISCAL CRISIS OF THE STATE

1. For further discussion of the Sierra Leone case, see the contributions in D.F. Luke and S.P. Riley (eds), Economic Decline and Prospects for Adjustment in Sub-Saharan Africa: the Case of Sierra Leone (Westview, 1989).
2. 'Introduction', in Luke and Riley (eds), Economic Decline and Prospects for Adjustment; and D.F. Luke, 'Continuity in Sierra Leone: from Stevens to Momoh', Third World Quarterly, 18: 1, (January 1988).
3. 'Africa's submission to the Special Session of the United Nations General Assembly on Africa's Economic and Social Crisis', Economic Commission for Africa, (1986); and N. Harris, The End of the Third World? (Harmondsworth, Penguin, 1987).
4. S. Kamara, 'The genesis of macroeconomic problems'; O. Johnson 'The economic performance of Sierra Leone, 1969-85: analysis and lessons'; and S. Funna, 'Government finances and expenditures'; in Luke and Riley (eds), Economic Decline and Prospects for Adjustment.

5. This is now a much discussed concept in African political studies. For an introductory comment, see R. Sandbrook, *The Politics of Africa's Economic Stagnation*, (Cambridge, Cambridge University Press, 1985).
6. J.F. Medard, 'The underdeveloped state in Africa: political clientelism or neopatrimonialism?', in C. Clapham (ed.) *Private Patronage and Public Power*, (London, Pinter, 1982); M. Szeftel, 'Conflict, spoils and class formation in Zambia', PhD thesis, University of Manchester, 1978.
7. James S. Butty, 'Liberia's foreign debt crisis', *Liberia-Forum*, 2: 2, (1986); J. Haynes, T.W. Parfitt and S.P. Riley, 'Debt in Sub-Saharan Africa: the local politics of stabilization', *African Affairs*, 86: 344, (Oxford, July 1987), pp.343-66; and World Bank, *World Debt Tables, 1986-7*, First Supplement, (1987), p.166.
8. R.H. Green and S. Griffith-Jones, 'External debt: Sub-Saharan Africa's emerging iceberg', in T. Rose (ed.) *Crisis and Recovery in Sub-Saharan Africa* (Paris, OECD, 1985), pp.216-19.
9. Ibid.
10. J. Mathonnat, 'The impact of external factors and of domestic policies on external debt', in Rose (ed.), *Crisis and Recovery*, pp.231-40.
11. T.W. Parfitt and S.P. Riley, 'Africa in the debt trap: which way out?', *Journal of Modern African Studies*, 24: 3, (1986); and R. Brown, 'International responses to Sudan's economic crisis', *Development and Change*, 17, (1986), pp.487-511.
12. B. Sutcliffe, 'The world recession and the crisis in Africa', in P. Lawrence (ed.), *World Recession and the Food Crisis in Africa* (London, James Currey, 1986).
13. World Bank, *Sierra Leone: Prospects for Growth and Equity* (Washington DC, 1981) p.6.
14. *Africa Economic Digest*, (10 February 1984), p.15.
15. C. Clapham, (ed.), *Private Patronage and Public Power: Political Clientelism in the Modern State*, (London, Frances Pinter, 1982).
16. 'Sierra Leone: salaries in kind', *Africa Now*, (December 1982), p.23.
17. *West Africa*, (4 March 1985), pp.404-5.
18. *Africa Economic Digest*, (25 July 1980), p.17.
19. R.J. Bhatia, 'Stabilization Program in Sierra Leone', *IMF Staff Papers*, 16, part 3, (November 1969), pp.504-28.

20. Africa Economic Digest, (8 January 1982), p.22; this was equivalent to the cost of three weeks imports.
21. African Business, (May 1981), p.53.
22. C. Payer, The Debt Trap, (Harmondsworth, Penguin, 1974), p.34.
23. Africa Economic Digest, (7 January 1983), p.16.
24. Interviews carried out by Stephen Riley with government officials and politicians, 1982-3.
25. West Africa, (4 March 1985), p.428.
26. Payer, The Debt Trap.
27. Chernor Maju, a Minister of State, was sacked in August 1984 after being caught attempting to smuggle gold dust and currency: West Africa, (27 August 1984), p.1754.
28. Economist Intelligence Unit, Country Report on Sierra Leone, 4, 1986; and 1, 1987 (London, The Economist).
29. T.W. Parfitt, 'Sierra Leone: out of order', and A. Hoogvelt, 'IMF crime of conditionality', both in Review of African Political Economy, 38, (1987); and R. Dowden, 'Cure that kills the patient', The Independent (London, 14 April 1987), p.15.
30. But there have been student demonstrations: see West Africa, (9 February 1987).
31. World Bank, Accelerated Development in Sub-Saharan Africa: an Agenda for Action, (Washington DC, 1981).
32. West Africa, (18 February 1985), pp.309-10.
33. National News Bulletin, (Freetown, 25 December 1984).
34. S.P. Riley and T.W. Parfitt, 'Party or masquerade? The all people's congress (APC) of Sierra Leone', Journal of Commonwealth and Comparative Studies, 25: 2, (July 1987).
35. West Africa, (25 February 1985), pp.348-9.
36. Africa Confidential, (London, 28 November 1984).
37. Economist Intelligence Unit, Quarterly Report on Sierra Leone, 4, (1986); and 2, (1987) (London, The Economist).
38. Liat is a firm with interests in other African states, including the small homeland of Bophuthatswana, and is headed by a Russian Jewish emigré, Shabtai Kalmanowitch. In 1987 and 1988 Kalmanowitch had a series of encounters with the law in Britain, the United States, and Israel, thus effectively ending his business operations in Sierra Leone. See 'Liat scandal', West Africa Hotline, 9, (London, June 1987).

7 EXTERNAL DEBT AND FRANCOPHONE AFRICA: THE EFFECTS OF A SPECIAL RELATIONSHIP

1. R. Sandbrook, The Politics of Africa's Economic Stagnation, (Cambridge, Cambridge University Press, 1985), p.107.
2. Reagan is quoted in W.J. Foltz, 'Libya's military power', in R. Lemarchand (ed.), The Green and the Black: Libyan Policies in North and Sub-Saharan Africa, (Bloomington, Indiana University Press, 1988).
3. R. Luckham, 'French militarism in Africa', Review of African Political Economy, 24, (1982).
4. M. Staniland, 'Francophone Africa; the enduring French connection', The Annals, 489, (January 1987), pp.53-5.
5. T. Golan, "A certain mystery: how can France do everything that it does in Africa - and get away with it?', African Affairs, 80:318, (1981).
6. D.K. Fieldhouse, Black Africa, 1945-80: Economic Decolonization and Arrested Development, (London, Allen and Unwin, 1986), p.187.
7. See Sandbrook, Africa's Economic Stagnation, ch.5.
8. Boigny's home village, Yamoussoukro, has been extensively developed and much discussed. Another entertaining example - which is hardly likely to have amused Ivory Coast's external creditors - is a news report of 4 January 1984 which read: 'Ivory Coast president Felix Houphouet-Boigny went for a walk through Abidjan, handing out CFA10,000 (US$22.34) bank notes to passersby and wishing them a "Happy New Year"', Africa Economic Digest, (7 September 1984), p.22.
9. R.M. Price, 'Neocolonialism and Ghana's economic decline: a critical assessment', Canadian Journal of African Studies, 18:1, (1984).
10. S. Amin, Neocolonialism in West Africa (Harmondsworth, Penguin 1971), p.51.
11. Fieldhouse, Black Africa 1945-80.
12. B. Campbell, 'Ivory Coast', in J. Dunn (ed.), West African States, (Cambridge, Cambridge University Press, 1978).
13. B.A. Tuinder, Ivory Coast: the Challenge of Success, (London, World Bank, 1978), tables; and P.H. Blackburn, 'Côte d'Ivoire', Africa Review 1988, Saffron Walden, 1988), p.74.
14. Blackburn, 'Côte d'Ivoire'.
15. R.M. Hecht, 'The Ivory Coast economic miracle: what

benefit for the peasant farmers?', Journal of Modern African Studies, 21:1, (1983).

16. J. Loxley, 'The IMF, the World Bank and Sub-Saharan Africa', in K.J. Havnevik (ed.), The IMF and the World Bank in Africa, seminar series 18, (Viisala, Scandinavian Institute of African Studies, 1987), p.57.
17. Ibid. On the significance of multi-year rescheduling agreements (MYRAs) and the Paris and London Clubs, see M. Martin, 'Crisis management: solving Africa's debt problem?', in O. Akinrinade and J.K. Barling (eds.), Economic Development in Africa, (London, Pinter, 1987).
18. Details in this paragraph are from: '"Le Sage" unleases shock for French', West African Hotline, (16 June 1987), p.6.
19. 'Côte d'Ivoire: at home and abroad', West Africa, (11 January 1988), p.16.
20. Such as the network of relationships between senior advisers to successive French presidents and African leaders. For a comment on such figures as Jacques Foccart and Maurice Robert, see Staniland, 'Francophone Africa', pp.57-8.
21. R. Joseph, 'The Gaullist legacy: patterns of French neocolonialism', Review of African Political Economy, 6, (1976).
22. J. Chipman, 'French military policy and African security', Adelphi Paper 201, (London, International Institute for Strategic Studies, 1985).
23. Staniland, 'Francophone Africa', p.55.
24. Chipman, 'French military policy', p.2.
25. Staniland, 'Francophone Africa', p.53.
26. I.W. Zartman, 'Africa and the west: the French connection', in B.E. Arlinghaus, African Security Issues: Sovereignty, Stability, and Solidarity, (Boulder, Colorado, Westview, 1985).
27. Joseph, 'The Gaullist legacy', p.4.

8 WAYS OUT OF THE DEBT TRAP

1. Special Report on Banking and Finance, Africa Economic Digest, (September 1986), p.2.
2. J.M. Nelson, 'The political economy of stabilization: commitment, capacity, and public response', World Development, 12:10, (1984), p.1003.

3. The American 'new right' have developed a particular line of criticism of major international institutions including UNESCO and the IMF. For a discourse on the IMF from this perspective, see 'World debt and the monetary order', Special Issue of The Cato Journal, 4:1 (spring/summer 1984).
4. Africa Economic Digest, (30 September 1983), p.10.
5. Ibid, p.10.
6. Africa Economic Digest, (21 October 1983), p.7.
7. Details from The Economist, (12 October 1985), pp.75-6.
8. Africa Economic Digest, (18 September 1987), pp.20-1.
9. All Party Parliamentary Group on Overseas Development, Managing Third World Debt; Report of the Second Working Party established by the All Party Group on Overseas Development, (London, Overseas Development Institute, 1987), p.37.
10. World Bank, World Debt Tables: External Debt of Developing Countries 1986-7 Edition, (Washington DC, World Bank, February 1987), p.24.
11. World Bank, World Debt Tables 1986-7, pp.22-5.
12. West African Hotline, 10, (1-15 July 1987), pp.6-7.
13. World Bank, World Debt Tables 1986-7, pp.32-4.
14. Ibid, pp.32-3.
15. World Bank, Address by Barber Conable to the Board of Governors of the World Bank and International Finance Corporation, (Washington DC, World Bank, 29 September 1987), p.11.
16. Africa Economic Digest, (18 September 1987), p.20.
17. Ibid, pp.21-2.
18. The Treasury, Economic Progress Report, 190, (London, July 1987), p.4.
19. South, 86, (December 1987), p.14.
20. Treasury, Economic Progress Report, 190, p.3.
21. Africa Economic Digest, (2 October 1987), p.2.
22. Financial Times, (20 December 1987), p.26.
23. South, 86, p.14.
24. Ibid, p.16.
25. Quoted in P. O'Brien, 'The debt cannot be paid: Castro and the Latin American debt', Bulletin of Latin American Research, 5:1 (1986), p.55.
26. Ibid, pp.56-7.
27. G. O'Donnell, 'Brazil's failure; what future for debtors' cartels?', Third World Quarterly, 9:4, (October 1987), pp.1157-66.

28. J. Ravenhill, 'Collective self-reliance or collective self-delusion: is the Lagos Plan a viable alternative?' in J. Ravenhill (ed.), Africa in Economic Crisis, (New York, Columbia University Press, 1986), pp.85-107.
29. Africa Research Bulletin, Economic Series, 23:5, (30 June 1986), p.8223.
30. United Nations, Progress in the Implementation of the United Nations Programme of Action for African Economic Recovery and Development, 1986-90: Report of the Secretary-General, (Geneva, 1987), pp.4-5.
31. Ibid.
32. Ibid, pp.24-5.
33. Africa Research Bulletin, Economic Series, 24:6, (31 July 1986), p.8732.
34. Such reforms are summarized in Latin America Bureau, The Poverty Brokers: the IMF and Latin America, (London, Latin America Bureau, 1983), ch.7.
35. H. Lever and C. Huhne, Debt and Danger: The World Financial Crisis, (Harmondsworth, Penguin, 1985), ch.9.
36. P. Korner, G. Maass, T. Siebold and R. Tetzlaff, The IMF and the Debt Crisis: a Guide to the Third World's Dilemmas, (London, Zed Books, 1986), ch.5.
37. Lever and Huhne, Debt and Danger, p.141.
38. See R.E. Galli and J. Jones, Guinea Bissau: Politics, Economics, and Society, (London, Frances Pinter, 1987), p.60; and J. McCulloch, In The Twilight Of Revolution; the Political Theory of Amilcar Cabral, (London, Routledge and Kegan Paul, 1983), pp.67-9.
39. A. Adams, 'The Senegal River Valley: what kind of change?', in W. Johnson and H. Bernstein (eds), Third World Lives of Struggle, (London, Heinemann, 1982).
40. Jean-François Bayart, 'Civil society in Africa', in P. Chabal (ed.), Political Domination in Africa: Reflections on the Limits of Power, (Cambridge, Cambridge University Press, 1986), p.125.
41. Bayart, 'Civil society in Africa', p.125.
42. A useful review of this literature is provided by J. Midgeley, A. Hall, M. Hardiman and D. Narine, Community Participation, Social Development, and the State, (London, Methuen, 1986).
43. R. Sandbrook, The Politics of Basic Needs: Urban Aspects of Assaulting Poverty in Africa, (London, Heinemann Educational Books Ltd, 1982), pp.241-2.
44. T.W. Parfitt, 'Tested to destruction? An evaluation of aid effectiveness in Sierra Leone's agricultural sector',

in D.F. Luke and S.P. Riley (eds), Economic Decline and Prospects for Adjustment in Sub-Saharan Africa: the Case of Sierra Leone, (Boulder, Westview Press, 1989).

POSTSCRIPT

1. IMF Survey, Supplement on Sub-Saharan African Debt, (June 1988), p.180 and West Africa, (23 May 1988), p.931.
2. Financial Times, (6 June 1988).
3. West Africa, (11 April 1988), p.653.
4. West African Hotline, 27, (1-15 April 1988), p.4.
5. Africa Analysis, 45, (15 April 1988), p.5.
6. Africa Confidential, 29:8, (15 April 1988), pp.4-6.
7. Africa Confidential, 29:8, pp.4-6 and Africa Analysis, 43, (18 March 1988), pp.1-2.
8. West African Hotline, 27, p.4.
9. Africa Analysis, 49, (10 June 1988), p.1.
10. Financial Times, (9 June 1988), p.1.
11. Financial Times, (21 June 1988), p.1.
12. West Africa, (4 July 1988), p.1206.
13. West Africa, (11 April 1988), p.653.
14. West Africa, (4 July 1988), p.1218.
15. Financial Times, (20 June 1988), p.1.
16. Financial Times, (22 June 1988), p.4.
17. West Africa, (11 April 1988), p.653.

Index

For Product Safety Concerns and Information please contact our EU
representative GPSR@taylorandfrancis.com
Taylor & Francis Verlag GmbH, Kaufingerstraße 24, 80331 München, Germany

www.ingramcontent.com/pod-product-compliance
Lightning Source LLC
LaVergne TN
LVHW011126300926
849160LV00008B/534

* 9 7 8 0 4 1 5 8 5 3 5 8 3 *